HORROR
in the
Heartland

HORROR
in the
Heartland

Strange and Gothic Tales from the Midwest

KEVEN MCQUEEN

AN IMPRINT OF
INDIANA UNIVERSITY PRESS
BLOOMINGTON AND INDIANAPOLIS

This book is a publication of

Quarry Books an imprint of
INDIANA UNIVERSITY PRESS

Office of Scholarly Publishing
Herman B Wells Library 350
1320 East 10th Street
Bloomington, Indiana 47405 USA

iupress.indiana.edu

The paper used in this publication meets the minimum requirements
of the American National Standard for Information Sciences—
Permanence of Paper for Printed Library Materials, ANSI Z39.48–1992.

Manufactured in the United States of America

Library of Congress Cataloging-in-Publication Data

Names: McQueen, Keven, author.
Title: Horror in the heartland : strange and Gothic tales from
    the Midwest / Keven McQueen.
Description: 1st [edition]. | Bloomington : Indiana University Press,
    2017. | Includes bibliographical references.
Identifiers: LCCN 2017011847 (print) | LCCN 2017024719 (ebook) |
    ISBN 9780253029126 (e-book) | ISBN 9780253029041 (pbk. : alk.
    paper) | ISBN 9780253028907 (cloth : alk. paper)
Subjects: LCSH: Haunted places—Middle West. | Ghosts—Middle
    West. | Curiosities and wonders—Middle West. | Middle West—
    Miscellanea.
Classification: LCC BF1472.U6 (ebook) | LCC BF1472.U6 M437 2017
    (print) | DDC 398.20977—dc23
LC record available at https://lccn.loc.gov/2017011847

1 2 3 4 5   22 21 20 19 18 17

Dedicated to my great in-laws,
Craig and Debbie Smith.

CONTENTS

ACKNOWLEDGMENTS

Thrown bouquets to:

Drema Colangelo; Gaile Sheppard Dempsey; Eastern Kentucky University Department of English; Eastern Kentucky University Interlibrary Loan Department (Stefanie Brooks, Heather Frith, Shelby Wills); Amy McQueen and Quentin Hawkins; Darrell and Swecia McQueen; Darren, Alison, and Elizabeth McQueen; Kyle McQueen; Michael, Lori, and Blaine McQueen and Evan Holbrook; Ashley Runyon and everyone at Indiana University Press; Mia Temple. Also: The Ancient of Days.

INTRODUCTION

FAMILIAR IMAGES ENTER THE MIND WHEN ONE CONTEMPLATES the American Midwest: fields of wheat waving in the breeze; cozy small towns with friendly, down-to-earth inhabitants; mighty rivers and verdant farms; terrain as flat as a table.

Certainly those mental pictures depict the Midwest—but they are not the whole story. Where, for example, are the hardworking body snatchers? What about the ghosts? The cemeteries full of wide tombstones with droll inscriptions? The colorful murderers, the practical jokes gone wrong, the rat attacks, the premature burials?

These things are part of the fabric of America's past as much as Valley Forge or the discovery of the Mississippi. They provide small, if sometimes dark, insights into history and human nature.

I love this unnerving Midwest as much as the idyllic version. It is a region teeming with real-life surrealism and historical horror-comedy. It is a region with a past that abounds with eccentrics, people who sneered at death in its many forms, and many mysteries, including a monster in every forest and a haunted house in every town. Let's explore it!

HORROR
in the
Heartland

1

EERIE INDIANA

A Booming Underground Industry

IN THE NINETEENTH AND EARLY TWENTIETH CENTURIES, midwestern medical schools were in perpetual need of cadavers for students to dissect. The gallows provided the schools with a steady supply of "patients," but there were not enough hanged felons to go around; the result was a thriving trade in grave robbery. A little furtive work with a shovel, a sack, and a lantern, and the intrepid snatcher could make enough money to keep himself comfortably in ale for a while. There are many examples of this lost folk art from Indiana history.

Persons entering a graveyard several miles from Indianapolis on October 20, 1877, spied the bodies of Mrs. R. and her child lying on the ground near their open grave. Why hadn't the body snatchers carried away their prize? The woman died of highly contagious tuberculosis several weeks before; perhaps her excavators were unaware of this fact until they already completed their laborious task, and they left the body out of fear and/or disgust at having done all that hard work for an unusable cadaver.

Sometimes people who objected to the shoplifting of their dearly departed would hire "grave watchers"—operatives who, exactly as their name implies, were paid to camp out at a gravesite until enough time had passed for the occupant to spoil, thereby becoming of no interest to any medical school. Rising Sun, Indiana, was plagued with body snatchings in early 1877; when a little girl was buried on February 13, her family and friends hired two men to watch the grave. Unbeknownst to them, the mayor hired two others to do the same. When the two sets of grave watchers spotted each other, they came to the natural conclusion and exchanged shots. Henry S., hired by the mayor, received slight wounds, but Joseph J. of the other party sustained a serious load of shot in his side.

Ghouls Just Want to Have Fun: Indiana

Sometimes furtive openers of graves weren't in it to steal bodies but rather to swipe valuables, plain and simple. There are cases in which their motives are undiscernible, and that may be for the better.

Ursula T. was buried in a graveyard near Taylorsville after her death on October 26, 1865. In May 1921 her coffin was unearthed and pried open by parties unknown—at least eight of them, judging from the footprints in the dirt. The reason was a mystery until one elderly resident remembered an old rumor that dated to the 1840s. Back then, Ursula and her husband, Zachariah, put up $10,000 in gold as bond for a friend who was being tried on a felony charge. The man committed suicide in the courtroom after a guilty verdict was rendered. The religious couple refused to use any of the money after it was returned them; rumor held that Ursula buried the money with Zachariah when he died. So the would-be grave robbers unearthed the wrong casket! Someone must have forgotten to bring a flashlight. There is no record of their taking a second go at it.

Lydia A. died in September 1933 and was buried in Hessville on the sixteenth day of the month. Everyone naively thought she had been laid to rest forever.

In April 1937, George B. and Lynn S., teenage boys respectively from Hammond and Highland, were discovered with Lydia's skull in their possession. They confessed to having stolen the body of the young tuberculosis victim from her grave on March 21, 1937, after fortifying themselves with gin. They opened the coffin with a crowbar and stuffed Lydia in their car.

The boys removed Lydia's head and tossed the rest of her in a marsh in a field near Warren G. Harding School in Hammond. George—who was a whiz at chemistry—boiled the head. As he explained to detectives later, "If I used acid to clean it, I would have softened it." Then he painted the skull white. Unfortunately for the youthful ghouls, they accidentally left a leather glove and a pen with the monogram "G" behind in the cemetery, clues that led authorities right to them.

Why did the teens swipe the skull? They wanted it for "secret society" initiation rites in the Hammond Youth Esquire Club. In fact, they were in a hurry to rob the grave before a rival club beat them to it. Their competitors already were using a really swell casket flanked by candles in their rituals. The Esquire Club did not want to be outclassed and thirsted to possess a neat-o, gen-u-wine human skull. It was like a really creepy *Our Gang* short.

George and Lynn could have gotten jail time, but authorities chose leniency since they considered the incident more of a prank than a crime; also, the late Lydia's husband, Frank, had remarried and moved out of the area, so there was no offended kin to press charges.

Buried Alive: Indiana

It is well known that our ancestors had a terror of premature burial. Was their fear founded in reality, or was the danger exaggerated? As the following unwholesome example demonstrates, they had good reason to be worried . . .

According to a story that appears to have originated in the *New York Sun*, George W., a forty-two-year-old Indiana farmer, threw a party at his house on June 18, 1886. Next morning his wife found him dead in bed. "Heart disease," opined the doctor. Better bury him as soon as possible! Over the course of the next several hours, some noted that George maintained a lifelike appearance and had no rigor mortis.

George was placed in a coffin and loaded in a hearse, which led a procession of vehicles. On the way to the country graveyard, a runaway wagon collided with the hearse, flinging the coffin to the ground. When mourners approached to lift the coffin, they heard a familiar voice within saying, "For God's sake let me out of this!"

According to press accounts, "With a little assistance he pulled himself out of the box and walked into the house and sat down in a chair." George told his no longer mournful friends that he had been in a waking coma, able to see and think but unable to speak or move. He added:

> Had a pistol been fired in the room I am sure the spell would have been broken. After the doctor's ultimatum I felt that I should be buried alive. But was I alive? All of a sudden this query flashed across my brain and I was troubled more than I can tell you. As I had never died before, how was I to know the sensations? Could the dead hear and think? Was the mind of the corpse in active operation? It was a problem I could not solve.

George could hear everything taking place around him, including his wife's weeping and entreaties, though he couldn't understand what she was getting so upset about. He listened to the clock in the kitchen ticking; he eavesdropped on a conversation two nearby friends had about his untimely passing (which they later confirmed); he even overheard two lowlifes break into his barn and make off with a horse's bridle.

And, once traveling to the cemetery, he clearly heard the sound of the runaway team of horses slamming into the hearse, which ended the fun: "As the collision came my eyes opened and my speech was restored, and from that moment I was all right."

Remains to Be Seen: Indiana

Ella P.'s candle flickered and went out at St. Anthony's Hospital in Terre Haute in September 1887. No one claimed her body. Ball's undertaking establishment embalmed Ella, so she would "keep" two or three weeks in case relatives should turn up. They didn't, and Ball's was stuck with an unwanted body. The embalmer thought to himself, *Why not use some experimental chemicals on it and see what happens?*

His tinkering proved of interest to doctors, scientists, and undertakers because Ella became mummified "hard as a rock," according to a reporter, who also wrote: "The color of the body is a dark brown, and the fingers of the hands are so hard that they cannot be bent, even with an unusual effort. . . . The tissues have fallen away considerably. The features remain very natural and retain a great deal of their original cast. No odor of any kind is emitted." Strangest of all, Ella's body made a hollow sound when thumped, "like an empty wooden box."

The proprietors at Ball's, knowing a good advertisement when they saw one, placed Ella on display in a glass case at first, then later in a coffin, so sightseers could drop by and take in the sight. These included people from the Rose Polytechnic Institute, the State Normal School, and representatives from the public schools.

Eccentric Interments: Indiana

Some rugged individualists can't even be *buried* normally. When Katherine H. of Medora died on March 10, 1916, she requested that her late husband, John, be exhumed and buried in the same grave with her. John had died in February 1912.

⊷⊶◦⊷⊶

Isaiah S., an ex-soldier, onetime stonemason, and former post-master of Pleasant Lake erected his own grave marker, a garish ten-ton monument made of red, white, and blue granite. He did not wish to be enclosed in a vault because, as he said, "When Gabriel blows the trumpet I don't want to be impeded by having a concrete overcoat on." He also listed the pallbearers he wanted to tote him to his final resting place—six former girlfriends, whom he described as being "all husky girls of about 160 pounds and good looking, too." They were Lottie, Nannie, Minnie, Addie, Josie, and Millie. Isaiah made these elaborate plans in 1926, many years before he began to slip from the memory of man on November 15, 1939.

Infidel Inscriptions, Indiana

Some religious skeptics of times past shocked their communities by having blasphemous inscriptions carved on their tombstones; as a rule, their sentiments were straight from the fusty "village atheist" school of argument that went out in the days of Robert Ingersoll and Clarence Darrow. For example, Martin Jenners's gravestone in Spring Vale Cemetery at Lafayette reads: "My only objection to religion is that it is not true. I Cor. XV, 52. Is. XXVI, 14. No preaching, no praying, no psalm singing permitted on this lot."

The two biblical verses referred to on the monument are "In a moment, in the twinkling of an eye, at the last trump: for the trumpet shall sound, and the dead shall be raised incorruptible, and we shall be changed" (1 Cor. 15:52) and "They are dead, they shall not live; they are deceased, they shall not rise: therefore hast thou visited and destroyed them, and made all their memory to perish" (Isaiah 26:14). Evidently Martin thought the verses contradicted each other in that the first promises a resurrection and the second appears not to. If he had read only five verses farther in Isaiah he would have come to 26:19: "Thy dead men *shall* live, together with my dead body shall they arise. Awake and sing, ye that dwell in dust: for thy dew is as the dew of herbs, and the earth shall cast out the dead."

Martin was asphyxiated on December 22, 1919.

Clubs You Wouldn't Have Wanted to Join: Indiana

Most high school students in the 1930s joined organizations such as the 4-H Club, the Glee Club, or the Latin Club. Howard S., who attended North Side High in Fort Wayne, joined a secret suicide club. The sixteen-year-old hanged himself in his parents' basement on June 17, 1934, to see how long he could dangle without losing consciousness. The whole point of the club's existence was "to find out exactly how long a person could hang without dying." Howard's parents, wise after the fact, said they noticed that he came home several times with rope burns around his neck.

Getting Stiffed, Part One

Walter M. died at Elkhart on December 4, 1920. His funeral expenses were covered with cash he had saved just for that occasion—but after the money was spent, bankers discovered that the bills were counterfeit. His widow had to cover the loss.

O'er Their Tomb No Trophies Raise

Charles Chase died in 1900 and was buried in Venter Ridge Cemetery in Sullivan. He is notable for the tininess of his grave marker, a piece of marble only four inches high, two inches wide, and seven inches long, and bearing a three-word inscription: "Chase, the Barber." Charles had used the wee stone as a doorstop.

Succinct Obituaries, Part One

On October 18, 1922, Samuel D. and another man were constructing a chicken coop in Terre Haute. They needed something to brace the structure on. "Why not use my head?" asked Samuel. The end result was a nail driven in his skull. His obituary noted: "The widow found the body after waiting [for] supper for more than fifteen minutes."

A Parrot Prognosticates

On May 7, 1917, a twenty-year-old parrot belonging to a married couple of Bedford called out, "Good-bye." Then it fell off its perch as dead as its counterpart in a certain Monty Python skit.

Boo! Did I Scare You?

It sounds like a scene out of Mark Twain: a group of boys see humor in making the schoolmistress think she's encountered a ghost. So on the night of June 22, 1888, a dark stretch of road at Birdseye was full of hiding, snickering boys—including the intended victim's younger brother—just waiting for Miss Josie C. to walk home from a neighbor's house. When she drew near, one of them covered himself with a sheet, jumped into the road, and gyrated his arms. The teacher screamed, fell to the ground, and died in convulsions a half hour later. When the boys heard the result of the practical joke they'd played on Miss Josie—described as "beautiful and accomplished" and "a very popular young school teacher"—they fled the neighborhood in shame, their little joke having lost its savor.

Creativity in Suicide: Indiana

Avery S. killed himself at his home near Columbus on March 18, 1920. He employed the same old muzzle-loading shotgun his father, Sidel, had used to end his own life twenty years before.

⊷⊶○⊷⊶

Some people find out the hard way that suicide is not always "the easy way out." Peter V., a coal miner from Washington, Indiana, stabbed himself several times in the neck with a table fork on September 1, 1896. When that didn't do the trick, he bashed himself repeatedly over the head with the blade end of an ax until the Death Angel stayed Peter's hand. After all that work and bother he might as well have lived.

⊷⊶○⊷⊶

Searle J., a nineteen-year-old high school student in Evansville, went to the family kitchen on June 8, 1900, and "told the cook a funny story." After thus entertaining the domestic, the young man produced a pistol and a moment later Searle's head had gained a couple ounces in weight. His death was blamed on "being jilted by a young woman and the use of cigarettes."

⊢•⊕•○•⊕•⊣

Lucy W. died in Kokomo on September 1, 1901, after flinging herself down a flight of stairs and then starving herself. She had tired of life at age 122.

⊢•⊕•○•⊕•⊣

An unknown (and totally nude) fisherman practiced the gentle Japanese art of hara-kiri on an island below Henderson, Kentucky, on June 30, 1907. He disemboweled himself with a six-inch-long cut in the belly and slashed his throat twice with a razor—but not before making his appearance presentable, as testified by a shaving mug found near the scene and a mirror dangling from a bush. He was identified next day as the ironically named Finis G. of Newburg, Indiana.

⊢•⊕•○•⊕•⊣

"I will be dead tomorrow. I am going to kill myself," said John L. to Ernest R., bartender at a saloon in Jeffersonville on October 12, 1907.

"No, you are not," scoffed the barkeep. "You haven't the nerve."

"If you don't believe I am game, just watch me," retorted John, who proved his point by drinking an ounce of carbolic acid. Before he expired horribly, John offered to buy a pint of whisky for Albert C., whom he had sent to the druggist to purchase the poison. Albert declined the kind offer.

⊢•⊕•○•⊕•⊣

Workers at the Globe Handle Company in Evansville were surprised on April 21, 1910, to find that a monkey had hanged itself with a chain from a rafter in their plant. It was believed to have escaped from a traveling circus that visited the city on April 15. Some imaginative souls conjectured that it committed suicide out of loneliness after being separated from its mates.

><

John Helms, a farmer who has a claim to fame as the founder of Helmsburg, employed a uniquely unpleasant way to kill himself on May 26, 1916: he jammed a sharp stick at least a foot down his throat repeatedly until he bled to death.

Bitter Ironies, Part One

John M. murdered Carl S. in August 1916 and was sentenced to life in prison. Five years later the governor of Indiana gave him a parole. John celebrated by returning to his home ten miles west of Petersburg on June 13, 1921. He was there less than a half hour when he was stricken with paralysis and died.

><

A doctor was noted for his lecture titled "Why Worry?" He committed suicide by poison in Kokomo on July 20, 1921.

Impressing Their Congregations: Indiana

A storm gathered as a congregation of Free Methodists held an outdoor revival at Springville on August 9, 1920. "If lightning should strike this tent tonight how many would be ready for it?" asked the reverend. The question became more than rhetorical a few moments later, resulting in the deaths of two other reverends.

Closing Remarks, Indiana

Miss Beatrice C. drowned herself in a lake in Oak Ridge Cemetery, Evansville, on April 18, 1911. Her suicide note said, "Among the goldfishes."

What Calvin Saw and What Happened Afterward

Calvin Z. of Fort Wayne saw a man named Dolan run over by a train on the night of November 4, 1910. The sight so unnerved him that when he went to work at an asphalt plant next day, Calvin lost his footing and fell into a grinding mill. His obituary noted: "His body came from the outlet as part of the mixture."

When Nightmares Become Real, Part One

Conrad K., a Southern Pacific railroad clerk, survived the San Francisco earthquake of April 1906 without injury. One night, however, he dreamed he was experiencing the quake. Thrashing about, Conrad kicked his bedpost with such force that he snapped ligaments in his leg. He contracted pneumonia while recovering and died in Logansport on November 5, 1906.

<hr />

Harry C., marshal of Jonesville for six years, was found dead in bed on April 14, 1918. It was thought that he smothered himself in his pillow while in the midst of a nightmare.

Slaying the Audience

John C. went to the movies in Petersburg on August 18, 1923. His choice was *Out of Luck*, a comedy starring Hoot Gibson and Laura LaPlante. A little too funny: a witness saw John laugh and then fall out of his seat. The coroner ruled that John died of apoplexy triggered by laughter.

Initiating the Dead

The Pi Beta Phi chapter at Indiana University in Bloomington wanted Margaret P. of Saint Petersburg, Florida, as a member, and they weren't deterred by the fact that she died after an operation for appendicitis the day before. On October 8, 1928, forty members trooped to the Bloomington home of Margaret's grandparents. There they pinned their official badge on Margaret's dress and sang the sorority song. Margaret's mother, also a member, was present.

It Must Be Monday

One fine day in 1881, Edward M. of Jeffersonville met up with his friends Patrick, John, and Barney, and they got stinking drunk. Alcohol makes trivialities seem like matters of vast significance, and intoxicated men fight over pointless issues. This quartet was no different. Edward insisted that a passing cat was named (get this!) Garfield. Patrick and Barney begged to differ and attempted to settle this important dispute in time-honored Irish fashion: Patrick knocked Edward down but was surprised when his foe arose with a knife in hand. In the following melee Edward missed Patrick but stabbed John in the jugular, killing him instantly. Barney tried to take Edward home but ended up dead himself from a knife wound in his side.

Edward was sentenced to prison at Michigan City. But the attorney who prosecuted him felt pangs of guilt since the prisoner had been so darn drunk when he'd slaughtered his friends that he didn't know what he was doing. The judge agreed that the sentence was too harsh. Starting around 1889, the district attorney led a crusade to have the prisoner released. His efforts paid off in January 1901, when the governor issued a parole for Edward. He spent nearly twenty years in jail because four drunks couldn't agree on a name for a cat.

A Prolific Victim

Just three days before Christmas 1895, someone murdered the elderly widow Hester C. of Lafayette. Her gory corpse was found sitting upright in a chair with a bloody bank book clutched in her hand. She had a crushed skull from a clubbing. The best anyone could figure was that burglars had broken in, and her last act on earth had been to show them her bank book to convince the thieves that all her money was in the bank, not salted away in her house.

Hester was the mother of twenty-five children, including seven sets of twins, so perhaps death came as a sweet relief.

Dear Diary

William H., a farmer and Civil War veteran who lived at Tennyson, long believed that his much younger wife was unfaithful. He had suspicions about two men in particular, later identified in the newspapers only as "a preacher living near Tennyson" and "a prominent Boonville businessman." William's wife complained to her friends about her husband's attitude and insisted that he had no grounds for jealousy.

Starting on May 5, 1906, William kept a secret diary in which he vented his spleen daily about his unhappy domestic life and permitted his imagination to run amok concerning his wife's alleged infidelities. On the night of June 23, the elderly man emptied the contents of a shotgun into his wife as their thirteen-year-old son, Minor, escaped.

Bad news travels swiftly, and hundreds of neighbors spent their night standing on William's lawn although a crazy man with a loaded gun was inside the house. No one dared enter, however, because every time someone tried it the homeowner's voice warned them away. With every passing hour the cheery old sun slowly rose, and when the morning light became sufficient, the neighbors peeped in a window and saw William sitting calmly in a chair with his weapon in his lap. Around noon he got up and walked into the inner recesses of the house. A shot rang out, but it was another hour before a half dozen people worked up the nerve to enter. They found William lying dead from a self-inflicted shotgun blast near his wife's corpse. The diary lay next to his body.

The coroner refused to divulge the contents of the dead man's journal, but his prudence only served to make the diary an object of speculation, wild imagination, and unfounded rumor all over the county. "He admits, however," said a news report, "that it contains the names of several prominent citizens against whom William makes charges. The parties are among the most prominent in the county and the double tragedy with its possible further sensational developments has created a tremendous sensation." In an excerpt from the diary that did get released to the press, William wrote that he wanted to assassinate the suspected preacher and businessman: "Had it not been that I feared the preferment of a charge of murder I would long ago have killed these men." He ended the diary: "Good-bye. I will close but with half untold." He added an unhealthy prayer that his descendants would track down the two men he deemed guilty and kill them.

Clearly, William was a man of determination with a thirst for vengeance. It comes as no surprise, then, that nine months after the murder-suicide, William's house was reputed to be haunted. The residence was left untouched since the night the old man's temper got the better of him but passersby claimed that although it was unoccupied, they occasionally saw a dim light shining from within and the sound of immaterial feet walking.

Death Row Dramas: Indiana

George D. beheaded his common law wife May M. in Gary in spring 1911. For this, he was sentenced to be hanged on February 9, 1912. The prisoner wasn't perturbed—in fact, he looked forward to his execution since he regarded hanging as a "mark of honor." The governor robbed George of this peculiar distinction by commuting his sentence to life imprisonment.

꜒꜔꜖

Charles S. was on trial for murdering Stephen M., the town marshal of New Albany. On January 25, 1919, as the jury deliberated,

Charles cut his throat in his cell. But the jury, unaware of his suicide, intended to acquit him on grounds of insanity.

>+++0++++

For murdering his wife at Bloomingdale on July 21, 1921, the state sentenced William D. to take a load off his feet in the electric chair. May 31, 1922, was the date set for the execution. The governor considered commuting the sentence to life in prison—until he heard from the condemned man's seventeen-year-old daughter, Mabel, who lived in Harrodsburg, Kentucky. Mabel urged the governor not to interfere, saying, "Death is surely what he deserves." William walked to the death chamber in Michigan City right on schedule.

Consumed by Rats, Part One

Margaret T., a seventy-five-year-old paralyzed woman, was found dead in her bed at Walkerton on December 28, 1923. At first the police thought she had been slashed by a home invader, as she had a long jagged wound extending from her right ear to her chin. The coroner determined that the helpless Margaret actually had been—shudder!—gnawed to death by famished rodents.

Rough Justice for a Train Wrecker

In days of long ago, when Americans were more dependent than now on trains for personal transportation and delivery of goods, antisocial miscreants sometimes intentionally wrecked the engines—sometimes for profit, as they would pick the pockets of injured passengers while pretending to help them; sometimes just for the sheer fun of seeing a locomotive jump the tracks and crash. Railroads offered big rewards for the capture of these villains, but one impatient engineer took the law into his own hands.

On a section of track running into the countryside outside of Indianapolis, a certain passenger train wrecked every night for a week, sometimes with loss of life. Someone was getting his jollies by placing obstructions on the track. One evening the engineer said to the fireman: "If this train jumps the track at that place tonight you follow me; don't stop for anything, but keep close after me. Somebody has been throwing this train off the track, and I'm going to catch him."

The train hit a misplaced rail at the usual spot but stopped before incurring any serious damage. The engineer and the fireman jumped out of the cab and ran into a nearby cornfield, where they overtook a man. He confessed, possibly expecting nothing worse than a drubbing, but the railroad men forced him back to the train. The passengers had exited by then and expressed a desire to lynch the miscreant who had risked their lives, but the engineer coolly told them that he would handle the situation and urged them back on the cars.

The train started back on its route, with the terrified wrecker riding in the cab with the engineer and fireman. Once the engine was on a straight stretch of track, the engineer clobbered the vandal over the head with a stick of firewood and shoved the stunned man into the train engine's furnace. Then he closed the furnace door, and the train had some free extra fuel that night. When the *Indianapolis Sentinel* told the story to its readers in February 1873, it discreetly omitted the, by then deceased, engineer's name.

Silent Types: Indiana

As a very young man, George S. whiled away hours at the Indiana Hospital for the Insane sitting in the same position, with his head in his hands. He became famous around the hospital for his absolute refusal to speak, even at meals. It sounds as if George had autism in the days before it was a known disorder and was simply considered madness.

He was discharged around 1875 as incurable and sent to the County Poor Asylum in Vincennes. There he continued his campaign of total silence.

On July 3, 1885, when George was about thirty years old, he got up out of his chair and walked to the poorhouse well and stared down into it. The sight of an ambulatory George was so astonishing that the superintendent and a couple of attendants followed him. The superintendent told the men to take George back inside, whereupon the taciturn pauper sprinted up the road, forcing the three men to chase him. When they finally caught up with him, the superintendent chastised him with a slap in the face. Then George said the first words he was known to have spoken in more than a decade: "Don't you do that again."

The ice was broken, and after that George spoke as rationally as anyone else—though he seemed afraid of the sound of his own voice.

Mad Medics, Part One

Dr. Orin A.'s friends and family members in Marshfield had known he was insane since April 1885; in fact, he was scheduled to go to the State Asylum on August 5. And yet they allowed him to keep his black bag full of very sharp medical instruments.

Late on the night of August 4, Dr. A. got out his case of tools, ostensibly to show them to his assembled watchers, but he took a double-edged knife in hand and started for his wife's room. She wisely fled the house. He pursued her, couldn't find her, and returned to the house, where he encountered his longtime friend Dr. B.

Dr. A. greeted his professional colleague by slashing Dr. B.'s throat with the knife, then stabbing him in the chest, the back, and under the arm. In the fight that followed, Dr. B. managed to grasp the blade with both hands—but the sharp double edge cut his hands nearly in half.

Dr. B. escaped when Dr. A. stopped for a breather. After resting, Dr. A. stalked around inside the house for a while by himself—no one dared enter. At last he stepped outside, plunged a knife into his own throat, and drank some iodine. Neither physician survived, and everyone learned a valuable life lesson about permitting crazy people to have access to sharp tools.

Faithful until Death, Part One

Many are familiar with the story of Greyfriars Bobby, the Skye Terrier who allegedly guarded his master's grave in Greyfriars Cemetery, Edinburgh, Scotland, for fourteen years until the dog died in 1872. The American Midwest provides similar examples of the boundless devotion of man's best friend.

For example, in spring 1914, a farmer, David Hershman, was buried in the Anderson Cemetery a few miles east of Petersburg. His shepherd dog followed the funeral procession to the cemetery and lay down next to the grave when the mourners left, and would allow no one near. David's neighbors brought food to it. As of May the dog was still there.

2

OUTLANDISH ILLINOIS

Missing from the Vault: Body Snatching

BOHEMIAN IMMIGRANTS VISITED THEIR ETHNIC CEMETERY in Chicago on December 28, 1878, and were outraged to find that a twelve-year-old girl named Mathilda S. was missing from her vault. She was located in the Chicago Medical College—and she wasn't exactly there on a scholarship.

⊢·◆·○·◆·◄

Cyrus McCormick, developer of the mechanical reaper, met the nonmechanical Reaper on May 13, 1884. As of May 4, 1885— nearly an entire year later!—a hired watchman still guarded his tomb in Graceland Cemetery, Chicago, to thwart body snatchers who might be tempted not to sell his long-dead remains to a medical school but rather hold them for ransom. The million- aire's family offered a generous salary but had difficulty finding someone willing to watch over the grave every night. At last they hired a superstitious man named Mike A.—but he was so spooked by the nature of his job that the strain killed him in the spring of 1885 and the McCormicks had to hire a second watchman.

Ghouls Just Want to Have Fun: Illinois

Were Chicago cemeteries plundered by a syndicate of professional grave robbers in the 1930s? Such was the charge made by the Cook County coroner in July 1934. He claimed that for several years undertakers and racketeers had joined forces to exhume the newly dead, strip them of their clothing and finery, steal their coffins, and rebury them wrapped in newspapers in cheap wooden boxes. Their clothing and caskets allegedly were reused by dishonest undertakers. He further claimed that the ghouls got away with it because they were politically connected.

Animals as Grave Robbers: Illinois

A hyena named Jim gnawed through the door of his cage in Chicago's Lincoln Park Zoo in mid-June 1897 and—being a scavenger of carrion—made a beeline for Graceland Cemetery, where he unearthed a number of graves. People who lived in the vicinity of the graveyard had to spend the night of June 15 with their hands over their ears, since Jim "made [the] night hideous with his howls."

The zoo's head keeper and a number of men spent June 16 trying to capture the animal with no assistance from the Chicago Police Department, the members of which expressed a preference for battling burglars.

Buried Alive: Illinois

Three Sicilians were hanged in Chicago on November 14, 1885. They had been convicted of murdering a man, cramming him in a trunk, and sending him on a free trip to Pittsburgh at baggage rates. The hanged men were Giovanni Azari, Agostino Gelardi, and Ignazio Silvestri.

After the execution, a weird rumor made the rounds that Giovanni did not actually die when hanged and that when the three coffins were opened at the cemetery, the attendants noticed that Giovanni's body "had changed its position and showed signs of life." The story continued, saying that the attendants feared that if Giovanni's resuscitation became public knowledge he would suffer the indignity of being hanged twice—so they humanely screwed the lid down and placed the coffin in the vault and let him suffocate. Was the rumor true? The president of the Society for the Burial of Indigent Italians—and that must have been some club—confirmed only that Giovanni's body had changed its position in the coffin.

The wife of Henry S., a prominent farmer in Atwood, died on March 1, 1889, and was on the verge of burial on March 3. At the graveside, the coffin was opened so everyone could have a last look at the deceased. Alarmed friends saw that her complexion was rosy and her limbs were supple rather than stiff. Fearing she might merely be in a state of suspended animation, they insisted the burial be postponed. Doctors tried to restore her to the land of the living. "Their efforts seem likely to prove successful, and the result is waited with great anxiety," said the newspapers, which neglected to tell us what happened next.

Wilhelmina S., age twenty-one, died of "rheumatism of the heart" in Chicago's Jefferson Park suburb on April 24, 1889. The burial was postponed because the girl displayed no signs of returning to dust—also, her nervous family noted, she had gone into a deathlike trance once before in Germany. Her family put her body in a bed and applied artificial heat in a forlorn hope of reviving her. The doctors did the best they could with the technology available to them at the time. They placed a mirror next to her lips: no vapor. They tried artificial respiration and abdominal pressure with no result. Then they performed a grim, drastic final test: they opened her tibial artery. No blood flowed, proving her heart was not pumping. Had she been alive, that test would probably have killed her.

But Wilhelmina's mother was so worried about premature burial that she ignored the doctors' findings and the young woman remained unburied more than a week after her death. In the meantime the family, which lived on the highway near the Northwestern Railroad station, was annoyed by travelers who wanted to enter their abode and gawk at Wilhelmina.

She was finally buried in Norwood Cemetery on May 3. And yet, noted a reporter, "Not the slightest discoloration or odor was detectable, although nine days had elapsed since death."

Upon hearing of the case, the physician Henry Tanner—who had achieved nationwide fame in 1880 by fasting for forty days—made remarks in an interview with the Associated Press that would scarcely provide comfort for relatives of the recently dead. Dr. Tanner said that the only sure proof of death was decomposition, "and an advanced stage of that." He added, "I take it that what I may say on this subject would have little weight because the enlightened public is aware of the utter unreliability of doctors' decisions that a person is dead. The cases of suspended animation in which the facts were discovered too late are entirely too numerous." Dr. Tanner estimated that at least one person was buried alive every week in the United States and recalled a couple such sensational occasions, including this one:

> I have a case in my mind where the body of a young man was buried in a vault, and in three years, the body was removed and found to be not decomposed. The physicians considered that fact strange, and laid the body on a dissecting table to study it. An incision was made with a scalpel, and instantly the man arose, being thoroughly resuscitated. He lived for years, too.

The embarrassed doctor called a press conference a couple of days later in which he stated that he had been badly misquoted.

Of course, he meant that the prematurely buried young man had lived three *days* in the vault, not three *years*.

⊱──────⊰

Close calls don't come much closer than the one experienced by Christina H. of East Saint Louis, Illinois. She sighed in her hospital bed on the morning of January 14, 1900, and afterward seemed to be dead to all intents and purposes. The doctor took her pulse, did other tests, and pronounced her deceased.

The undertaker came and performed his strange chores. He cleaned and partially bleached Christina's body and placed weights on her eyelids to keep them from flipping open during the funeral and giving onlookers a bad turn. He spread a cloth saturated with bleaching fluid on her face. Just as the undertaker was preparing to embalm the body, he heard the gentle clunk of some object hitting the floor. One of the eyelid weights had fallen off. As he replaced it, he thought he felt a slight movement of the eyelash. He double checked for a heartbeat, a pulse, and a sign of breath but detected nothing. He readied his hypodermic needles for injecting embalming fluid into Christina's artery when the eyelid weight fell off again. The shaken mortician "applied the most powerful test known to undertakers," in the words of a reporter who failed to tell readers just what this test entailed. This time there was a definite sign of life! The undertaker rushed Christina back to the hospital, where she was restored to her formerly grieving husband after having literally been saved by an eyelash.

Getting in the Last Word: Bizarre Epitaphs, Illinois

George Hays stabbed Harvey Telford in Centralia, Marion County. Harvey, age twenty-two, died the next day and George escaped. The dead man's family had the following inscription placed on his tombstone: "Murdered by George W. Hays. Harvey Telford died Jan. 18, 1879." They also included a carving of a butcher knife.

On Charles DuPlessis (d. 1907), Rosehill Cemetery, Chicago: "Now ain't that too bad."

A mysterious epitaph can be seen in tiny Pritchett Cemetery near Boulder. It is the subject of much folklore and speculation, but there is no confirmed explanation of its meaning:

> *Kiss me and I will go to sleep.*
> *Alice, first and last wife of Thomas Phillip.*
> *Talked to death by friends.*

The stone has no birth or death dates or any other information. However, it must date back to at least 1891 and appears to have been erected in a spirit of vengeance, as attested by an August 1891 news story from the *Pittsburgh Dispatch*, which states that Thomas purchased the stone from the Frazier and Leffel monument works of Centralia, Illinois. Allegedly, after dictating the strange inscription, Thomas said: "There now, I want it just as I write it; nothing more and nothing less. I propose to pay for just what I want." Then he walked away without a word of clarification, but with the air of a man who had just taken secret—and satisfying—revenge against someone.

Home Bodies: Keeping the Dead as Furniture, Illinois

In May 1912 Charles H.—overwrought with grief and not afraid of a little hard work—stole his wife's body from her grave in a Naperville cemetery and stashed her in her mother's barn. He threatened anyone who approached with a gun and an ax. Those who ventured close enough said Charles had the body propped upright and spoke to it for hours, trying to convince it to return to life. She didn't wanna, and the sheriff finally captured the distraught husband. For some reason, people suspected he might be insane.

Eccentric Interments, Illinois

It wasn't until Walter L. Newberry's widow Julia passed away in December 1885 that the true story of his burial became public knowledge. The wealthy Chicago merchant died at sea aboard the steamship *Pereire* on November 7, 1868; one of Newberry's acquaintances, New York banker W. A. Booth, urged the captain not to bury the body at sea but rather preserve it, at least until the ship reached its destination, Le Havre, France. Booth assured the captain that the dead man's family would pay any expenses incurred in keeping the body. A cask of Medford rum happened to be in the cargo, and Newberry was placed in it. The alcohol preserved his body and the barrel proved such a handy make-shift casket that Newberry was buried in it—rum and all—in Chicago's Graceland Cemetery. Meanwhile, much of Newberry's fortune went to build a library.

That's the fun version of the story, as told by eyewitnesses. The killjoy version—as told by W. E. Morris, the New York Health Department authority who signed off on the body's shipment from New York to Chicago—is that Newberry was packed in a boring lead case, as required by French law. Believe whichever version you choose.

━┼━━O━━┼━

John M. of Ellington loved his dog Honey so much that his will requested that he and the dear, deceased dog be cremated and their ashes placed in the same jar to mingle together forever. At some point John changed his mind and ordered instead that he and Honey simply be buried in the same coffin when his end came—which it did in November 1903.

━┼━━O━━┼━

Eliza S., an invalid, spent the last five years of her life looking at a cornfield from the window of her home in Decatur. When she was buried on December 1, 1903, the coffin was decorated with cornstalks instead of flowers as per her dying request.

Israel R.'s funeral was halted in progress at Oak Woods Cemetery, Chicago, on April 25, 1921, with the news that his wife was on her deathbed and could live only a few more hours at most. The relatives held a conference and decided it was only proper to bury husband and wife together. The hearse was sent back to the family home and mourners waited until the stricken wife's end came. The couple were buried in the same grave on April 27.

Strange Wills, Illinois

At Brushy Fork, near Rockford, there lived a woman—the press preserved her anonymity—who was disappointed in love in 1849. She spent the rest of her life, like Dickens's Miss Havisham, taking revenge on the male gender. The "man hater" had enough money to live a comfortable life but refused to speak to any man. On the rare occasions when she came to town, she did all her shopping with female clerks. In 1897 she bought a cemetery plot and made her will, in which she instructed that there should be no male preacher, no male pallbearers, and no men in the procession. She ordered that a woman should drive the hearse and women lower the coffin and fill the grave.

Breakneck Burial

"The dead travel fast."—Bram Stoker.

Mary L., described as "winsome and beautiful," died in Chicago on August 18, 1880. Her remains were taken first to Godfrey for services at the Episcopal church there, and then by fast freight train to Carrollton, where she immediately received a midnight burial on August 24. The moonlight ceremony was not intended to be romantic. Mary died in the height of summer in the days before widespread embalming or refrigeration, and she had been dead nearly a week before she arrived in Carrollton. All was in haste by necessity.

Boneyard Boorishness

After six-year-old Willie G. drowned in Lake Michigan in July 1886, his body was taken to Chicago's Calvary Cemetery for burial. It was the grieving mother's desire to lay him beside her husband, John. But when the funeral procession arrived, it was found that they forgot to bring the deed to the family plot. The cemetery superintendent responded to the technicality in this admirably understated fashion: he forbade burial—he even forbade a grave to be dug!—until the deed was produced; he called the police to help kick the mourners out of the graveyard and threatened to fire a shotgun. One mourner knocked the weapon from his hands; it discharged, resulting in a general panic but no injuries. The superintendent's son fired a horse pistol and a mourner got a flesh wound. The angry party defiantly placed the boy's coffin in a vault and then "roughly handled" the superintendent.

This was not the first time the superintendent fancied himself autocrat of the cemetery. On Memorial Day 1886, he ordered a contingent of Union veterans off the grounds simply because one of them had referred to God in a speech at the grave of Col. Mulligan. ("Only priests are allowed to say prayers here," he said.) After the veterans chased the superintendent to his office, they were heard to mutter something about giving him a ride on a rail.

Tomb Treasures

In April 1891 a woman in Chicago received the welcome news that she had inherited two million dollars from the estate of her uncle Isaac P., who'd died in 1834. Why the long delay? Other relatives were unable to prove they were related to Isaac because they had no record of his birth. As the years passed, someone

remembered that the birth record was in the family Bible—
which had been passed down to Isaac's brother Jacob—who in
turn buried it with his daughter Susanna on June 4, 1866. The
family got permission to open the girl's grave in Washington
Street Cemetery, Easton, Massachusetts, and there in the coffin
was the Bible. Fortunately for the woman—*very* fortunately!—
the record of Isaac's birth was legible.

Baggage Blunder

Mary W. of Chicago journeyed to Pittsburgh on June 22, 1911,
to bury a brass urn containing the ashes of her husband, who'd
died a month before. But because of a railroad baggage handler's
mistake, she ended up with a box of mechanics' tools. In the
meantime, a New York chauffeur received not the tools he was
expecting but an urn full of her husband's ashes. Presumably the
mix-up was resolved to everyone's satisfaction and they all had
a good laugh over it years later.

Clubs You Wouldn't Have Wanted to Join: Illinois

A man sang a hymn before his fellow club members in February
1912: "There is a land of pure delight / Where saints immortal
reign." This was an accomplishment because that man had been
dead since 1906. His voice warbled from a phonograph record.

That was rather the idea behind the Borrowed Time Club of
Oak Park, formed in 1902. It consisted of men, all over age seventy, who recorded their voices. Then when a member died, the
others gathered to listen to his voice laughing, making witti-
cisms, and/or singing. Sometimes they even sang along, and the
voices of the living and the dead joined to form an inspiring, and
slightly creepy, chorus.

Timely Ends, Part One

Some lucky midwesterners have predicted with uncanny accuracy the dates of their own deaths. For example, Fred H. of

Rockford said, "I think I'll die today," to his coworker Frank as they commuted to their factory on November 7, 1922. It was not merely idle workplace chatter. Fred—who had been complaining of heart trouble—hit the floor dead three hours later.

To Avoid Gaucherie, Sip Your Wine

One morning in December 1888, Richard B. of 106 McHenry Street, Chicago, saw a bottle of enticing red liquid in his cupboard. Thinking it wine, he chug-a-lugged every drop of it. He drank it so fast that he didn't even taste it, because only after the bottle was empty did he notice that the contents had an awful flavor. Had he sipped it like a gentleman, he might have avoided the awful thing that happened next.

When his wife found out what Richard had imbibed, she shrieked and sent for a doctor. The stuff was embalming fluid, left behind by an undertaker who'd used it to preserve cousin Charles's remains there in the house. (In those days, embalming often was done at home rather than at funeral parlors.)

The unlucky Richard went to bed, where he underwent fever, convulsions, and pain despite the doctor's ministrations with stomach pump and emetics. He died after five hours spent in the perfection of misery. Essentially, he was embalmed alive. The *Chicago Herald* remarked: "The doctor said the man's stomach had been burned out by the fluid."

Impractical Jokes

Pranksters knew Peter K. of Norris City believed in ghosts and was afraid of the same. They drove a nail in his roof, attached a tin can to the nail, and ran a string from the can to the ground. By rubbing the string with rosin, the jokers could produce unearthly noises. This they did on the night of January 11, 1904. Peter was found dead in bed the next morning with "a look of horror frozen on his face."

><+<>+<>+<

Joseph G. of Chicago was an obedient husband. When he came home drunk on August 11, 1905, his wife jokingly told him to jump in the lake and drown himself. He took her suggestion; rescuers fished Joseph out of the water alive but he died in the hospital two hours later. The coroner found a note in his pocket reading, "This is to certify that my wife, Maggie, told me to leave the house and go to the lake and drown myself. Goodbye and God forgive her." Maggie was left to explain that she had been only making a funny.

Creativity in Suicide: Illinois

George B., a self-styled atheist, published a bulletin on July 21, 1878, telling the residents of Capron that he would deliver an "infidel lecture" at Thornton Hall on July 23, at the conclusion of which he would shoot himself onstage. Admission was a dollar a head and the proceeds were to be used to pay for his funeral. If any money was left over, George stipulated that it be used to buy volumes by Charles Darwin and Thomas Huxley for the local library. Naturally, the hall was packed to the rafters on July 23; let us be charitable and assume that the townsfolk thought George was only bluffing. But he wasn't: after delivering an oration "of wonderful power in manner and tone," he produced a derringer and scattered his gray matter hither and yon—mostly yon. His body was sent to friends in Cincinnati, and the way was paved for further survival of the fittest.

A man who lived on West Jackson Street in Chicago was despondent because he couldn't get work. So he found work of another sort on the night of November 20, 1888, experimenting with ways to kill himself. These included shooting himself in the head, severing the arteries in both wrists, cutting his throat, and slashing his temple.

His name is lost to history, but the staff at Chicago's Palmer House hotel long remembered a "drummer" (traveling salesman) who left a note in July 1876 stating that he meant to kill himself in a spectacular fashion that would never be forgotten. The man filled the bathtub in his suite with scalding water; tied a rope around his neck; soaked his clothes with kerosene; tied one end of a string to a revolver pointing at his heart and the other end to his vest; held a dagger to his chest; and then attached a fuse to his clothing. After making these Rube Goldberg preparations, the drummer stood on the edge of the tub, took a dose of morphine, and lit the fuse. Flames enveloped his clothes. When the string burned up the gun went off, shooting him in the chest. He lurched forward, tightening the noose and stabbing himself in the chest. The fire burned through the rope and he fell into the tub. The coroner had his work cut out for him in trying to determine whether the salesman died by poisoning, hanging, shooting, burning, stabbing, scalding, or drowning.

⊢⊣◦⊣◦⊢⊣

Some days you just can't win. On May 23, 1914, Reginald B. killed his girlfriend, Florence, by breaking her neck at Downer's Grove. Immediately afterward he felt remorse and went to Aurora, bought some poison and returned to Florence's body so he could journey to the Garden of Spirits while lying beside her. He took the poison and survived, much to his disappointment. Reginald went back to Aurora, purchased more poison, returned to the corpse, and survived his second attempt at a suitably dramatic suicide. Peeved, he waited a few days. On May 26 he leaped into a quarry pit at Naperville with a view to drowning himself and found to his amazement that he couldn't sink. Finally deciding that it was time to stop fooling around, he jumped under a moving train. That accomplished his purpose. He left a note claiming the death of Florence was accidental.

⊢⊣◦⊣◦⊢⊣

Judging from the meticulous method of suicide he chose, one suspects that Louis W. was a neat freak. On the night of September 16, 1889, the former cabinetmaker put on his Sunday best, got a shave, polished his shoes, lit a stogie, and selected a pleasant spot on the bank of the river at Rockford. He lay down on his back, crossed his feet, tied a handkerchief around his neck so his nice shirt would not be bloodstained, and shot himself in the temple. He was found two days later "resting peacefully in death, cigar in his mouth, and a satisfied look on his face."

▸◂●◂▸◂

"If you will come tonight, you will find me dead and have a good story." So said the note Walter H. sent to a Chicago woman reporter on January 26, 1892. Unable to resist a scoop, she hurried to the address given and found that Walter was as good as his word. He was dead from poison.

▸◂●◂▸◂

A young man who signed the register at Chicago's Kimball Hotel with the pseudonym "E. L. Bryan" went to his room on November 29, 1896, and drank laudanum. He tore the labels out of his clothing so his identity could not be discerned, but he entertained himself during the twenty minutes it took to cross the Jordan by writing notes on his dying sensations for the benefit of medical science:

> To M.D.—Drank one ounce of laudanum. After five minutes feel little or no pain. Heart action now pronounced. A slight pain in stomach. (Note—My stomach is very weak, having suffered for years from acute dyspepsia.) Ten minutes— Condition about the same. Pulse rapid and pains in wrists and slight pain in region of heart. Hand trembles. A feeling of dullness with more pain in all parts of the body. (Note—Will keep up this description of effects as long as possible. Hope it will be of use to medical science.) Eyes show change. A feeling of drowsiness coming on. A sort of a feeling of intoxication

accompanied by slight fever. Twenty minutes—Pain increasing. A slight perspiration started. Am getting sleepy. Have a sort of a numb feeling and no pain.

There was more, but after writing the last sentence the anonymous man's handwriting was impossible to decipher.

>⊷⊶⊷O⊷⊶⊷<

Eighteen-year-old Marie S. of Louisville gassed herself in a Chicago hotel room on June 29, 1903. She was to inherit $10,000 when she turned twenty-one but her suicide note explained that she found it too hard for "a good girl" to make a living in Chicago until then. In modern currency, her inheritance would have been equal to over $200,000.

>⊷⊶⊷O⊷⊶⊷<

Anna P., a twenty-four-year-old actress, was having a philosophical conversation with her roommate Sally in Chicago's Inter-Ocean Hotel on July 29, 1903.

"What would become of my soul if I killed myself?" asked Anna.

"You'd go to hell," replied Sally.

"What have I done that my soul should be tormented on earth and go condemned into the next world? I don't believe it," exclaimed Anna, who punctuated her sentence by shooting herself.

>⊷⊶⊷O⊷⊶⊷<

Fifteen-year-old John S. of Fordville was accused in early March 1907 of stealing a calf hide. He avoided arrest by hiding in a church for nearly a week and then killed himself by propping up a heavy rolltop desk, positioning himself under it, and dropping it on his neck. He was found on March 10 with pockets full of grains of corn—his only food for a week—and a knife in his hand, evidently a backup means of suicide if plan A did not succeed.

In February 1923 Marietta C. of Chicago schemed up a clever way to kill herself while masking the true cause of her death: she put poison in a bottle of laxative salts. The plan worked to perfection, but had an unintended consequence when, on March 14, her sister Anna unsuspectingly went to the medicine chest and . . .

Betty L., a twenty-five-year-old blonde who had ties to a ring of jewel thieves, was beaten and strangled by a hit man in her deluxe apartment in Chicago's North Side on January 13, 1928. Investigators found a suicide note written by Betty, which meant that the hit man could have saved himself the trouble had he waited a bit longer.

August J., a Chicago janitor, committed an absurd suicide on August 2, 1931. He bought a coffin, a cemetery plot, and a bottle of embalming fluid for the convenience of the undertaker. After donning his best clothes, August turned on the gas, climbed into his coffin, and strummed a harp until he took his place among the silent majority. When the authorities found August's body, his fingers were resting on the strings.

Phil H., an unemployed Chicago iron worker, used his amateur electrician's knowledge to put a creative end to his own existence on May 11, 1932. He made electrodes by soldering razor blades to the ends of two wires, which he placed on his chest. He covered them with a damp cloth and held them in place with a belt. Phil attached the other ends of the wires to coils to conduct current from the B-battery eliminator—in effect, turning his radio into an ersatz electric chair. He switched on the current in the radio's receiver and electrocuted himself on the spot. Phil's triumph was thought to be the nation's first case of "suicide by radio." His high-tech death occurred during a radio show called *Beautiful Thoughts*.

⊢•⊕•○•⊕•⊣

Julius J. wanted to drown himself in the Chicago River. Problem was, he was just too good a swimmer. He spent weeks practicing tying his hands behind his back until he thought he could render himself helpless. His father identified the body on August 8, 1932.

⊢•⊕•○•⊕•⊣

On October 3, 1938, Valentine H. lit a fire in his Chicago backyard, placed a length of pipe—with a twelve-gauge shotgun shell inside—in the flames and sat in front of it. A few minutes later the heat made the shell discharge. It flew out of the pipe as though expelled from a shotgun barrel, killing him instantly. A crowd of curious boys peeping over the fence watched the rare spectacle unfold.

An Inventor Proves His Point

William S. of Chicago was obsessed with the idea of inventing an explosive that packed the punch of dynamite but would be safer. On July 14, 1932, he told friends, "I believe I've almost got it!" A few hours later his machine shop was blown to particles. William's decapitated body was found beside his workbench.

Bitter Ironies, Part Two

One doctor in Carbondale diagnosed his own illness and filled out his death certificate. It was signed by another doctor after he passed away on March 10, 1922.

Romantic Suicides, Part One

On May 23, 1911, widower Charles B.'s daughter encountered him on the streets of Bath, walking toward the cemetery. He handed her a note and made her promise not to read it until she got home. When the child opened the note, it read: "You will find me down at the cemetery over mother's grave." Charles's daughters later found that he had written his self-chosen death date in the family Bible.

While Charles ended his life atop a grave, the reverse happened on September 19, 1913, when a woman attended her husband's funeral in Mount Greenwood Cemetery, Chicago. A few minutes later she gave birth to their son. The undertaker gave mother and infant a ride home in his carriage.

What Gave It Away?

Casper S. was a Chicago baker who worked the night shift. When he came home at five in the morning on June 10, 1882, his wife greeted him at the door, dressed in white and saying, "Come see how the children have all died and gone to Heaven! See how pretty they are with nice flowers!"

Casper stepped into the house to find his four children stretched out on the floor, holding flowers and dressed in white grave clothes and gaily colored ribbons their mother had gotten for them. His wife herself died two hours later. She had poisoned all of her children and herself.

The oldest daughter, age twelve, left several notes. One, addressed to her father, said: "Forgive me; we have to leave you. Mamma thought it was the best we could do." Another asked him to bury them decently and told him that she left some money so he could purchase flowers. She also wrote several notes to schoolmates, one of which read: "Mother was always sick, you know, and thought of dying often, and how we would be treated, and so thought it best all of us die at once, and bought something to kill us—baby first, Annie second, Tony third, I after and then mother. We did not suffer much, and now we are all out of trouble."

It was suspected that Mrs. S. was insane.

Even Anarchists Should Read Labels

The Chicago anarchist riot of May 1886 is the stuff of history textbooks. One incident of the fracas is not so well known: On May 5, a group of anarchists and labor activists—who obviously thought nothing of cheating a hardworking shop owner—broke into a drugstore on the corner of Center Avenue and Eighteenth Street, grabbed every bottle containing alcoholic beverages they could find, and carried them away to have free drinks. The anarchists may not have believed in laws or rules, but they would have been better served if they had paid closer attention to the labels on the bottles. One contained carbolic acid and since it closely resembled whisky, each triumphant rioter took a swig and passed the bottle to the next. By the time they realized something wasn't quite right with the bottle's contents, a half dozen had taken a drink. Within a few days, two were dead and three more were pounding on Death's door.

Poor Jessie Is Driven to Her Grave

When would those threatening anonymous letters ever cease? Poor Jessie Z. White, daughter of respected carpenter James S. White of Joliet, got them on a regular basis starting in 1886, when she was sixteen. And she wasn't the only recipient. Every young man she met at a dance or social function got a letter from the fiend. All of them were written in the same hand, and all told the most horrible lies about her. Jessie theorized that the letters came from some boy whose attentions she had rejected in the past, but she had no idea who it might be.

It all started when a Joliet newspaper printed an obituary mailed on a postcard: "October 13, 1886. Miss Jessie White, adopted daughter of J. S. White, of quick consumption. Funeral notice later." The card was signed "Her mother," but it was actually sent by the unknown letter writer who would make Jessie's future life a torment. He also mailed a notice to Chamberlain's undertaking firm.

He repeated his "prank" in April 1887, this time sending notices to young men of the town, requesting them to serve as pallbearers at Jessie's funeral. The undertaker got a weird letter too, written in a confessional tone and strongly suggesting that the writer was angry because the aloof Jessie would not bestow her romantic favors upon him. It concluded with an unsubtle hint that he planned to murder her:

> Mr. Chamberlain: I have now laid my plans so that the family will have to grieve the death of their daughter Jessie. It seems as though she wants to live in single blessedness, for no strange man can win a smile from her. She passes us young fellows on the street without even looking at us. She is a little above medium height, has black hair, blue eyes, and a lovely figure; in all, she is a prepossessing young lady, or rather a blushing maiden of "sweet sixteen." I have persecuted her by sending notes concerning her death to many prominent men in this city, all bearing the signature of her mother; but since that has failed to humble her I will pursue a different course. I always respected her for being shy of the men, but she carries her independence too far. This city is too quiet. It needs something like a murder case to make excitement, and it's always catching before hanging. Your service will be needed soon, I think, if the execution of my plans are carried out all right. So look out for a tradgide [sic]. I am on the safe side, for my writing and spelling furnishes me a disguise.

A newspaper carried the story of Jessie's strange persecution—and then the letter writer, who seemed to relish notoriety, really took the gloves off. The White family found black funerary crape tied on their doorknob one morning. A letter dropped on their doorstep read:

> My Dear Little Jessie: I wish you all that happiness affords you this week, but next week you will be lyeing [sic] under the sod, just where you ought to have been before you broke any hearts. I intend to take your life with my own hands, and I am willing to hang for your own

sweet sake. I have been attending the opera-house this spring quite regular, but only saw you there at a matinee with your sister. I would have shot you then, but fearing your sister might receive the bullet, I put the shooting off for another time, but you will get it yet. [Then began a passage censored by the press.] I once more tell you that your young life will be brought to a close next week. I knew I could make an excitement in this city! Well, goodbye, dearest, but I must tell you that this is written with many tears, for I love you, but still I hate you for your independence. Please excuse bad writing, but I dare not write with my own hand, for fear of detection.

The letter was published, and then he sent another.

My Precious Doomed Darling: I did not intend to write to you any more persecuting letters, for your time of living is short without anything else to torment you, but I want to warn you again to be on your guard for I am going to shoot you this week. I think it is no more than right that I should let you know what danger you are in every day and night. You are a young and innocent girl, and I know that by shooting you I will be committing the most horrible crime that can't be forgiven by God or man. I well know that I will be lynched, and I know I will richly deserve to be, but the sooner you and I are out of the world's way the better it will be for both of us, for I don't care to die if I had to to-morrow. The papers state that the villain ought to be lynched for what he has already done, but if they catch me it won't be until I have accomplished my ends. I had a grand chance to pop you over last night when you was in the parlor with your sister but just as I was making aim at your heart you suddenly turned and left the room, but any way I stood where I could not be seen and listened to your sister playing "My Grandfather's Clock" on the piano. I dropped my note when the front rooms were vacated. Well, this is my last letter to you, my doomed Jessie. You won't receive letters after this week. Good bye, darling.

For all his murderous braggadocio, the persecutor seemed content to write threatening letters. He neither showed himself to Jessie nor physically harmed her. And although he said he would write no more letters, he continued to do so.

The unknown tormentor escalated his cruelty: he sent letters slandering Jessie's character to the young men of Joliet and to local newspapers, which of course weren't about to print such libelous screeds. A comparison of the letters proved they were all written by the same person.

The mayor sent two policemen to watch the family's house. One night a buggy pulled up and a young man got out. He was Jessie's cousin David. When the cops pounced on him, he pulled a gun, thinking he was being robbed. The fact that David was armed was good enough evidence for the police, who arrested him although he swore he was only there to play a game of cards.

At David's trial in circuit court, Jessie's father expressed bafflement. He swore that his daughter had never had a serious boyfriend, had never turned down a marriage proposal, seemed popular, and had no known enemies. There was no solid evidence against David and he was released under a peace bond.

The author continued his war against Jessie. Letters were flung on the family's porch and pushed under the doors. The family became afraid even to step outside. In desperation, they sent Jessie out East for a while. To no avail: the villain figured out where she was and sent his threats to her even there.

At last Jessie could stand the torrent of abuse no longer. On March 19, 1890, she put on her best clothes and went for a buggy ride, beaming at any acquaintances she passed on the street. When nearly in front of the Hotel Monroe, she stopped the horse, produced a revolver, and shot herself in the heart. Some nearby gentlemen caught her body before it hit the ground. She left a note addressed to her long-suffering family—a final cry of despair—in the same box that held the revolver:

I am tired of life and am going to shoot myself and deny the letter-writer the pleasure of doing it. Three years is long enough to be tortured by him, and there is no prospect of any peace for us as long as I live, and inasmuch as he has promised to take my life, I really think he means to, but now he never shall. If he found any pleasure in torturing me I hope he will be satisfied now, for he has driven me to destroy my soul. All I have to say now is for you to forget and forgive me for the wicked act I am about to commit. Now, dear folks, I love you all so dearly I could not live if any of you were to be taken from me, so I want you to think it was all for the best I should leave this world.

In a separate letter she named the undertaker and pallbearers she wanted—all of whom, perhaps significantly, had received slandering letters about her from the poison penman. Poor Jessie was borne to her grave, and the only consolation was that her strange persecution finally ended.

But that's when things got really interesting.

In February 1890—six weeks before Jessie committed suicide—a mutual friend introduced her to a young man named Hice, a doctor's son. The very next day, Hice got one of the by now infamous letters blackening Jessie's character and calling her immoral. Funny thing was, absolutely nobody knew of his introduction to Jessie except Hice himself, the mutual friend, and Jessie. Hice, formerly a total stranger to Jessie, swore he didn't write it. He regarded the mutual friend as "above suspicion." That left only one suspect.

A few weeks before Jessie's death, her cousin from Chicago, W. H. Parks, suggested the family turn the anonymous letters over to the postal authorities. Her father thought that was a great idea and alerted the post office in Chicago. The matter was kept top secret—no one in Joliet knew about it except the family—yet at this juncture the constant stream of letters mysteriously ceased, and Jessie started avoiding the company of Parks. She also became noticeably emotionally unbalanced.

A newspaper reporter wrote with maddening vagueness: "Many of the letters to young men accused Miss White of acts of immorality. The phrases used by the anonymous letter writer were those which a woman would use." (Whatever that could have meant!)

In addition, the mayor revealed that he had secretly personally watched the family house for three weeks. He also hired other men for surveillance. And although they saw no one approaching or leaving the place, the threatening letters came anyway.

Yes, it was true: the disturbed Jessie had spent three and a half years sending anonymous threatening and libelous letters to herself, to male acquaintances, to newspapers. Was it a desperate cry for attention? Did she have a persecution complex? Was it a demented scheme for meeting boys? (The young men who received those letters about her made a point of coming to her residence and sympathizing with her torments like gentlemen.) Had she been planning suicide all along and thought that an elaborate campaign of fake persecution would make her act somehow easier for her family to bear? These were all questions fit for psychiatrists to answer—but as psychiatry was in its infancy in 1890, modern therapists will have to diagnose the strange workings of Jessie's mind from a distance.

The Gambler Who Folded

Folding beds are an endless source of amusement in French farces and Three Stooges comedies, but on at least one occasion the furniture proved fatal. On August 25, 1897, Chicago gambler Al H. entered his apartment at 398 Cottage Grove Avenue and sat down on the edge of his folding bed. It folded and broke Al's neck, killing him nearly instantaneously.

Somnambulistic Slayings, Part One

Is it possible to murder and maim while asleep? The magic of backbreaking research has turned up several examples ranging from laughable to convincing. John M. of Chicago shot to death his wife and two children and then attempted to take his own life by shooting himself and slashing his throat. His explanation: "I did it in my sleep!" But the prosecution proved that John was a habitual domestic abuser and on August 5, 1905, the jury sentenced him to hang. On February 16, 1906, John walked onto the scaffold and "raised his head up," as Joseph phrased it in Genesis.

Power of Suggestion

Elderly Virginia J. of Chicago drank from a bottle containing "some kind of brownish fluid." She felt poorly afterward and concluded that she had been poisoned. Her terror was so intense that her heart burst and she died of fear. The coroner's verdict at the autopsy held on December 22, 1903: "Not poisoned, but dead because she thought she had been poisoned."

A Hard Choice

On September 2, 1905, Nels A., a motor inspector for the Illinois Steel Company in South Chicago, was repairing the arm of a crane that dangled directly over a pit full of hot metal. When the arm moved, Nels lost his balance. The only thing within reach was an uninsulated live wire. He had a split-second decision to make: should he fall into the molten metal below or instantly electrocute himself by grabbing the wire? He chose the latter course of action.

Closing Remarks, Illinois

Joseph H. of Chicago drank carbolic acid on June 26, 1912. He had some idea that his wife might be a trifle upset by the news; his suicide note included this line: "Only have Mr. A. Rus, saloonkeeper at 1946 South Center Avenue, tell it to my wife in a roundabout way so she will not get scared too much."

Warren P., twenty-one years old, engaged to be married, and heir to a million-dollar fortune, found the prospect of self-destruction more attractive than youth, love, or money. He poisoned himself in Chicago on November 11, 1915, leaving a note to his fiancée, which, like the peace of God, passeth understanding: "I have gone. You must not look for me, for it will be useless. I love you. You must be brave. It won't be long. I will keep you warm and happy in the land of the great forest and the rolling prairies. I will always think of you and you will know."

A traveling salesman from Portland, Oregon, drank poison in the Burton Hotel in Aurora on August 6, 1921. He left a note for the coroner stating his paramount concern: he requested that he be buried wearing his stylish bone rim glasses.

Karl G. of Chicago, a hit-and-run driver, felt such guilt after injuring two girls that he felt suicide was the only honorable choice. Before joining the majority in August 1938 he wrote a note: "As judge, jury and executioner, I have heard the evidence and passed sentence upon myself. There is no appeal."

Picture This

Orla C., a photographer from Mattoon, wanted to prove that the chemicals he used for his work were harmless. On November 25, 1913, a skeptic double dog dared him to drink them, and he complied. That's what the coroner's jury determined, anyway.

Let the Unpleasantness Ensue!

On the evening of October 22, 1922, H. P. Zimmerman's maid Marie C. was struck by a car as she walked on the Lincoln Highway near Batavia. But because it was the Halloween season, motorists thought her body was just a straw dummy. For an entire night, an estimated hundreds of gleeful drivers sped up and ran over the "effigy." In the morning a pedestrian named Cora realized that the dummy was no dummy. The victim had to be identified by her clothes because, as the coroner determined, every bone in Marie's body was broken and "her flesh had been churned to jelly."

History Repeats Itself

Somebody murdered Earle E. in Richmond on February 24, 1907, and left the gun beside the body. The weapon was acquired by the dead man's brother Charles, who carried it with him for the rest of his life. Charles thirsted for revenge: "Someday I'll find the man who killed Earle," he would say, "and when I do I'll kill him with the same gun." Charles, a wealthy Chicago attorney, gave up his practice and dedicated the rest of his life to avenging his brother.

Only one thing interested Charles as much as tracking down and killing his brother's murderer: his private island in Nippersink Creek. That's where a reverend found him dead in his own forest on the Fourth of July, 1931.

The unnerving part was that Charles, age sixty-four, was shot to death with the same gun that killed his brother Earle twenty-four years before, and in nearly identical circumstances. He was shot once below the heart, just like Earle; the 1907 homicide also had taken place on the private island; rumors held that both Earle and Charles were assassinated by a poacher. (Both brothers were game wardens.) The coroner remarked, "That's just the trouble. The circumstances are entirely too similar."

Had the object of Charles's search found him first and gotten the drop on him? There were signs of a struggle at the death scene and the gun was found a hundred feet from the body, so suicide was ruled out.

Charles's murder is still unsolved.

Bad Advice from the Spirit World

Louisa Lindloff *saw dead people*, provided it was made worth her while: she was a professional Spiritualist medium and healer. Her alleged powers made her the wonder of her Chicago neighborhood. Folks were especially impressed by her most beloved possession, a crystal ball that was worth five hundred dollars, according to newspaper reports published after she became famous in a way that was not to her liking. Skeptical persons claimed the item was worth more in the nature of fifty cents. Louisa said that the ball contained a tear shed by Cleopatra, which gave the crystal its occult qualities. She explained: "When I gaze into the ball I see the tear in its center expand in size and within it I see what will happen in future years." Gossips wondered how she could have afforded to buy such a priceless artifact, even as they lined her pocketbook with payments for readings and séances.

This exotic woman was born in Colmar, Germany, on February 4, 1871. In 1888 she married her first husband, Julius Graunke, and a few years later they immigrated to Milwaukee, where he became a saloon keeper. They had three children, Frieda, Alma, and Arthur. Despite Louisa's claim that she was blessed with the Gift, misfortune seemed to dog her every step. When the run of bad luck finally ended, she was the sole survivor in her family. Julius died on August 12, 1905. His symptoms baffled physicians, who at length decided that he met his end from sunstroke. Fortunately for the bereaved widow, the late Julius was insured for $2,300. The thirty-five-year-old psychic married her second husband, twenty-year-old William Lindloff, on November 7, 1906.

Tragedy struck again with the illness of John Otto, William's brother and one-time boyfriend of Frieda. Louisa disapproved of her brother-in-law's courting her daughter because John Otto was a heavy drinker. Nevertheless, she thought enough of the fellow to buy him a generous insurance policy with herself as the beneficiary. She emerged $2,000 richer when he died foaming at the mouth on October 12, 1907.

The family's bad luck got worse. Eighteen-year-old Frieda died on June 11, 1908, of what the doctors took to be typhoid fever. Her mother's grief was assuaged somewhat by the $1,350 worth of insurance she collected. Afterward, Louisa, her children, and second husband moved to Chicago.

The marriage to William was short-lived, as was William himself despite his youth. He died a raving maniac on August 3, 1910. The supposed cause of death was heart disease. His widow weathered the tragedy $1,625 richer thanks to the friendly folks at the Prudential life insurance company. Neighbors were scandalized by the lack of decorum Louisa showed at her relatives' funerals, which she arranged to resemble "pleasure parties."

No doubt putting her psychic powers to work, Louisa realized that her seventeen-year-old daughter Alma would be the next to go and insured the girl for $2,300. Alma died almost a year after William, also allegedly of heart disease. A doctor was called in to see the sick girl and later testified that several days before Alma's death, Louisa told him that she would die on August 4, 1911, and—lo!—her prophecy proved correct. The spirits gave her the information, she said. No one ever seemed to ask why Louisa, who made her living as a psychic healer, was unable to heal her own ailing relatives, but we shall let that pass in a spirit of charity.

All of these calamities illustrated the necessity of having a good life insurance policy in this world of uncertainty, so Louisa insured her last surviving child, Arthur, for $3,375. The agents at Prudential seemed unwary even though she was always the sole beneficiary of the policies and dressed in mourning more frequently than the law of averages dictated. She had taken out a mere $1,000 policy on herself, reserving for others the privilege of being insured for larger amounts.

Fifteen-year-old Arthur took ill on June 2, 1912. He complained about the sandy, weird-tasting water his mother gave him. Louisa again brought in the doctor, who performed an examination and told the mother that he suspected it was a case of poisoning. "Impossible!" she said—unless he had been poisoned by the chemicals in his wallpaper. The doctor found her explanation farfetched and consulted another physician. Over the mother's strenuous objections, the doctors insisted that Arthur be taken to a hospital. As she had with her daughter Alma, Louisa accurately predicted the exact date her son would die: June 13. The initial verdict was pancreatic trouble, but the doctor requested that the body be taken to the morgue and inspected by the coroner.

Arthur's death was one coincidence too many for the police, though perhaps they should have started getting skeptical three or four corpses earlier. Within a mere seven years, the seeress had lost two husbands, a brother-in-law, and three children but had gained nearly $13,000 in insurance. At the request of the coroner, on June 14 the police picked up a very indignant Louisa—did Cleopatra's mystic tear see that one coming?— and grilled her at the station for a couple of hours. She stoutly maintained that all the deaths in her family were from natural causes, and what was more, she had *no poison* in her house. Not content to take a lady's word as her bond, four ungallant detectives searched her house at 2044 Ogden Avenue and found rat poison, a box of mercury, some suspect brown powder, several bottles clearly labeled "poison," vials of white powder, and many empty bottles for chemists to examine. This was plenty enough evidence to have Louisa arrested on suspicion. Detectives also discovered some of the tools used in her trade. In addition to the soon-to-be-famous crystal ball, they found a typewritten letter from a New York astrologer who'd cast her horoscope. I quote it verbatim, for most of its prophecies would come true in spades with the notable exception of the last sentence: "You shall have a little trouble during the year 1912, and one of your immediate relatives will die. You will fall heir to some property and cash, but you will have trouble in collecting it. After you have received your legacy you will spend the rest of the year in traveling." On a less cosmic note, the detectives also found a trunk catalog and a wig among Louisa's possessions. She admitted that she had been planning to leave the city, hence her eagerness to buy a trunk, but she refused to state the intended purpose of the wig.

At the time of her arrest, Louisa had only thirty dollars and no bank account, apparently having squandered her vast fortune on such things as wigs, horoscopes, and crystal balls. Her public image was not burnished when it was revealed that she was so eager to collect her son Arthur's insurance money that she sent her boarder, Henry K., to the Prudential office to pick up a death claim certificate the day after the boy's death. The police arrested Henry just to be on the safe side but released him days later.

The authorities at the Fillmore Street police station permitted Louisa to take liberties that they probably would not have allowed the average male prisoner. For example, they let her attend Arthur's funeral at Oak Ridge Cemetery on June 16, accompanied by a police guard of course. Possibly nervous about the impending results of the autopsy, she glossed over her earlier wallpaper explanation with a brand new story. She claimed that she fed Arthur a can of tuna the day before he took sick and that if any poison was found in his body, it must have come from the bad fish. She told reporters with a straight face: "Because I carried insurance on his life is no reason why I should be arrested. I will consult the spirits in the crystal, and they will direct me as to what steps to take in order to obtain justice." And she did exactly that, since the indulgent police allowed her to keep the prized crystal ball in her cell. According to Louisa, the ghost of Arthur communicated with her through the crystal and reassured her that, with help from the spirit world, she would be exonerated. When telling a *Chicago Tribune* reporter of these wonders, she made a personal remark about one of her persecutors: "I have not been able to convey a message to my last husband, William, but Arthur will find him. My son declared the police had made a great mistake and the spirits will punish Capt. [Bernard] Baer for his part in my arrest."

When the coroner questioned Louisa in her cell, he could not resist staring into her crystal ball. "Do you see anything?" she asked.

"Yes, I see your two dead husbands and your three children standing at your right side. They are accusing you of killing them."

Perhaps the coroner thought that would scare a confession out of her, but she was equal to the occasion. "You lie!" she shouted. "They are standing to my left, and they are saying that I am innocent. If they were at my right I would be guilty." Her logic was impeccable, at least by her own standards, but she was booked on a charge of murder anyway and held without bail. She proclaimed that the ghost of Arthur protected her constantly: "I am not afraid. I will go to jail and await the consequences, as the police cannot terrorize me when I have the aid of the spirits." Furthermore, she crowed, "In the sign language with which I communicate with my boy I learned that I will be released the latter part of this month." It was not the last time the spirit world would give Louisa bad advice. After a few days of this foolish talk the police took the crystal ball away.

In the meanwhile, chemists had been examining the strange liquids and powders found at Louisa's home and in Arthur's internal organs. The results were announced on June 18: Arthur was teeming with arsenic, and neither wallpaper nor spoiled tuna could be considered plausible sources. The coroner obtained a court order to exhume the bodies of Louisa's second husband, William, and her daughters, Frieda and Alma. Even before tests were performed, physicians observed that the bodies were all in mint condition—a telltale sign of arsenic poisoning.

At the request of the Chicago police, Milwaukee authorities disinterred the bodies of Louisa's first husband, Julius Graunke, and her brother-in-law John Otto Lindloff. Arsenic was found in their livers and kidneys. The remains of second husband, William, and daughter Alma contained the drug in "deadly quantities." Frieda's body contained some mineral poison, though not as much as the others. Physicians compared notes and found that most of the family suffered from the same symptoms when dying—parched lips, headache, aching legs and back—all symptoms of poisoning by arsenic, although they allegedly had contracted a variety of ailments.

As if all of this were not enough to make things warm for Louisa, she was beset by her former boarder, Henry K. After the police set him free, he claimed that he had been the Spiritualist's lover. She had even promised to marry him—provided he took out $6,000 worth of insurance on himself. The jilted Henry claimed that her wandering eye turned in the direction of the undertaker who buried her daughter Alma. Perhaps she thought that marrying a mortician would provide a thrifty way to dispose of the ever-accumulating bodies in her household. The undertaker protested that his relations with Louisa were strictly business.

As Louisa's attempt to sweet-talk Henry into taking out insurance indicates, her murderous career may have been even more extensive than the law could prove. Poisoners tend to push their luck by doing away with friends, family, acquaintances, and enemies until they finally exterminate one person too many and get caught. Until that day comes, however, they rack up quite a body count. In addition to the six members of her family, investigators noted that four of her acquaintances died under mysterious circumstances. Bertha H. of Milwaukee claimed that her six-month-old infant took ill and died right after her then next door neighbor, Louisa, babysat. Bertha entertained no suspicions at the time, but she noticed a tendency of Louisa's dogs to get sick and die. The supposition was that the poisoner had been experimenting on dogs with doses of arsenic and then decided to try it out on a baby. Another possible victim was Charles L. of Milwaukee, Louisa's former boarder. His body was exhumed and examined at the request of the Chicago police. A third was a friend of Alma's, nineteen-year-old Tessie F., who died just before Christmas Day, 1911. Neither Charles nor Tessie was insured to Louisa's benefit, so it is difficult to see what motive she would have had for murdering them unless it was simply to keep her hand in. But with the unexplained death of the fourth acquaintance, Eugenie C., we can detect Louisa's profit-oriented thought processes at work. Eugenie came down with liver trouble. Her health took a downward spiral; Louisa insisted on acting as her nurse. Eugenie willed money and property to her daughter Mabel, and after Eugenie passed away on July 19, 1909, the seeress unsuccessfully attempted to convince Mabel to move into her house. Mabel's aunt opined that had she moved in with the family, she would have joined the long parade of the clairvoyant's friends and relatives whose passings were doubtful.

On October 24, Louisa went on trial for murdering her son, Arthur. The judge sensibly ruled that the prosecution could present evidence that Louisa had poisoned other family members in order to strengthen its case. All too often in murder trials evidence demonstrating a clear pattern of behavior from the accused is dismissed as "remote" or "irrelevant," and the result is that many an archcriminal has ended up walking the wide, open spaces free to commit more mischief.

Early in the trial the defense claimed that Arthur died from overindulging in cucumbers. When this contention went nowhere, the defense conceded that Arthur's remains were indeed full of arsenic, but argued that the poison could have gotten there in a number of ways ranging from the ridiculous (wallpaper fumes) to the plausible; in the latter category, the defense noted that some contemporary patent medicines included arsenic as a minor ingredient, and some brands of embalming fluid were generously spiked with it. (Arsenic in embalming fluid was outlawed around 1920.) But the extravagant amount of arsenic found in the bodies ruled out ingestion via medicine or the embalming process. One-fourth to one-half a grain of arsenic is sufficient to preserve a body, but the toxicologist told the court that he had found more than two grains apiece in William, Alma, and Arthur. The toxicologist testified that Arthur's entire system might have contained as many as three or four grains. (To put it in modern terms, a grain was about sixty milligrams.) The toxicologist had examined the mysterious powder found in the accused woman's house and declared that it contained 80 percent mineral poison. A small red box full of rat poison was thought to be Louisa's source of arsenic. The toxicologist further denied the defense a leg to stand on when he analyzed the fluid used by the undertaker to embalm Arthur and determined that it contained no arsenic. It should be noted that a chemist found that the embalming fluid used on three of the alleged Milwaukee victims (Julius, John Otto, and Charles) did contain arsenic. But this meant only that the causes of their deaths could not be accurately determined. It was still quite possible that Louisa poisoned them.

Depending on the victim's size and weight, as little as half a grain of arsenic can prove fatal. Because it takes some time for arsenic to work its diabolical magic, the poison collects in the fingernails and hair through a slow process of absorption. The presence of so much arsenic in the bodies indicated that the victims ingested it for weeks or months, not days as one would expect if the arsenic were consumed in patent medicine. It is true that Arthur took ill and died in only eleven days, but it is probable Louisa got greedy and gave him a few large doses rather than many small ones over time, the usual method of the clever poisoner. That would explain the boy's complaints about the odd taste and consistency of the water she brought him. Sadie R., Louisa's housekeeper, testified that while on his sickbed, Arthur often complained that when his mother brought him water to drink, it tasted like salt and contained a gritty, sand-like substance. Sadie also testified that her employer tried to get her to take out a life insurance policy. On one occasion Sadie and a woman named Katherine D. ate a meal at the family home and were stricken with nausea and stomach cramps afterward. Sadie got so sick, in fact, that Louisa predicted she would die and even named a date. Sadie took no more meals at Louisa's, and the prognostication failed to come true. The "coincidence" is instructive.

The two doctors who tried to save Arthur testified that he had shown symptoms of poisoning by arsenic. The doctor added that William and Alma suffered from similar symptoms. A doctor from Milwaukee tended to Julius Graunke, Louisa's first husband, and testified that she gave her afflicted spouse her own medicine rather than the drugs the doctor left for him. When the physician insisted that she give him the proper medicine, she replied: "Oh, what's the use? He's going to die anyway." Stuart W., Alma's boyfriend, testified that the accused predicted Alma's death and at her funeral the distraught mother predicted that Arthur too would be dead within a year. She knew because the spirits told her so. Similarly, the undertaker bore witness that when he buried William, the widow told him that he would be making a return visit within a year. One cannot avoid the impression that Louisa was trying to profit twice from her relatives' deaths: through insurance payoffs and also by "predicting" their untimely ends to boost her reputation as a seeress. The defense could counter only that Louisa had not objected to Arthur's autopsy (though they did not mention that she objected to his being sent to a hospital as he lay dying), and that she "volunteered the information that another physician had told her [Arthur] had symptoms of poisoning"—as well she might, since the fact of his poisoning was bound to come out anyway after the postmortem.

The reader will have noticed the bold confidence Louisa placed in the spirit world, and this characteristic did not leave her in her times of woe. From her less-than-mystical jail cell she made a prediction about her own fate. According to her Spiritualistic visions, the jury would acquit her: "The spirits come to my cell at night and comfort me. They know I am innocent." She also attempted a little damage control by telling journalists that she had been predicting the deaths of others with uncanny accuracy ever since she was eight years old. Various fortune-tellers, crystal gazers, and spook communicators filled the courtroom to show support for their psychic sister. On October 28, the assembled necromancers claimed they saw spirits of the dead floating around the courtroom, taking in the proceedings, and offering more of their invaluable advice to Louisa. Bolstered by the ghosts' goodwill, she again announced to reporters: "It is only a question of a few days and I will be walking out of here a free woman."

The prosecution suffered a setback on Halloween, when former housekeeper Sadie R., who had testified for the state, abruptly changed course and testified in Louisa's favor. She scored some points for the defense when she noted that Arthur suffered from a skin disease, and the medicine he used contained some mineral poison. Her testimony lost its effectiveness during cross-examination, when she answered many questions with "I don't remember," making it seem as if she were shielding Louisa. The defense attorney was reduced to claiming that the multitudinous dead all suffered from a hereditary disease that caused them to be sensitive to the mineral poison in patent medicines. Considering that William and John Otto were not related by blood to Louisa and her children, the theory was something of a stretch.

Louisa's attorneys had her take the witness stand on November 1—a risky move, but having the accused tell sob stories about his or her personal tragedies sometimes plays well to jurors who think living a hard life gives a murderer an excuse to avoid appropriate punishment. In fact, at least one juror was visibly moved by her tale of woe. Louisa told of her impoverished childhood; her early marriage to Julius Graunke; how the ungrateful Julius had been unfaithful as she toiled in the fields; how she took him back; how she at last left him and took up residence in a haunted house, presumably for the company; how Julius tricked his absent dove into returning, then became ill and died soon after they bought a saloon; how daughter Alma was a flighty girl, full of sass, who caused untold worry for her poor mother by going to dances even as she was dying; how all the family suffered from a hereditary disease—unnamed—and how she watched heartbroken as her loved ones dropped like flies around her, one by one. (Somehow it never occurred to the family to stop taking that patent medicine that obviously disagreed with them, even as the body count rose within the family.) In the process of relating this soap opera, Louisa let it slip that a previously unmentioned child of hers, Erick, died many years before, in June 1891. This came as news to the police and prosecution.

Either Louisa was guilty or Fate took special pleasure in contriving coincidence after coincidence that cast her in a dubious light. To believe in her innocence is to believe that six of her relatives (to say nothing of several acquaintances) just happened to die within seven years, each insured to her benefit, and that each died of natural causes or by taking patent medicine, all of which mimicked symptoms of poisoning by arsenic. Two pathologists who spoke for the defense noted that arsenic in a compound (i.e., medicine) can sometimes transform into an inorganic, deadly form in the system. Fair enough—but to believe the phenomenon would kill so many members of the same family in so short a period of time strains credulity. As the assistant state's attorney observed with admirable sarcasm, the compound most consistently encountered in the case was the amalgam of arsenic and insurance.

As the trial wrapped up, the defense attorney made a foolish, grandstanding ploy by demanding that either his client be freed or given the death penalty. No doubt he hoped that he had raised some reasonable doubt against the state's case and that if challenged to select one of two options, the jury would choose the side of mercy. He miscalculated. The jury was in a compromising mood, and on November 4, after five hours' deliberation, they found Louisa guilty and recommended that she receive twenty-five years in prison. The clairvoyant registered her displeasure by laughing hysterically, protesting her innocence, and crying out, "There is no justice here!" She also fainted like a heroine in a drawing-room melodrama. The record does not state what the ghosts packing the courtroom thought about the verdict. Louisa was sent to the county jail's hospital ward under a suicide watch in case she decided to consult with the spirits face-to-face.

As she often had done before, Louisa declared that she would be acquitted at her retrial, "for the spirits have told me. They have never failed me." But fail her they did. While imprisoned at the Cook County jail, Louisa Lindloff became ill with cancer and entered the world of ghosts on March 15, 1914.

That's Show Biz

Bob R. made his living as a professional carnival sword swallower. During his performance at Jacksonville, Illinois, on June 2, 1936, he thought he'd give the crowd a little something extra. He swallowed a twenty-gauge shotgun barrel and lit a fuse at the end, thinking the crowd would hear an interesting explosion issuing from within his stomach. The audience witnessed this and so much more. Bob expired two days later.

Through a Glass Darkly

Around August 1889, a woman from Stockton went to visit friends in Mankato, Minnesota. During a conversation, she glanced at the window and shouted with surprise at the face of her sister peering through. Her friend also saw and recognized the face. Next morning came a telegram from Stockton bearing the sad news you are fully expecting, and which occurred at the same day and time that the woman saw the image.

House of Suicides

The three unmarried sisters lived at 126 Langley Avenue, Chicago. They were Elizabeth, age forty-three; Anna, age forty; and Nora, age twenty-five and uncharitably described as "half-witted." On July 21, 1879, the curtains were drawn and disturbing rumors were afoot. So a policeman entered the house accompanied by several men from the neighborhood.

The policeman was probably grateful for the company, because by the light of his lamp he found the two elder sisters hanging from a second-floor archway. It seemed they had screwed hooks in the woodwork for the specific purpose of hanging themselves.

At the inquest Nora, the family "simpleton," said her sisters became suicidal from fear that their dissipated, villainous father would find some way to seize their property, including a house they owned on Halsted Street. Nora intended to hang herself too but decided not to so she "could be there and tell how it all happened." It was Nora who told neighbors that Elizabeth and Anna were dead; before starting the rumor, she walked around for two hours in the room where her sisters swung.

The house was for rent within a week but nobody wanted to live there. People passing by early in the morning said they saw the wraiths of the sisters moving about in the abandoned rooms. Sophisticated types sneered at the very idea that the house was haunted—yet the place remained empty for years until it was rented by a family from the east, who were ignorant of the house's history.

They moved right back out a week later. The family's father said he didn't like the smell of sewer gas in the place, but the maid claimed that the furniture was rearranged every morning and that invisible feet could be heard in the hallway and on the stairs.

The house was tenanted several times but never for long. Fleeing occupants said the rent was too high, or the rooms were badly arranged, and things like that. By 1888, the man who purchased the house after the sisters' suicide had taken a major financial loss on it: not only did he lose rent because no one would stay there, he had to tear it down and rebuild it "from the foundation up."

But Nora—who at that time was still alive—was financially well-to-do thanks to the value of the Halsted Street lot, worry over which had inspired her siblings to stretch their necks. She might not have been so stupid after all.

Ghostly Trio on the Tracks

The folks in the area encompassing Hallsville, Beason, and Midland City were in a funk of fear during the winter of 1890. The problem was ghosts that didn't behave the way ghosts were widely supposed to act.

Beginning in early March, they appeared every night around ten o'clock on a railroad bridge just east of Hallsville—right around the time the Illinois Central was due. As the train approached, the three figures would wave their arms as though trying to stop it. Every night the train ran into them and they seemed to be hurled into the river below. No bodies of rekilled ghosts or practical jokers were ever found.

Paradoxically, the ghosts seemed physically real enough to be bumped off the tracks yet sufficiently incorporeal to be impervious to bullets. One night several Hallsville men waited for the figures and fired many shots at them to no effect, hence the community's panic. Whatever the ghosts' object was, it must have been pretty important to them if they were willing to be kissed by a locomotive and flung off a bridge nightly.

Roamy Ghost and Joliet

Joliet, Illinois, is famous for its prison where many a murderer "danced a jig at the end of a rope," as the Irish used to say. These slightly elongated killers—and prisoners who died of natural causes—were buried in a cemetery on Fairmont Hill (a.k.a.

"Monkey Hill"), which overlooked the jail. A few decades into the twentieth century the graveyard was in sorry shape. Over a thousand were buried there, yet there was only one legible marker—a marble stone reading "Hartman, 1895," a mystery because there is no record of anyone by that name having died at Joliet in that year.

The cemetery gave citizens who lived near the prison a serious case of the creeps starting on the night of July 16, 1932. Many insisted that a ghost wandered the grounds at night—a spirit clad in a white shroud, which sang old hymns such as "Rock of Ages" and "Onward Christian Soldiers" in a voice described as "dismal" and "sepulchral."

On two occasions, complaints about the ghostly troubadour led the sheriff to spend the night in the graveyard watching for it. The second time, on the night of July 25–26, the Sheriff was accompanied by a posse of seventy-five men armed with shotguns and clubs. The ghost didn't show up. "It's just a silly notion," scoffed the lawman. "There's no ghost in this cemetery. These women just see shadows and hear the wind moaning through the trees."

The sheriff and posse abandoned the graveyard in disgust in the predawn hours—but a few minutes after they left, the ghost showed up and did its usual wandering and crooning for an hour and then vanished into thin air with a shriek. At least, that's what many neighbors swore they witnessed.

So many parishioners were alarmed by the ghost's appearances that a reverend, pastor of the nearby Trinity Evangelical Church, told the press that he did not know how to reassure them.

Said Anthony G., a grocer: "Once while the voice was issuing from the graveyard, I turned my automobile headlights upon the graves. The song kept on but it came from a different part of the cemetery. As I'd move my lights, the ghost would flit one jump ahead of them."

One night a crowd of three thousand gathered to see if the ghost would come out and favor them with a few tunes. It didn't.

At last prison officials claimed to have solved the mystery: the "ghost," they said, was merely William C., a trustee who liked to while away the lonely hours by singing to himself as he walked to the rock quarry a mile from prison where he had a job manning the pumps. But why would prison authorities allow William—an unaccompanied prisoner—to dawdle about in a cemetery for hours at a time on his way to work? While wearing a shroud? That was their story and they stuck to it.

Evidently, Ax Murdering Doesn't Count as Work

Chicago police were skeptical when Joseph B. walked into a station on Monday, January 16, 1939, and told them he had ax murdered a woman yesterday—but chose to wait a day before confessing "because Sunday is a day of rest." Investigators checked out his story and found it true.

Death Row Dramas: Illinois

George Jacks was once chief of police at Muskegon, Michigan, but in time he became a criminal himself and acquired an impressive rap sheet. His career culminated in the Chicago murder of Andrew M., for which George was sentenced to hang. Before his execution, George wrote a singular letter to the jailer:

> —My Dear Sir: Please do not let any of the clergy in to see me. If I, an innocent man, be hanged today without the right to have the highest court in the land pass upon my case, which is all prepared at great expense to myself and labor to my friends; if I am refused this right, which every man is entitled to, there certainly can be no God above us, and in that case the clergy can do no good. So please do not allow any to see me.

Perhaps George's dubious theological assertion was only a ruse to get his case retried. In any case, when he walked to the gallows on October 14, 1898, he was accompanied by a priest with whom he prayed fervently.

Chris B. strolled into the Chicago sheriff's office on August 21, 1905, and offered to let himself be hanged in place of Henry

Heusack, scheduled to be executed that day for murdering his father-in-law. Chris offered this brilliant argument: "I am tired of life and Heusack wants to live. Why not let me die in his place? He would be better satisfied, I would be better satisfied, and the law that demands an eye for an eye, a tooth for a tooth, would be satisfied. Besides, I do not believe this man is guilty. This looks like a legal murder to me." He was crestfallen to learn that Henry already had been hanged ten minutes earlier.

Robert G. murdered his fiancée, Agnes, in Chicago on June 15, 1905, but he escaped the death penalty because he suffered from ossification of the vertebrae and tissues of the neck. The attorney explained to the court when his client was arraigned on October 9: "This is a case where it won't do you any good to ask for the death penalty. They can't break this man's neck if they do try to hang him, and you may lose him altogether by hanging him and failing to execute the sentence in full." A professor from Rush Medical College testified that only five similar cases of such severe neck-stiffening were known to medical science. Robert's name does not appear on lists of those who paid the ultimate penalty in Illinois, so it appears the legal system recognized him as a man who could not be hanged.

Sam Cardinella (or Cardinelli) was sentenced to hang in Chicago on April 15, 1921. The mobster complained that thanks to Daylight Saving Time, he'd be losing an extra hour of his life. He refused to walk to the gallows and had to be carried to the noose in a chair. He was hanged while still strapped to the chair.

Sam must have desperately wanted to cling to life. After his hanging, jail officials became suspicious of the ambulance his family hired to carry his body away. The vehicle contained a heating pad, hot water bottles, an oxygen tank, an electric battery, and syringes containing who knows what. The warden kept Sam's body for an extra hour and a police car detained the ambulance as it drove away, thus quashing any hopes the mobster's family may have had of bringing him back to life.

In 1923, a Chicago newspaper held a contest in which readers were invited to submit a funny caption for a picture. The winner was announced on September 14: William J. Cramer, a death row inmate who shot a man the previous March.

While robbing a Chicago grocery in 1922, seventeen-year-old Bernard Grant allegedly killed a policeman. No one knew for sure because his accomplice Walter Krauser kept changing his story as to which of the two pulled the trigger.

By 1924, Bernard had been reprieved from going to the hangman seven times. The strain told in his appearance: his many close calls made his hair turn white. January 16, 1925, was chosen as his new death date. Bernard's attorneys appealed for the eighth time and a petition with nearly a million signatures was sent to the governor, who extended Bernard's execution date to April 17.

On April 14 the governor gave Bernard another reprieve until August 14. Would Bernard have received reprieves indefinitely? Would he eventually have been hanged? Would he have been pardoned? All such questions became moot when Bernard's partner in crime, Walter, stabbed him five times in the neck and chest on June 20. Bernard refused treatment, telling the doctor: "I'll be dead in a little while if you'll let me alone, so why prolong my life when it's going to be taken from me anyway?" The prisoner died a half hour later.

When Walter was told Bernard had died, he said, "Is that so? Well, there might be some more that will die soon." The world found out what his cryptic statement meant on June 30, when Walter attempted to kill himself by setting his prison uniform and mattress on fire. He survived. On November 28, 1925, he was sentenced to serve two life sentences concurrently.

Frank Lanciano stood on the scaffold at Chicago's Cook County jail on October 16, 1925. His final words were philosophical: "When everything's fine, no God. Then comes trouble and we remember God."

Nineteen-year-old Charles Shader, three-time killer and one of six criminals sentenced to be hanged at Joliet, was noted for his dark sense of humor. On February 4, 1927, he saw workers in the prison yard constructing a board wall to enclose the gallows.

He asked the sheriff, "Have you completed that little playhouse you're building for us in the back yard? There won't be much playing for us fellows, though. All we got to do is just walk out there and jump through a hole."

Charles also requested a fur collar if he should be hanged on a cold day. He was executed on October 10, 1928.

The Woman in the Furnace

It was the morning before Halloween 1928 in Lake Bluff, a town thirty-five miles north of Chicago. At seven in the morning, workers arrived at the building that served as both city hall and police station; they found it locked securely. When they unlocked the door and went inside, they noticed a strange and sickening smell drifting up from the boiler room in the basement. An intrepid janitor went downstairs to investigate and found a naked woman leaning against a pipe that ran alongside the red-hot furnace from which she had emerged.

All her clothing had burned to ashes; her face was scorched black; her hair was gone; her forearms were charred to the bone; both of her feet were roasted, and the toes on one had burned off. Her horrific burns were bad enough, but even worse was the fact that she was alive and cognizant of her condition. She was rushed to the Alice Home Hospital in Lake Forest with all the speed that was humanly possible. Meanwhile, the police had to figure out who she was and how she came to be roasted alive in the furnace.

The first question was quickly answered. The woman's purse, wristwatch, and shoes were the only personal items left intact, and though she refused to identify herself when asked, a letter in the purse revealed her to be twenty-nine-year-old Elfrieda Grace Knaak, attractive, unmarried, and well educated. She attended the University of Illinois in 1917 and 1918, Michigan State Teachers College in 1920, and the University of Chicago from 1921 to 1923. She lived with her family in Deerfield. Formerly she had been a schoolteacher at Glen Flora Public School in Waukegan, but at present she worked as a saleswoman for the F. E. Compton Publishing Company of Chicago, printers of the famous *Compton's Encyclopedia*. The second enigma proved much tougher to crack.

On the first day of Elfrieda's hospitalization, the police stood near her bed. Whenever she was conscious, the police would ask, "Who did this to you?" She refused to answer. She was no more forthcoming with her three brothers, to whom she would say only that she went to the building alone. But every now and then she would cry out, "Oh, Hitch, where are you?" The visiting policemen exchanged glances, for they knew that Hitch was a popular fellow officer, Charles Hitchcock, fifty-two, a married man with four children. He functioned as Lake Bluff's night policeman.

Hitchcock was no run-of-the-mill cop. A decade earlier he was an actor on the vaudeville stage and in silent movies. He appears not to have been a major star—his résumé includes such inconsequential-sounding roles as "Gardener," "Hotel Clerk," "Train Brakeman," "Detective" and "Woodpile Thief"—yet he was successful enough to have appeared in twenty-seven films between 1912 and 1915, according to the Internet Movie Database. He may have directed a 1918 film called *The Sunset Princess*. It is not clear what course of events resulted in Hitchcock's going from Hollywood actor to small town Illinois policeman, but he remained a redoubtable physical specimen, as proved by a photograph that appears in a Redpath Chautauqua pamphlet in the University of Iowa Archives, dating probably from around 1920. News accounts at the time of the furnace incident refer to him as "the village Adonis," "Lake Bluff's handsomest man," a "Beau Brummel," and the "local Demosthenes."

Naturally the authorities wondered if Officer Hitchcock had been having an affair with Elfrieda. They discovered that on the night of her ordeal, Elfrieda traveled from Deerfield to Lake Bluff to see Hitch. He had keys to the city hall/police station, which would explain the mystery of how Elfrieda got into the locked building. The police tactfully asked the injured woman about the nature of her relationship with Hitch. "Oh, you don't understand," she said. "We are friends in a spiritual way." But at other times she confessed that she was in love with Hitchcock. The embarrassed officer denied that he had been involved with Elfrieda in any capacity other than having "a fatherly interest" in her, and said he was unaware of her true feelings for him. He explained that in addition to police work, he moonlighted as an instructor of elocution, expression, public speaking, and salesmanship at the Waukegan YWCA. He first met Elfrieda in 1924, when she was still a schoolteacher. He spent two years instructing her in the art of salesmanship, and every few months she made a friendly visit to Bluff Lake to discuss the progress she had been making in her current career as a bookseller for F. E. Compton.

The police had few facts but an overabundance of theories. Some thought Elfrieda had attempted suicide in the most painful and gruesome way imaginable. Her siblings derided that theory but also doubted that she was involved in a romantic fling. They described her as being exceedingly timid and not given to love affairs. Her pastor agreed and added a farfetched conjecture in response to rumors that Elfrieda had been raped. The reverend thought that she was so religious that if she were attacked at the city hall, she "might desire to kill herself or to purify herself in flames." But her doctor stated that there was no evidence of sexual assault.

It was much more likely that someone tried to murder her by pushing her into the furnace after knocking her unconscious. This was the theory favored by the police; as the state's attorney said to the press, "Some maniac attempted to burn her alive." In fact, there were signs of a struggle in the city hall basement, including a puddle of blood near the furnace and bloody handprints on the furnace room door and one of the building's locked outer doors. This evidence pointed to someone other than Elfrieda having been at the scene. But if a fiend tried to murder her, why did he only push her head, arms, and feet into the flames, and why did he not stick around to make sure she was dead?

Why did he take the trouble to burn her dress in the furnace, as proved by metal buttons and beads found inside it? And how did he drag his victim into the locked city hall?

The case got "curiouser and curiouser." It occurred to the police that nobody heard screams issuing from the boiler room on the night Elfrieda was burned. On the second day of her hospitalization, October 31, the semidelirious Elfrieda told the police that she intentionally stuck her limbs in the furnace as part of a strange ritual. Specifically, she told the following absurd story to a detective:

After attending a sales conference in Chicago for her publisher on the afternoon of October 30, she traveled to Bluff Lake. Showing disregard for the fact that all the doors to the city hall/police department were locked when workers arrived in the morning, Elfrieda claimed she entered the building the night before by a back door "but did not know why she went there." She spent the night alone in the building, and when dawn came, it occurred to her that she ought to burn herself piecemeal in the furnace. She stuck her right foot into the inferno first, then her arms, shoulders and head, and then finally her left foot. By this point her discomfort was not inconsiderable, and she attempted to flee the basement but found the door locked. But, asked the detective, how came the door to be locked since you entered the room freely? Elfrieda answered that "a mysterious hand" locked it. Then she refused to answer any more questions.

Despite Elfrieda's excellent education, she was not impervious to superstition. She was a Spiritualist and claimed that she tortured herself in the furnace as part of a rite out of obsessive love for Officer Hitchcock: "I did it myself for faith, for purity, for love." Later she called him a "spiritual sweetheart." She implied that their relationship was platonic, but they communed in spirit by means of astral projection. Those with a bent for abnormal psychology thought she "punish[ed] herself for actual or imaginary sin." One theory was that Elfrieda felt such guilt for falling in love with a married man that she burned herself as part of a purification ritual. Dr. Clarence Neyman, a psychiatrist who'd testified in the notorious Ruth Snyder-Judd Gray murder trial in New York the previous year, stated: "There need not necessarily have been any pain. Persons may get into a mental condition like a hypnotic state where they dissociate themselves with the world and enter a dream world." By way of illustration, the psychiatrist recalled a case in which a man wrote the cheery message "God bless you all" in the snow with his own blood after slashing an artery in his throat.

The more practical-minded cops and Elfrieda's doctor believed that her explanation was the product of a mind unbalanced by pain. They thought it impossible for a human, sane or otherwise, to subject herself to such agony. The doctor told the detective:

> To believe her story, you would have to believe the following seemingly incredible acts. First, she placed her right foot in the furnace and kept it there for several minutes. Then she stood on the burned foot and put the other one in the fire. After this, standing on the two injured feet, she thrust her head and arms into the fire. The pain would have been excruciating and she probably would have fainted after the first feeling of the flames.

Sometimes Elfrieda claimed that she burned herself; at other times she dropped dark hints about an agreement she made with an unnamed person. To her brother Alvin she said, "We had a pact, but the other one did not go through with it. I went through it alone." Later she added cryptically, "I didn't think the other girls would put it over on me." At one point Elfrieda said "We did it," but when pressed as to whom "we" referred, she said she meant herself and a spirit who aided in the torture. On yet another occasion she muttered, "Frank threw me down." The only man named Frank who could be even remotely connected with the case was a violin instructor who shared a studio with Hitchcock. Frank told the police that he had never even met Elfrieda, and evidently his denial was convincing or else he had an ironclad alibi, since detectives pursued the lead no further.

To say that Elfrieda's story did not add up would be a gross understatement, and it is hard to escape the feeling that she was lying to protect someone. A second person must have let her into the locked city hall. There is no reason to think she had a key. There were signs of a struggle in the boiler room, indicating that she was attacked just before her adventure with the furnace. Bloody handprints (evidently not hers) were on the door. Her bloody footprints were found on the floor. How had she walked on charred feet?

If Elfrieda were trying to protect someone, the obvious candidate would be the object of her infatuation, Hitchcock. But if he were guilty, he must have had help, because he had a broken leg at the time of the murder and was confined to his house in a plaster cast. (A doctor confirmed that Hitchcock's broken leg was authentic and had an X-ray to prove it.) Hitch provided detectives with a list of three men, none named by the press, whom he suspected could have harmed Elfrieda. One was a Cornell graduate who recently had been released from an insane asylum. The second was a gardener who "molested women along the north shore between Lake Bluff and Waukegan." The third was a prominent local married man who also was a child molester.

None of these suspects appear to have panned out—perhaps the policeman named them to draw attention away from himself—and Hitchcock remained the number one person of interest. As an experiment, the state's attorney told Elfrieda that he was going to have the night patrolman arrested. She became hysterical and cried, "You would be doing a rank injustice."

On November 2, the state's attorney brought Hitchcock to the hospital room to see how the dying woman reacted to his presence. The police hoped for revelations but got only disappointment. Referring to Elfrieda by her nickname, Hitchcock said: "Fritzie, Fritzie, you didn't mean to do this terrible thing." She replied, "No." That was pretty much the extent of their conversation. After Hitchcock left the room, Elfrieda murmured, "I wonder, I wonder, I wonder."

As one of her brothers took notes, the nurse asked, "What do you wonder, Elfrieda?" Contradicting her earlier statement that she tortured herself, Elfrieda replied, "I wonder why they did it."

"Who did it?" asked the nurse.

"I can't remember."

"Why did you go to the furnace room?" asked her brother Theodore.

"It was cold and I wanted to get warm."

"How did you get in?"

"I had a key. You'll find it in my coat pocket." (While remnants of her dress were found in the furnace, her coat was missing and never was found. Who took it? And if it were true that she had a key to the city hall, who gave it to her?)

Theodore asked more questions about the key, but she slipped again into unconsciousness. She awoke a few minutes later and muttered, "I didn't do it," repeatedly. She added quietly, "They did it."

"Who are they?" begged the nurse.

Elfrieda said her final words: "I can't remember." Death ended her suffering but also destroyed any chance of finding out what actually had happened to her. The police could only theorize based on what little evidence they had, including the woman's sometimes conflicting statements. The authorities did not believe she spent a night in the city hall basement. It was agreed that she had arrived in Lake Bluff from Chicago around nine thirty in the evening on Monday, October 29, and was found in the boiler room at seven thirty in the morning on Tuesday, October 30. The police were certain the riddle would be solved if only it could be conclusively shown where she spent the intervening hours, but no answers were forthcoming.

When on her deathbed, Elfrieda told her brother Alvin that she visited the city hall/police department earlier in the evening, searching in vain for Hitchcock. This may or may not be true, but it was confirmed that she had called the Lake Bluff Police Department from Highland Park at quarter to ten and that someone answered her call—exactly who was never determined. Hitchcock was home with a broken leg, or so he said, and the officer on duty that night claimed that when he locked up a little after nine, nobody remained in the station.

In a case riddled with contradictions, it seems only appropriate that after Elfrieda's body was autopsied two completely opposing reports were issued. The coroner's physician announced that the body bore "no evidence of violence" except a broken arm, and that apparently had been caused by a fall. Though it seemed to go against all common sense, some detectives who at first were certain that the woman had been murdered now believed that "her immolation was voluntary and due to depression amounting to self-hypnotism." They overlooked the evidence that Elfrieda bled profusely in the furnace room and that a second person must have taken her coat. Perhaps overt signs of violence on her body, such as cuts or abrasions, were obliterated by the fire.

But on the same day the coroner's physician made his announcement, another coroner expressed a firm belief that Elfrieda was murdered. "I have reason to believe she was struck in the back of the neck," he told reporters. The detective confirmed that he found a depression on the back of Elfrieda's neck, suggesting that she was struck with an iron bar.

The state's attorney was not convinced that Elfrieda had intentionally committed suicide via furnace and told the press that he would look into the possibility that someone forced her to burn herself, or at the very least witnessed the act. The state's attorney was undeterred even when a coroner's jury declared on November 10 that the burns were self-inflicted. The doctor who'd earlier told detectives that it would be "incredible" for Elfrieda to have voluntarily injured herself so now testified that he had reversed his opinion.

Elfrieda's relatives agreed with the state's attorney and hired their own detectives. Alvin flatly told the police that he thought Hitchcock knew more than he was telling. He told a reporter pointedly: "Someone else at least had a moral responsibility if not a physical responsibility for Elfrieda's burning." Despite a $1,000 reward for any relevant information concerning the true nature of Elfrieda's death, no new clues surfaced until November 13, when police searched her personal effects.

They found books on religious topics. One of them, *Christ in You*, referred to "the refiner's fire." The following passage was underlined: "It is grander to suffer because, rightly viewed, it is sure to perfect the soul. It is impossible to know true joy—the heights of joy—until you have known the corresponding depths of pain." Some thought that Elfrieda took the book literally and had indeed performed the daunting act of scorching herself one limb at a time.

The police also found a letter from a woman in Libertyville, Illinois. The note was dated just a few days before the incident with the furnace. This woman and Elfrieda shared an interest in matters mystical, and the former mailed many religious tracts to the latter. Apparently the two underwent a recent quarrel, however, and the letter writer asked for forgiveness. The sheriff wondered if Elfrieda met the woman in the furnace room on the fatal night, since Libertyville and Bluff Lake were only ten minutes apart by trolley. But the letter was a dead end. In early December the woman was found to be a woman from Waukegan. She had no new information to share with the police other than that she thought Elfrieda exerted a hypnotic influence over her.

As in all high-profile investigations, the mentally unbalanced and the foolish came out to confuse matters or otherwise put in their two cents' worth. In the former category was a deranged army deserter in Texas who called himself Edward though his real name was Ezra. He confessed that he forced Elfrieda into the furnace, but could provide no earthly reason why he would have done so. His story was quickly disproved and he recanted, stating that he only wanted to humiliate his relatives. In the second category—the foolish—was a depressed young woman in Chicago who thought it a grand idea to duplicate Elfrieda's feat. In February 1929 she stuck her head and shoulder into her home furnace and received severe burns. She could bear the pain only for a few seconds, which throws doubt on Elfrieda's claim that she slowly and methodically burned herself one limb at a time.

After the nuts had had their say, all was quiet for several months. The bizarre case was largely forgotten everywhere but in Bluff Lake. A few weeks after Elfrieda was found in the furnace room, the chief of police came down with a heart ailment and retired to recuperate. The local paper blamed his ill health on the stress and overwork caused by the notorious case: "The excitement caused by his finding Elfrieda burned in the basement of the Lake Bluff police station augmented by the strain connected with attempts to solve the puzzling case proved too much for his weakened condition." He was troubled also by idle gossips on the street who whispered that he "knew more than he was telling." By mid-December he was near death and spoke about Elfrieda while in a delirium. He died on December 16.

Due to the suspicion surrounding Hitchcock, the Lake Bluff village board adopted a resolution in December 1928 "requesting [his] resignation" from the police force—a roundabout way of firing him. His resignation took effect on January 1, 1929, after which he took up work as a bill collector, a job that well suited his brawny physique.

In August 1929 the case was abruptly reopened. Hitchcock and his eighteen-year-old son were arrested on charges of burglary. The pair confessed to having secretly stolen from their fellow citizens since 1927 in order to "keep up appearances." I don't know what decision the court handed down regarding Hitchcock, but in November his son was sentenced to one to ten years in the state reformatory at Pontiac.

The new chief of police told reporters that Elfrieda's mystery would soon be solved, which implies that he learned some new and critical information while Hitchcock was held for questioning. But no more information came to light and the case remains unsolved. A few years ago a Lake Bluff police officer, seeking to review the case, discovered that all the evidence has disappeared.

The most popular local rumor held that former night patrolman Hitchcock and his wife conspired to murder Elfrieda. The story goes that once Hitchcock had a chance he fled Lake Bluff, never to return. Census records confirm that he remained in the area until at least 1930, after which he vanishes. Despite the rumor assigning her a share of the blame, Hitchcock's wife remained in Lake Bluff until her death in January 1981. She was almost one hundred years old.

Jail Bird

Late on the night of April 14–15, 1934, somebody shot Chicago divorcee Margaret S. in the heart and placed her body sitting grotesquely upright on her doorstep. That somebody was her boyfriend, Charles W., who tried to kill himself several hours later by taking poison and shooting himself in the head. Charles had dated Margaret for six years but somehow forgot to tell her he was married.

Charles survived and went on trial in August. The defense must have been desperate because they scraped the bottom of the logical barrel on August 8. As the murdered woman's mother testified as to the position of the body on the doorstep, a white pigeon flew into the courtroom through an open window and landed at Charles's feet. The killer's attorneys claimed it was an omen of Charles's guiltlessness. "That proves my client is innocent!" shouted Charles's attorney.

It might sound like a stupid defense but, according to a news account, "Court attaches said that when a similar incident occurred several years ago the jury returned a verdict of acquittal." The pigeon was no lucky portent for Charles, however; two hours later the jury found him guilty and recommended life in prison.

Practicing

Samuel E. of Chicago was in a mood to kill himself on November 3, 1937, but first he shot three siblings. He was disarmed by two other brothers before he could fulfill his original goal of suicide. Samuel explained to the police: "I put the gun to my head but I guess I didn't have the guts to kill myself. Then I figured if I killed somebody else first, I'd have guts enough to kill myself."

Mad Medics, Part Two

A doctor from Chicago suspected his wife of trying to gain possession of his property. On October 7, 1896, the physician settled an argument by stabbing her in the abdomen with a surgical instrument. He sat down beside her and stabbed her a second time, this time fatally.

The doctor, a man of science, saw his wife's death throes as an opportunity to further humanity's store of medical knowledge. For the next four hours the doctor made notes on her symptoms as death slowly approached, and every now and then he stabbed her again just to see what effect it would have. At one point he left the dying woman so he could eat oyster stew at a restaurant and purchase a gun.

The doctor ended his busy day by shooting himself in the head. His deaf father sat in an adjoining room the whole time, unaware of the atrocity taking place a few feet away.

Phantom Limb

In June 1886, Frank Cave of Arcola felt distinct discomfort in his arm although the limb recently had been amputated and buried. He complained that it felt just like his missing thumb was doubled up under his hand. The arm was disinterred and the thumb was found to be in exactly the position Frank described. The digit was straightened and Frank felt immediate relief.

Death's Domicile

In 1903, butcher Jacob W. opened a meat market at 2359 Wentworth Avenue in Chicago. Shortly afterward his family died and Jacob committed suicide.

Jacob's clerk Fred K. took over the business. In short order his daughter fell into a pickling vat and was scalded to death. A week later Fred died "under mysterious circumstances."

Then a man bought the house and was murdered there.

A few weeks later an Italian committed suicide under the porch.

The house was destroyed on March 19, 1913, in a fire that killed a woman and her two children.

Stink in Zinc

Friendly tip: when purchasing a secondhand trunk, you should look inside before buying it because there might be a body in it. That was the lesson learned at an auction held on March 26, 1896, at Wakem and McLaughlin's warehouse at 594 North Water Street, Chicago. A large rough zinc box was one of the pieces of unredeemed property on the block. Two men from the suburb of Austin, Philip G. and Charles H., made the winning bid. They bought the box out of sheer curiosity, having no idea what was inside.

The box contained a trunk and inside the trunk was a murdered man, much the worse for decomposition. "G. M. Morgan, 164 Jefferson Court, Chicago" was written on the top of the trunk, but the name and address proved no help in determining the identity of either killer or victim.

A representative of the warehouse firm stated that his company auctioned abandoned railroad baggage after a certain time limit expired. He thought the trunk came from the Michigan Central Railroad Company and that it might have sat in the warehouse with a festering corpse inside for up to a year.

An undertaker said the killer added some material to the body to speed up decomposition, and that the body was so far gone that it was impossible to say anything about his appearance other than that he was of medium height and was middle-aged.

On March 28 the trunk man was tentatively identified as Oliver P. of Fayette, Ohio, who had vanished from Seattle three years before. However, there was an opposing faction: friends of a Frenchman shared an ironclad certainty that the body was his, and were displeased when the coroner's jury declared on March 31 that the body was Oliver's. The Frenchman's compatriots were so miffed that, according to a news account, "[they] declare that they will yet secure possession of the body, even if they have to call on the Republic of France to protect their rights." And yet somehow war with France was averted.

Dora's Long Nap

Dora Meek, age seventeen, had a lover's spat with her boyfriend on September 28, 1902, after which the Centralia girl slipped into a deep and mysterious trance. She slept eighteen hours a day on average and spent her few "waking hours" sitting silently with her head drooping and eyes half closed; for the first ten days of her slumber she didn't eat. Loud noises, zaps from electric batteries, needles, and good hard pinches could not bring her out of it, though she registered mild discomfort during experiments with these and other unpleasant stimuli. Medicine and hypnotism didn't help either.

Joshua Meek, her father, was deluged with offers from every crank under the sun, including clairvoyants, Spiritualists, and osteopaths, all of whom wanted the glory of reviving Centralia's famous Sleeping Girl—for a fee, of course. John C. of Saint Louis wrote to say that a friend of his could cure her while he was "under the influence of the spirit of the celestial sphere." He offered to bring his cosmic friend if Joshua would pay. Joshua sagely replied that he'd pay after the cure.

Dora was still asleep on January 7, 1903—one hundred days after the quarrel—reportedly in fair physical condition though eating little.

On January 26 she woke up long enough to write a note to her mother—"I want to go to [my friend] Kate's house; I am tired of town"—and then she went back to sleep. Doctors took this as a sign that she might be recovering.

In December, Dora revived enough to go back to work. But without any warning symptoms, she fell asleep again for a few more weeks.

In March 1904 she caught the measles, triggering a physical decline that led to her death on October 16. She had been interested in hypnotism; doctors, having nothing else to blame, assigned this as the cause of her extraordinary sleeping habits.

Unnerving Adventures in Chicago

Joseph K. was a watchman for the Chicago and Eastern Illinois Railroad yard, so he was just doing his job as he walked along the tracks early in the morning of October 4, 1912.

As Joseph made his rounds, his left foot got stuck in a "frog" on the track. Here was a ticklish predicament: he knew that a fast passenger train was due in thirty minutes. He spent most of that half hour yanking, tugging, twisting, and wrenching his leg to set his foot free, accomplishing nothing more productive than breaking his leg in two places.

Joseph was desperate, so he took his pocket knife and commenced cutting his foot off. Just as he started, his luck turned: a coworker came by, opened the switch, and set Joseph free. Three minutes later the express train roared through.

⊱─━━─◦─◈─◦─━━─⊰

A similar event occurred in Chicago on September 1, 1919, but without a happy ending. William T., a cashier for the Baltimore and Ohio Railroad, was walking the tracks with his wife when she got her foot caught in the track. As a Chicago and Northwestern train approached, William said, "I'll stay with you, Mary." He embraced his wife and closed his eyes. Both were killed and William's bravery was the subject of much press speculation nationwide the next day. The couple left behind three orphaned children and a flagman who lost his left leg trying to rescue them.

⊱─━━─◦─◈─◦─━━─⊰

Chicago newspaperman John H. went to a barbershop on February 3, 1913, for a close shave—and that's precisely what he got! John got to experience the incomparable sensation of having a madman brandish a razor close to his throat.

"It's a fine day," said the barber as he lathered his customer's face. Then he added: "And it's a fine edge I have on my razor today. In fact—" At this point in the conversation he rested the razor's edge on the reporter's Adam's apple. "In fact, I could cut your throat without any trouble. I don't believe a drop of blood would show on the blade, it's so keen."

What could John do except try to joke his way out of the predicament? "Maybe not," he said, "but think how it would muss up the towels."

"Yes, yes!" cackled the barber. "Sure! Nobody would blame me, though, if I did cut your throat, would they?"

"Oh, no," replied John. "But we're old friends, so put it off a few days."

The rest of the transaction went without incident, and as soon as John wobbled out of the barbershop he sought a cop.

Faithful until Death, Part Two

The story of the faithful dog Shep comes closest to paralleling the legend of Greyfriars Bobby. On August 24, 1924, Francis McMahon of Erie fractured his skull in a fall and was taken to St. Anthony's Hospital in Rock Island. His Scotch Collie puppy came with him. As attendants wheeled Francis into the elevator, he patted Shep on the head and said, "Wait."

And wait he did. Francis died the next day but the dog, uncomprehending of his master's fate, remained in the hospital lobby and wouldn't leave. At first Shep refused to eat but gradually he made friends with a few sisters and nurses. The dog's vigil ended on December 19, 1936, after twelve years of waiting, when he was hit by a car in front of the hospital.

3

ODD OHIO

Body Snatching: Ohio

PASSERSBY NOTICED AN UNPLEASANT ODOR WAFTING from a cemetery in Columbus during the centennial summer of 1876. Inspection by a citizen and a policeman who likely held their noses with one hand revealed that the smell came from a shallow mound. They dug up a barrel that was buried so shallowly that the lid was practically level with the surface of the ground. Whatever was inside smelled so badly that the two had to abandon their excavation. When they worked up the courage to look in the barrel, they found putrescent human remains, including but not limited to bowels wrapped in tissue paper, a man's chin—or so it appeared to be—covered with gray whiskers, the intestines of three or four others, part of a woman's right side, and a human liver. These sad fragments were the leftovers of a dozen bodies that had been stolen from their graves and dissected. The medical students reburied the unneeded parts, though why they went to the great risk of hiding the remains in a cemetery instead of the middle of nowhere, no one could say.

▻╍╼◦╾╍◅

A rash of body snatching occurred in the environs of Fostoria in autumn 1884. An eighteen-year-old tuberculosis victim had been buried for some time in a temporary grave in the village cemetery; on October 2, her family opened the grave to move her to a new address. They lifted the coffin lid to see her face once more and found naught inside but rags. Suspicious persons examined two other recent graves and found that one contained only the corpse's clothes and the other a lonesome handkerchief. Twenty more graves that had been dug within the previous two years were then opened, and eleven were empty.

▻╍╼◦╾╍◅

In mid-January 1878, a man was arrested in Toledo for robbing the graves of an eighty-three-year-old woman and a thirteen-year-old boy and sending them to a medical school in Ann Arbor, Michigan. They were intercepted by the law and sent back. While in custody, the man broke out in eruptions that appeared to be smallpox. He was quarantined in a pesthouse by nervous health officers, from which he soon escaped; officers discovered that the wily doctor had faked smallpox, most likely by applying croton oil to his body.

▻╍╼◦╾╍◅

Edwin F. died in Willoughby on September 14, 1878. His body was buried in Willoughby Cemetery on September 16 and snatched in the night. Detectives found the body the next day at the Homeopathic Medical College in Cleveland. Somebody undertook considerable work: after going through the trouble of stealing the body, the thief hid it in a tank under a floor—which means the floor had to be removed and then nailed back in place. The staff improbably swore they had *no idea* how Edwin got under their carefully, laboriously nailed-down floor. Their denial became even more improbable when detectives looked in a vat and made the acquaintance of Angeline H. of Garrettsville.

The developments at Cleveland caused a sensation. A columnist for the *Louisville Courier-Journal* predicted that medical schools everywhere would receive unwelcome scrutiny, and "any effort of [resurrectionists] toward usurping the authority of Gabriel in causing a premature uprising is calculated to get them in trouble."

⊢•◆•○•◆•⊣

As grim as the business of robbing graves could be, sometimes the activity bordered on slapstick comedy. Eugene J. and F.O. were determined to steal the body of Mrs. Samuel B., a young married woman from Louisville who was buried in Bedford, Ohio, after dying of consumption there in August 1878. Eugene and F.O. were strangers and unfamiliar with the town, so they resorted to subterfuge: one of them pretended to be sick and went to see a local physician, Dr. S. Once they had the doctor in their confidence they revealed to him the *real* reason they were in Bedford. The doctor winked and told them to come back in a couple of hours and he would give them directions to the young woman's resting place.

When Eugene and F.O. returned to the doctor's house as directed, he informed them that the lady was buried next to her grandfather, Thomas P. Darkness fell; the men got their shovels and went to work. Soon they unearthed a coffin with a glass window. By accident or design, they broke the window and a stink radiated from the coffin that fairly knocked them back on their heels. The grave robbers looked at each other. The young woman had died very recently; she shouldn't smell *this* bad so soon! What if they stole the body and then found it was too decomposed to sell? They decided to test her for freshness. One of them reached into the dark coffin, located an ear, and gave it a tug. The auricular appendage came off in his hand. The thoroughly disgusted ghouls quickly put all the dirt back in the grave and gave up on their get-rich-quick scheme. I don't know what they did with the ear.

Somehow word of the aborted heist got out the following November. Investigators found that Eugene and F.O., working in pitch blackness, had opened the wrong grave—instead of unearthing the young woman, they invaded the tomb of her grandfather, who had gone to the Garden of Souls almost a year before! Authorities exhumed Thomas P. and found that his coffin was broken, his glass shattered, and his ear missing. They also checked on Mrs. B., whose remains were undisturbed.

The doctor was lucky; he died just before his role in the depredation became public knowledge. Eugene and F.O. were not quite so fortunate, and to escape a harsher sentence Eugene betrayed his friend by turning state's evidence. Moral: if you must rob a grave, bring a lantern.

⊢•⊕•○•⊕•⊣

Early in the morning of November 14, 1878, a policeman stood on a bridge in Zanesville. He became suspicious of a wagon heading his way and ordered the driver to stop. Instead, the driver whipped his horses and crossed the bridge as quickly as possible. The officer got some backup and chased the wagon fourteen miles into the countryside. One man aboard the wagon fired at his pursuers. At one point the fugitives hopped out and made an escape by hightailing it into the forest.

If an analogous scenario happened today involving a high-speed chase and the armed occupants of a suspicious car abandoning it and running away, we would expect to find drugs in the car. But this was November 1878, and the police found in the wagon the bodies of four prominent Zanesville citizens who had been buried in Woodlawn Cemetery over the previous three days.

⊢•⊕•○•⊕•⊣

In May 1883 "a prominent physician of northern Ohio" told a story to a *Cleveland Herald* reporter, in which the names of the persons involved were prudently omitted. In autumn 1882 "a young gentleman, son of a prominent resident of a town not a hundred miles from Cleveland," went to medical school in New York. He was called home after two months to attend the deathbed of his beloved sister.

After her passing, the grieving brother went back to his studies in New York. His anatomy professor instructed the young man to attend a demonstration involving the dissection of a corpse. Said the reporter:

> After the first shock incident to the horrible sights which greeted his gaze had passed away, he wandered curiously through the long room, with its sawdust-covered floor and plain deal tables covered by human bodies in the various stages of decomposition and mutilation. Faint and almost overcome by the deathly odor which permeated the room, he was about to take his departure, when his attention was attracted by the ribald remarks of two of the students who were busily hacking away at the subject before them.

You can guess who the subject turned out to be. The young man lost first his interest in medicine and then his mind.

────

Railroad baggage handlers were accustomed to dealing with all sorts of nameless horrors shipped by express, but the trunk that arrived in Toledo on September 11, 1886, reeked so prodigiously that the baggage man ran away from it. The suspicious trunk arrived via the Wheeling and Lake Erie Railroad, and the folks at the station must have had a pretty good idea what was in it because they notified the police. Shortly after the cops arrived, so did the fellow who came to collect the chest: a schoolteacher of Ithaca, Ohio. He was immediately arrested; the trunk was opened to reveal an emaciated twenty-year-old unanimated woman packed in hay. The schoolteacher refused to explain why he was using a trunk as a portable casket, but it was noted that he had been a student at the Toledo Medical College the previous winter.

On September 13, a Norwich Township farmer named John B. came to Toledo and identified the body as his seventeen-year-old daughter, Belle, who'd died of consumption on September 8 and was snatched from her lonesome grave by the schoolteacher and his medical school preceptor. John swore out warrants against the two men, not only for stealing the girl's corpse but also for taking her expensive silk dress—which was considered grand larceny.

⊱──❖──⊰

A doctor who worked at the Summit County infirmary in Akron, was accused in January 1887 of sending patients who died at his establishment to medical schools in Cleveland. It was said that he buried coffins full of rocks in the graveyard and shipped the bodies elsewhere; or he would simply let corpses lie beside open graves until the sun set, and then would pack them in boxes labeled "Glass."

But there was a more serious charge against the doctor. He was accused of neglecting patients so they would hurry up and die. Allegedly he allowed a man to die of scurvy and permitted another to die unattended with sores over his body. To top it all, there were "charges of promiscuous immorality among the inmates and other irregularities"—but what exactly those phrases meant the puritanical newspapers of the era do not permit us to know. According to Kimberli Hagelberg's book *Wicked Akron*, it meant that female inmates became pregnant with surprising frequency as the fruit of unwholesome relations with randy hospital employees. The doctor didn't admit guilt but he did resign from the infirmary. He was cleared of grave robbing charges—also, one assumes, cleared of neglecting patients—and later became Summit County's coroner.

Buckeye Burkers

There were occupational hazards among those who made their living by stealing bodies from graves: What if there were an outbreak of good health and pickings were slim? What if the subject's family kept watch at the gravesite until the merchandise spoiled? What if your team of resurrectionists were beaten to the punch by rival gangs? Some body snatchers driven to desperation created their own trade by *murdering people* and selling the bodies to medical school faculty who paid without expressing the slightest curiosity as to how the corpses were obtained. The practice became known as "burking," after the infamous Scottish entrepreneurs Burke and Hare who discovered in the Glasgow of 1828 that it was easier to manufacture bodies than to snatch them.

Fortunately, burking was rare in America, but an authentic incident occurred in Ohio when a two-man team—Allen I. and Benjamin J., both black—clubbed a black family consisting of Beverly T., his wife, and their adopted daughter Lizzie in their log cabin near Avondale on February 15, 1884. The family's neighbors knew something strange was afoot when they found the family's cabin on fire but with no bodies inside.

Allen and Benjamin sold the corpses to the Ohio Medical College in Cincinnati. The doctor asked no questions even though the deliveries were "still warm and bleeding." Even so, the burkers got cheated; they had been promised fifty dollars apiece but instead were given thirty-five to split.

As was usual in cases like this, the killers faced prosecution but members of the medical school faculty didn't. Riots broke out when the burkers were jailed in Cincinnati; in fact, a mob nearly battered down the door to Benjamin's cell when he was rescued by the militia and a squad of policemen.

Rather than face trial, Allen strangled himself to death in his cell on April 30, 1884. He left a note to his wife, written on the same day: "If anything happens to me, please don't fail to take me home." Another note was discovered in the rim of his hat beseeching the sheriff to send his body, "just as it is," to his wife. It appears the body snatcher had a mortal fear of his own precious cadaver going to the dissecting table.

A glum Benjamin went to trial at the end of May, was convicted of first-degree murder, and hanged on September 12. The *Louisville Courier-Journal*'s headline: "A Burker Jerked."

But even the suicide and the hanging may not have been the end of it. A month after Benjamin's execution, the *Courier-Journal* reported that "several thousand" poor Kentucky blacks were being lured to Ohio by men of their own race on a pretense of being paid to vote Republican, and then murdered and their bodies sold to medical schools. The newspaper didn't provide a scintilla of evidence, nor did it run any follow-up stories, so it appears to have been an irresponsible rumor in a Democratic paper.

Ghouls Just Want to Have Fun: Ohio

In June 1881 a miscreant unsealed a vault in a Canton cemetery which had not been opened in a quarter-century. The bones of the occupants were strewn about willy-nilly. Best anyone could figure, the invader was looking for jewelry.

In June 1934 two men broke into the tomb of President William Henry Harrison at North Bend, near Cincinnati. They stole neither jewelry nor other riches, but rather a grindstone and a tool chest stored beside the casket by landscape gardeners. It might say something about Harrison's standing in history that cemetery workers had no qualms about using his tomb as a spiffy toolshed.

The Relatives Fight Back!

Naturally, many combative persons did not appreciate the notion of marauders stealing their relatives' bodies for profit, and sometimes they set ingenious traps for grave robbers.

In 1878, Columbus artist Phil C. applied for a patent for a torpedo that would make things warm for anyone who violated the sanctity of the grave. Described as a six-inch "miniature needle-gun," half of the torpedo was to be nailed inside the coffin and hidden under the lining. Two small chains led from the device to the arms of the corpse. "So far the invention is harmless," chuckled a contemporary account. "But just before the final closing of the coffin, the second piece, containing a cartridge, and arranged on the needle-gun plan, is to be screwed on to the section containing the spring. The torpedo is now ready for action." A resurrectionist could dig down to the coffin and open the lid without harm, but as soon as he manhandled the body he'd get a face full of buckshot from the upward-aiming torpedo. It was recommended that *several* torpedoes be placed in the same coffin in case the body snatcher was quick on his mud-encrusted feet.

On at least one occasion, the invention did exactly as it was intended: in April 1881, resurrectionists who attempted to swipe the daughter of Russell C. in Plain City, Ohio, were frightened away after they detonated a torpedo. One wonders if any persons who were required to exhume a coffin for legitimate reasons (for example, to move a body or to do an examination in the course of a murder investigation) ever found themselves on the business end of a grave torpedo that they didn't know was there. One wonders additionally how many rusty grave torpedoes still lurk below the surface of our peaceful graveyards just patiently awaiting a chance to do their thing.

Animals as Grave Robbers: Ohio

Don M., Gustav J., and Stephen and Alfred W. were hunters in Mount Blanchard. In February 1901 they shot a pair of gray wolves in a cave. The hunters saw a wealth of bones in the cave and assumed at first that they were the remains of chickens and other livestock, but upon closer inspection many were scattered parts of human skeletons. Among these relics was the skull of a child, with the skin half eaten and a bead necklace tangled in the hair.

The human remains came from an old cemetery at the edge of the woods where the wolves roamed. Nine graves were dug up and the meat within stolen by the carnivorous canids. The wolves raided the potter's field section of the graveyard, where the impoverished were buried; the wolves' superior olfactory senses had sniffed out the easy meals that lay in shallow graves, and they easily unearthed and rent asunder the cheap coffins. The depredations had not been detected sooner because no burials had occurred within the last month, and mourners seldom visited the cemetery during the cold of winter.

No attempt was made to put the widely dispersed remains back in their proper graves, which probably would have been impossible anyway. Instead, all the bones were collected and buried in a mass grave—with the exception of the child's skull. Presumably its parents could identify it by the necklace.

Buried Alive: Ohio

Was Minnie H. dead or not? On November 28, 1883, she and her husband, Theodore, retired early at their home near Chester Cross Roads. Theodore was awakened at one a.m. by the sound of his wife struggling for breath. The terrified husband threw water in her face, hoping she had only fainted. But she seemed dead; Theodore called in the undertaker, who cleaned the body and delivered it to the Cleveland home of her father, Philip. An obituary was composed and published:

> Minnie H., wife of Theodore H., Wednesday, November 28, 1883, at Chester Crossing, aged twenty-six years and five months. Funeral from the residence of her parents, corner Kinsman and Herald Streets, Friday, at 1:30 o'clock. Friends are invited.

Problem was, Minnie—in the words of a reporter—was in "a condition strongly resembling death, [yet had] enough of the appearance of life to fan the spark of hope in the bosom of the heartbroken husband into a glow." She had no discernible heartbeat, yet her flesh became neither cold nor stiff. The family physician was puzzled. His prescription was to delay the burial and leave the casket open for a few days just in case. Also, lay off the ice and embalming fluid!

When the reverend preached the funeral sermon, eyewitnesses thought they saw Minnie's face flush. Someone placed a mirror to her lips; it clouded with moisture. But when a *Cleveland Leader* reporter performed the same test later that evening, "the clouding of the glass was almost imperceptible." The same reporter offered this description of Minnie: "There she was with her lips parted, as if half smiling, and with the flush of health in her cheeks as if the blood was still coursing through her veins."

Minnie hovered in the borderland between life and death until December 3, when signs of decomposition set in. But her body was placed in a receiving vault rather than consigned to the earth; someone, it appears, was not completely convinced.

<hr>

Miss Anna H. lived at 349 South Main Street in Dayton with her parents George and Theresa. "A young woman of high social connections," she passed away on January 9, 1884, at age eighteen. It happened on the day her brother Ed married a woman named Emma at Emmanuel's Church. Shortly after dressing for the ceremony, Anna slumped in a kitchen chair at home. A doctor was summoned and pronounced her dead just two hours before the ceremony. There was talk of postponing the wedding, but the reverend thought it best to continue, so the gloomy marriage took place despite the unpromising omen.

After examining Anna's remains, the doctor declared that when alive she had an "excitable temperament, [was] nervous, and afflicted with sympathetic palpitation of the heart." These medical terms made sense in 1884, perhaps, but are now considered so vague as to be nearly meaningless. Perhaps the physician was suggesting that the excitement of the wedding killed young Anna. She was buried in Calvary Cemetery on January 11. But one thing particularly bothered her friends: they thought her ears had a "natural color." Rumors got back to Anna's parents, who ordered her tomb opened. And then, according to the papers:

> It is stated that when the coffin was opened it was discovered that the supposed inanimate body had turned upon its right side. The hair of the head had been torn out in handfuls and the flesh of the fingers had been bitten from the bones. The body was reinterred and efforts made to conceal the case, but there are those who state that they saw the body and know the truth of the facts narrated.

⊱─━━━━━⊰

Mrs. George T. of West Pleasant Street, Springfield, had consumption. Her breathing became labored on February 2, 1891, and by two o'clock in the afternoon she was seemingly lifeless. The undertaker was called for, but the supposedly dead woman surprised everyone by sitting up in bed and saying, "I have come back to be baptized." The reverend was summoned, and he and her husband baptized her in a metal coffin full of water. Instead of dying, she revived and as of February 4 was said to be recovering. But she came very close to being buried alive.

⊱─━━━━━⊰

Henry K. was carried into the Cincinnati morgue in August 1892, placed in a cooling box, washed, covered with ice, and covered with a sheet. An attendant glanced through the half-opened door of the dead room a while later and saw sheet-clad Henry rising slowly from the box. Henry, a hostler, had been overcome by the summer heat while pitching hay. Next thing he knew he was in the morgue, scaring the wits out of the attendant. Henry died five days later—they were pretty sure.

Getting in the Last Word: Bizarre Epitaphs, Ohio

Isaac Thurston (d. 1914) slumbers in Walnut Grove Cemetery near Delphos under a gravestone shaped like a log. The monument facetiously observes: "He sawed logs for forty years but he won't saw this one."

⊳─⊹⊸─○─⊷⊹─⊲

When a stonecutter's wife died in Springdale in 1880, he realized that he had a golden opportunity to do a little free advertising: "Here lies Jane Smith, wife of Thomas Smith, marble cutter. This monument was erected by her husband as a tribute to her memory and a specimen of his work. Monuments of the same style 350 dollars."

⊳─⊹⊸─○─⊷⊹─⊲

August Hefner made an evidently precarious living as a professional sharpener of scissors, razors, and knives. He was buried in Evergreen Cemetery in Waverly in 1856; his epitaph suggests that he felt slighted by the community:

> *When your razor is dull*
> *And you want to shave*
> *Think of the man*
> *That lays in this grave.*
>
> *For there was a time*
> *It might have been whet.*
> *You was afeared of a dime*
> *And now its to late.*

Remains to Be Seen: Ohio

In 1862, Wallace B. of Carrollton buried his son in the local cemetery. In 1882, he had the remains exhumed for reburial in Lexington, Kentucky, and found to his astonishment that the child looked "as natural as the day it was buried." The *Cincinnati Gazette* stated: "A bouquet of choice flowers, which lay in the coffin, gives no evidence of its having been in the abode of the dead for twenty years, and each flower appears fresh and natural. The flesh of the child is a natural color, and the remains can be recognized at a glance by those who knew the little one while on earth."

Home Bodies: Keeping the Dead as Furniture, Ohio

Newton Gilkison may well have been one of the most accomplished weirdos and determined perverts of all time. It is amazing that he has been forgotten.

He was born around 1825 and spent his entire life in the environs of Ontario, Ohio, near Mansfield, where he owned a forty-acre farm. His neighbors considered him a prize eccentric. During the winter of 1859–60, Newton gave his ten-year-old son a violent beating because he denied stealing a trivial article. After the boy died a few days later, the farmer found that he had not stolen the article, and remorse unhinged his mind.

The child was interred in Mansfield Cemetery and remained there for several months until Newton informed cemetery trustees that he wanted to exhume the body and keep it. They refused. The undeterred father hired a gravedigger and marched to the burying ground, revolver in hand. The trustees thought it folly to argue, and Newton unearthed the coffin.

When the lid was opened . . . Well, here's how a reporter described the scene: "The water in the grave had somewhat preserved the remains, but a ghastly sight was presented to view. The hair on the child's head had grown to nearly a foot in length, and the body was in that horrible state of decomposition that might be expected under the circumstances." That didn't matter a whit to Newton, who constructed a zinc-lined coffin and slept with the remains under his bed for the next twenty-five years. The odor nearly drove his wife and daughter crazy.

Newton installed a round window in his son's coffin and occasionally peeked through it to see how things were going in there. The body eventually desiccated and "took on the appearance of a dried herring." In 1885, a visiting doctor was permitted to see it and found that some dust and bones yet remained.

The old man's daughter died in summer 1885, and at last he saw the wisdom in keeping the dead underground rather than at home. He consented to having his son buried beside his sister, which was done on June 18.

Newton committed depredations against the living as well as the gone away. In summer 1884 he adopted a fourteen-year-old girl from the local children's home. Neighbors suspected his motives weren't exactly benevolent and, as the press carefully phrased it, they "had the child removed before he accomplished his object."

As the story about his son's corpse proves, Newton had a stubborn streak. He applied to adopt another little girl from Butler County, but her parents were warned just in time what sort of man he was and the adoption didn't go through.

Then Newton placed an advertisement in the *Cleveland Plain Dealer* seeking to adopt a girl to "help his wife." He received ten replies, and the unlucky one chosen was eight-year-old Anna Francis W. of 317 St. Clair Street. He brought her to his home and did exactly what he had attempted to do twice before.

The crime did not long stay hidden and Newton was arrested just before Independence Day 1885. I have been unable to find out whether he went to prison; most likely he did, but if so, he was free again by September 1896. A news article of that date states that Newton still felt remorse for beating his son to death and, certain that he would never make it to heaven, planted lovely gardens all over his farm, turning it into a private landscaped park complete with elaborate stairways in the belief that his spirit would dwell there after death. He even reserved his own burial site on the farm, a large mound topped with a stake.

The article noted that children for miles around were afraid of old Newton Gilkison. They had good reason to be.

As Though by Magic

David C. of Zanesville was on trial for the crime of ax murdering his wife, who had had the temerity to remonstrate with him for beating their son. Immediately after his arrest and during the trial, David made a show of being deaf, dumb, and insane—which was interesting because he hadn't been so afflicted *before* committing the murder. Some observers wondered if he might be feigning insanity to gain sympathy and earn a lighter sentence. One person whose curiosity knew no bounds even applied a heavy shock to David with an electric battery to see if he would speak. He squirmed but said nothing.

The judge passed David's sentence on October 30, 1885: guilty of murder in the second degree, for which he would receive a life sentence. The "deaf," "dumb," "insane" prisoner suddenly found his sanity restored as though by magic, and his sight and hearing as well. He shouted some choice oaths at spectators and added, "I have got more sand and backbone than any of you, and if you can stand it, I can too." He screeched abuse and invective even after he was removed from the courtroom.

Eccentric Interments, Ohio

Philip H., a wealthy farmer who lived near Port Washington, had planned his own funeral since 1896, when he had a swanky coffin with black velvet upholstery constructed. But by the time he died on September 29, 1901, Philip had gained so much weight that his friends had to force him into it. His coffin was placed in a rough box he constructed himself, on which was attached a card he inscribed: "I am a stranger here; Heaven is my home." As he requested, he was not buried until five days after his spirit was freed. Also at his request, two men sat on the box containing his coffin as it bounced along to Philip's final resting place in a spring wagon. He was buried in Benton Cemetery, a long-abandoned graveyard. Philip's friends were afraid not to comply with his strange wishes, because he assured them he would haunt them if they didn't. They believed him.

Strange Wills, Ohio

The will of Rebecca Y., who died in Twinsburg in spring 1900, directed that her heart or brain be removed before burial, or, alternately, that she be shot twice in the heart and brain. Motive: mortal terror of being prematurely buried.

———○———

David B., a bachelor and member of a prominent Toledo family, died on February 8, 1927. His will, filed in probate court on March 12, ordered that $50,000 be set aside to construct a home in 1977 for "women between the ages of sixteen and twenty-eight, of small stature (no fat women need apply), bright, ambitious, stylish and good to look at."

———○———

William P., a sports editor for the *Cincinnati Times-Star*, was noted for his eccentricities and practical jokes. He made a mental note of the fact that a player for the Cincinnati Reds was a Cuban with "a horror of funerals or anything pertaining to death." After William's death on August 19, 1925, the executor of his will found that the sportswriter left instructions that his body be cremated and the ashes given to the superstitious Cuban.

Secondhand Stone

Henry W. of Mount Auburn was worth $65,000 when his first wife died in 1870, largely due to her frugality. Soon afterward the widower married Mattie P. of Hamilton, who proved such a spendthrift that she went through Henry's fortune. He was in such financial straits that in December 1878 he removed his first wife's $1,400 tombstone in Linden Grove Cemetery in Covington, Kentucky, and resold it to a Cincinnati marble shop as a secondhand monument.

By then, Henry was living in Portsmouth, Ohio. The *Cincinnati Commercial* and the *Louisville Courier-Journal* reprinted a couple of heated letters on the subject between Henry and his son William. William thought the hocking of his mother's gravestone a disgrace and an affront to higher human sensibilities; his father insisted that he intended to have his first wife exhumed and reburied in Portsmouth, and believed the rest of the family should just shut up.

Weird Wake

Devout Spiritualist Mercy Murch of 932 Poplar Street, Cincinnati, frequently held séances at her home. She and her husband Chauncey shared a primal terror of being buried alive, and when he died in 1887, his body was kept aboveground a week before it was sent to the bone orchard.

Mercy's soul fled her body on January 14, 1896, but like her husband she decreed that she should not be buried for a week. In the meantime, a reception was to be held at her house and everyone was invited to come in and stare at her remains. By "everyone," she meant *everyone*.

Cincinnatians were not about to turn down an offer to see an unembalmed corpse, and they spent the next week passing through the mansion by the hundreds. The family of the deceased even invited passing strangers inside. The "remarkably lifelike" Mercy lay in a copper casket in the house's double parlor. A musician pounded away on a reed organ to set the appropriate mood.

A photographer snapped a candid photo of Mercy on January 20, almost a week after her death, for undisclosed reasons.

She lay in state until January 21. On that day all the former servants were invited to a dinner at the mansion, after which brief funeral services were held in the parlor. Mercy was taken to Spring Grove Cemetery in a hearse followed by seven carriages. Her airtight copper casket was placed in a black cloth-covered casket, which was then placed in a burglarproof steel box. The whole shebang was sealed in slate one and a half inches thick. Evidently Mercy feared body snatchers as much as she dreaded premature burial. Three thousand residents of the Queen City passed through her house to see her body, but only three relatives attended the graveside ceremony.

Infidel Inscriptions: Ohio

Chester Bedell of Berlin prided himself on being an outspoken "free thinker"—the nineteenth-century euphemism for an atheist. He was the author of *Twenty-One Battles Fought with Relatives and Presbyterian Intolerance* (surely you've read it). In 1899 he erected a statue in his own honor in Hartzell Cemetery in Deerfield Township, Portage County. The statue featured the sort of less-than-subtle symbolism one usually sees in editorial cartoons: a smug-looking Chester stands on a sheet labeled "Superstition" while holding aloft a scroll bearing the words "Universal mental liberty." He underwent the ultimate test of his theories on September 1, 1908. His bullet-riddled statue was removed from its site by the Berlin Center Historical Society in 1998.

⊱━━⊶◦⊷━━⊰

Benjamin Godsell, an atheist who lived in Ashmont, was reported in February 1905 to have recorded his own funeral oration on a phonograph—to be played at the needful time—because he was so strongly opposed to encomia from the clergy. Benjamin considered this document so precious to benighted humankind that he stored it in a safe deposit vault.

Succinct Obituaries, Part Two

From a Cincinnati newspaper, circa August 1886: "A resident of Fourth Street last evening tried to drive a nail into a can of nitroglycerine."

⊱━━⊶◦⊷━━⊰

Obituary notice for Robert W. of Columbus, December 30, 1937: "[Robert] wondered if kerosene a companion threw on his trousers would burn. He lighted it. Funeral arrangements were being made tonight."

The Laziest Man Gets Lazier

Who was the laziest man in Jones Station, Ohio? Had you asked this important question many decades ago of the residents of this town, located near Hamilton, they would have replied: W. S., a strapping young man of twenty-five who was never known to do a lick of work in his life. He was content to lie around all day and be supported by his family, and for this he was the butt of the townsfolks' jokes. It was said of him—in fact, he said it himself—that he'd rather die than perform manual labor.

By February 1892, W. S.'s long-suffering family had had enough. They told him he had to get up off his lazy posterior and go to work like everyone else. He muttered, "Well, I'll go to a country where work is unknown."

What he meant by this became clear when he bought a container of morphine at a drugstore, slugged it down in a saloon, and went to the Country Where Work is Unknown.

Timely Ends, Part Two

Warren G., a prominent resident of Clark County, told his wife and neighbors in May 1910 that he would die on August 21. Despite his seeming good health, he was so certain the end was near that he tied up all of his life's loose ends. On the date predicted, Warren was found sitting dead in a chair, a victim of heart disease. To augment the eeriness, in 1886 his father, John, also predicted the date on which he suddenly died.

A Fictional Character Takes a Real Victim

Jeremiah W., an employee of the Hudson Hotel in Upper Sandusky, saw the play *Dr. Jekyll and Mr. Hyde* on the night of March 1, 1889, and afterward came home to bed and troubled dreams. Jeremiah dreamed that Mr. Hyde was out to get him, and he took a fatal leap through a third-story window in panic.

Juuust a Little Joke

It was well known in Somerville that a certain man had threatened to shoot elderly farmer A. J. W., and as a consequence he was in a constant state of terror. Three village boys thought of a splendid practical joke; on the night of March 5, 1883, two of the boys persuaded A. J. W. to walk with them to a neighbor's house on a pretense of repairing a clock. The third boy, hiding in the dark, shot a pistol into the air and one of the young geniuses with A. J. W. pretended to topple over dead. The alarmed old man ran to the neighbor's house and dropped to the floor. Unlike his companion, A. J. W.'s death wasn't feigned.

Emma M., a young woman who lived in Mellott's Ridge, Monroe County, played a practical joke that did not end to her advantage. One Sunday evening in March 1883, she spotted someone walking up the road that passed her front gate. In the murk of twilight she thought it was a young man of her acquaintance, and deemed it the height of hilarity to crouch by the gatepost and then jump out screaming as he approached. This she did—but to her surprise, the figure turned out to be a total stranger. More surprising, he had a long knife in his hand. He wondered aloud, "Are you ready to die?" and stabbed Emma twice. She was seriously injured but might have been hurt worse if her corset's steel had not deflected the villain's blade. Who was the ill-tempered stranger and why did he attack Emma? Possibly he couldn't take a joke? Nobody found out.

Young Joe H. worked as a telephone exchange operator in Cincinnati. Some of his coworkers, "for a joke," sent an electrical charge through his ear. "He fell as if shot," said a contemporary report. "Ever since he has been losing his mind gradually until now he is violently insane." The coworkers' delightful jest culminated in Joe's attempt to butcher his entire family with an ax. He was sent to the asylum on the day after Christmas 1891.

Creativity in Suicide: Ohio

Josh M., age twenty-eight, hanged himself in Toledo on November 18, 1881. He used the same rope with which his father had hanged himself from a bridge the previous summer.

⊱────⊰

On January 5, 1886, a man named Morrison of Shreve found a complicated way of accomplishing what could have been done simply. He tied his feet to a tree, looped a chain around his neck, hitched a team of horses to the chain, and then whipped the horses. The result was as slick a decapitation as you could wish for!

⊱────⊰

Richard B., a Cleveland barber, decided that life held no more joy and that he should end it all. He happened to be at work when he came to this decision. On May 10, 1890, after shaving only one of his customer's cheeks, Richard opened a drawer, produced a revolver, and committed—ahem!—barbicide before his terrified, half-finished patron.

⊱────⊰

Edward C. of Washington Court House, near Greenfield, had a girlfriend named Mary H. He saw a prime opportunity to show off for her as the sweethearts strolled near the Baltimore and Ohio train tracks on July 19, 1896. He said, "Did you know that you can tell if a train is coming from miles away if you put your ear on the rail?" As he demonstrated, a train came into view. Mary screamed for Edward to get off the track. He wouldn't budge, explaining, "I want to show you how game I am." A few seconds later, Mary could not help being impressed with the bravery of Edward—or to be more accurate, "Edwards" (note, plural).

⊷•◦•⊶

James B. and Nellie G., star-crossed lovers in Zanesville, entered a suicide pact. Unlike most persons who form such an agreement, they did not go out together. On September 17, 1904, Nellie killed herself in her bedroom; meanwhile, James shot himself three miles from the city. It was a rare case of synchronized suicide.

⊷•◦•⊶

John T. got carbolic acid on credit at Fisher's Pharmacy on Spring Grove Avenue, Cincinnati, on October 17, 1905. He promised that his wife would pay for it next morning. When he got home, he drank the stuff and expired, but not before telling his wife, Bertha, about his little outstanding debt. Thus did John force his widow to pay for the poison he used to kill himself. She went to Fisher's and paid the debt next morning just as promised, but she fainted when the clerk handed her the change.

⊷•◦•⊶

On June 21, 1908, a woman from Sunbury flung herself in front of a southbound Cleveland, Akron & Columbus passenger train. Most of her remained in Sunbury, but her head—which lodged on the locomotive's coal car—went for a 340-mile journey through rural Ohio's lovely scenery before anyone noticed.

⊷•◦•⊶

At 7:55 a.m. on September 29, 1915, Edward G. of Louisville said to Tillie P., who lived in the same apartment building on Spring Street in Cincinnati: "When you hear that clock across the street strike eight, you will hear a shot; then come for my body." Tillie didn't alert the authorities because she thought Edward *might* be kidding; still, she spent a mighty suspenseful five minutes wondering what would happen next. At eight o'clock the bells commenced chiming. A shot rang out and Tillie realized that Edward was not the sort to make idle promises.

⊶⊷⊶⊷

Forty-nine-year-old mechanical engineer James G.—who had degrees from Oxford and Columbia—lived at 10600 Almira Avenue SW, Cleveland. He was found dead beside lonely Glenridge Road in Euclid on the morning of August 19, 1933. He had a slash mark on the back of his neck and was stabbed three times in the back with a seven-inch stiletto, which was found beneath his body. An autopsy revealed that he'd consumed corrosive poison.

It looked as though James was murdered and that his killer took special joy in leaving behind clues. A pair of glasses was left at the scene, as were James's empty wallet, his silver watch, and a notebook of chemical formulas. Strangest of all, a murder mystery novel, *No Other Tiger* by A. E. W. Mason, was placed a few feet from the body.

Investigators became convinced that James committed an elaborate suicide and cleverly disguised it to appear a murder. But how did James manage to stab himself in the back? The autopsy proved that the wounds were superficial. There was a post at the site where the body was found; could James have attached the knife to it and then backed into the blade three times, causing the shallow stabs? An examination showed marks on the post that corresponded to the height of the location of James's wounds. Detectives found capsules containing the same poison that killed James in his coat pocket mingling with candy capsules. It was theorized that James mixed them all together to make it look as though a murderer had tricked him into poisoning himself.

In addition, investigators discovered that James had been despondent and ill and, though unemployed for the last year, was insured to the tune of $35,000—also, he was a fan of murder mysteries.

Bitter Ironies, Part Three

Louise G. was the housekeeper for a judge in Cincinnati for many years. After he died on May 15, 1922, she learned that she inherited $100,000. Louise died the next day.

Prince Yogi Ram, a Hindu astrologer from Lakewood, New Jersey, was killed in Cincinnati when a train hit his car on April 9, 1939. Strewn around the tracks were copies of his book *Astrological Forecast*, which said April 9 was an "unlucky day."

The astrologer's fellow mystics had warned him that 5 was a deadly number for him. After the fatal accident, some noted that he was killed by train number 25 on US Route 25 at 5:05. The dead astrologer had 55 cents in his pocket and his wreck was coroner's case number 5500.

A Final Slander

The folks who lived near Alfred B., a manager of Cincinnati's Washburn-Crosby mills, smelled gas coming from his apartment on March 22, 1903. They entered and found three persons who had been dead for a day: Mr. B.; his wife, Lulu; and their twenty-month-old son, Harry.

An aura of mystery lay behind the tragedy: Mr. B. had manifestly committed suicide and left a note accusing his wife of murdering their son. But what was the cause of death for Lulu and the boy, who was found in a basin of water? Neighbors theorized that Mr. B. attempted to revive the child in the basin and, failing, asphyxiated himself.

The couple were known to have an unhappy marriage; they filed for divorce in 1901 but changed their minds after their son was born. Their domestic infelicity turned out to be the key to the puzzle. The coroner announced in April that Lulu and the child died accidentally by breathing gas, and then Mr. B. deliberately did the same when he came home and found their bodies. The note was a final attempt to slander his wife—the man wanted people to think she had murdered her child.

The coroner concluded: "She was abused during life and maligned at her death by the one who had promised to protect her."

Caution: Children at Play

A Wild West traveling show played at East Liverpool in September 1895, and afterward every little boy in town had a head full of cowboys, Indians, and thrilling escapes of the former group from the latter. On October 3, six boys played at "burning at the stake" using real fire. The outcome was disastrous for the son of Andrew V., who played the cowboy.

▻·◄▻·○·◅▻·◄

Bellefontaine, October 27, 1902: As Thomas W. passed an open knife to a friend at a football game a ball happened to hit his hand, causing Thomas to drive the blade into his own side. He died almost instantly of a severed artery.

▻·◄▻·○·◅▻·◄

Emory H. and his friend Leonard H. of Delaware, Ohio, played a bracing game of "William Tell" on July 31, 1932, by taking turns shooting tin cans off each other's heads. Leonard won and Emory lost—big time.

Romantic Suicides, Part Two

On December 13, 1896, Edmund W. shot himself in the heart on the Toledo grave of his sweetheart. He was found with a crucifix and rosary in his hands.

Ursa Majorly Stupid

P. W. C. kept a pet black bear in the back of his saloon at 1002 Sheriff Street in Cleveland. What could possibly go wrong? Nothing did for two years, until a child named Rosie ventured too close to the bear on October 25, 1886, with results that need not be dwelled upon. Mr. C. faced a manslaughter charge.

Let's All Drink to the Death of a Clown

Sam D. has two claims to fame: he was an early American circus clown (he entered the profession in 1860), and he was killed by his makeup. He mixed his own, and some chemical in it caused slow blood poisoning over time.

Sam died friendless in the charity ward at Cincinnati's City Hospital on November 11, 1888. His makeup triggered paralysis in his diaphragm, in his arms from the elbows down, and finally in his heart muscles.

Impressing Their Congregations: Ohio

"No one of you can tell at what hour death will come," said the Presbyterian minister at Poland, Ohio, on March 14, 1909. No sooner had he said it than Matilda W. fell dead out of her seat.

Somnambulistic Slayings, Part Two

It was early in the morning of April 28, 1898—the Spanish-American War had just been declared a few days before. Mrs. Charles H. of Blue Ball, near Lebanon, sleepwalked her way to the bureau, got a pistol, returned to bed, and shot her husband of three months right through the heart. She explained that she had been dreaming she was killing the hated Spaniards.

><

On August 13, 1917, Frank L. of Toledo dreamed there was a burglar in the house. While sleepwalking he found his gun and shot his wife fatally in the right side.

The Serial Killer in the Cemetery

Cincinnati's Spring Grove Cemetery and Arboretum is considered one of the most beautiful burial spots in America. Founded in 1845, the cemetery is the final resting place of such notables as Union General Joe Hooker, abolitionist Levi Coffin, and Lincoln's secretary of the treasury, Salmon P. Chase.

In the early twentieth century, Spring Grove housed not only the illustrious dead but also one of the infamous living. Nobody knew the name of the anonymous man who prowled among the gravestones, but many desperately wished to know. He was a serial killer who existed seventy years before the term was invented and Spring Grove was where he watched and waited for his next victim.

The first known victim was found at dawn on Monday, May 1, 1904, in Cumminsville, a suburb. Mary McDonald, a slightly deaf thirty-two-year-old buttonhole maker, was found unconscious and dying between the parallel tracks of the Big Four Railroad near Dane Street, her left leg severed above the knee, her face mutilated, her skull fractured, and her hair soaked with blood. An engineer noticed her and blew his locomotive's whistle until he attracted the police's attention. The unfortunate woman was taken to the hospital, where she lived long enough to give the police her name and mutter about "somebody on the tomb." The police dismissed Mary's statement as a product of delirium. Due to her extensive injuries and the location where she was found, and because her breath smelled of whisky and the neck of her dress had been liberally splashed with the same, at first police believed she'd gotten drunk and was hit by a train.

But a closer inspection of the site shook their certainty. Mary was found lying on the ground between two parallel tracks, but her blood was on the inner rails of both tracks. She sustained ghastly injuries to the head and was missing a leg, but presumably she would have been in even worse shape had she been hit by a train. Also, engineers were certain they did not run over anyone in the night. It began to look as though someone hit her over the head and then arranged her body to look as though it had been run over. (Presumably her leg had been amputated premortem by a passing train.)

Witnesses came forward who saw Mary in her final hours. Around ten thirty on Saturday night, a couple saw her board a streetcar heading in the direction where she was later found. She appeared to be sober. Though they did not see the woman's face, they were able to identify her by her dress. Passengers on another streetcar saw Mary around midnight near the spot where her body was found, a lovers' lane on Fergus Street next to Spring Grove Cemetery. She was accompanied by a tall man wearing a slouch hat. The two appeared to be drunk; the man had difficulty supporting Mary and at one point leaned her against a telegraph pole. Police conjectured that the witnesses might have seen the killer feigning intoxication.

A railroad employee who looked at the telegraph pole noticed that the suspicious man's shoeprints were still there. He informed the authorities of his potentially important discovery, but when he and a policeman came back to the pole two hours later, the prints were gone. Someone had obliterated them with a large rock. Perhaps the killer had been watching the railroad man from a hiding place.

Because there was no solid evidence of foul play, Mary's death was officially ruled an accident. About five months later, at nine thirty on the night of October 1, a nineteen-year-old shop girl named Louise ("Lulu") Mueller walked down the lovers' lane on Fergus Street to meet her fiancé, Frank E. The next morning a machinist named Patrick found her body near the spot where Mary met her fate. Her remains lay near her parents' home and two hundred feet from Spring Grove Avenue. Lulu sustained injuries almost identical to Mary's except that neither of her legs had been severed. Although her body was found in the weeds seventy-five feet from the railroad tracks, the police's first instinct was to call Lulu's death an accident. They theorized that she was hit by a train and then crawled to the spot where she died, but the coroner declared that she had died instantaneously. The inevitable crowd gathered to watch the police carry away the remains, and many later recalled the jarring presence of a small bearded man who wrung his hands and cried, "It was an accident!"

An autopsy revealed that Lulu's skull had been crushed on the right upper side from the back of the head to the temple. In addition, her nose was broken and she was missing six front teeth. The killer left a thumb-shaped bruise on the right side of her neck. The deputy coroner found no evidence of rape, nor was the motive robbery since Lulu's purse contained money. A small box containing grains of cocaine was found a few feet from the spot where Lulu's body lay, but it was never determined whether the find had anything to do with the murder, since the police foolishly allowed thousands of curiosity seekers to wander the crime scene and play amateur detective. Undoubtedly evidence was trampled on, carried away, or destroyed.

Inspecting the death scene, the police noticed that the sidewalk leading to the lovers' lane went past Spring Grove, and a high embankment in the cemetery rose parallel to the sidewalk. A killer could hide among the tombstones on the embankment and peer down at passersby. Detectives thought that the killer may have thrown rocks down on the heads of his victims, an idea that led to the papers dubbing him "Jack the Brainer." (On October 8, Lulu's brothers found a bloody, sharp-edged rock hidden under a bush about forty feet from the murder site.) Near this high embankment the police found a pair of tennis shoes and a bare footprint in the mud, all size 7½. A bloody trail in the weeds and bushes near the embankment led to the spot where Lulu's body was found. The authorities questioned Frank E., who said that he had been detained in town and was late getting to the trysting place. When he did not see Lulu there, he assumed she'd given up waiting and gone home. His alibi was confirmed.

On October 5, police arrested two men, painter William W. and one-legged expressman Theodore S. The latter, who made his living by hauling freight in a wagon, owned a stable located near the crime scene. William and Theodore admitted they were acquainted with Lulu and Frank; in fact, Theodore and Frank were not on good terms. The suspects further confessed that they were drunk and in the vicinity on the night of the murder. Witnesses saw Theodore talking to a woman at the Spring Grove entrance to the lovers' lane about an hour before Lulu was murdered. The suspects told conflicting stories, which failed to match statements made by two women, Stella P. and Lily K., who were with William and Theodore earlier on the fatal evening. Theodore's crutch and wagon appeared to be spattered with blood. (A microscopic examination revealed that it was actually red paint.)

Things looked very dark for William and Theodore. They were formally charged with murder on October 8. While they were in jail, their innocence was proved beyond doubt when the killer claimed his third victim on the night of Wednesday, November 2.

The body of a young blond woman was found on the morning of November 3 in a vacant lot in Winton Place, near Spring Grove's entrance. Though they should have known better by then, some policemen believed she was struck by a train or streetcar. She bore wounds and mutilations identical to those of Lulu; her jawbone was crushed, several teeth were knocked out, and brain matter seeped from a vicious head wound. The dead woman's eyes were wide open. It appeared the murderer again attempted to make it look as though his victim had been killed in an accident. A streetcar transfer punched at 9:40 p.m. was found in her hand, and there was debate as to whether it had been planted. It seems unlikely that she would clutch the transfer while being beaten into unconsciousness. If the killer placed the ticket in her hand, he may have been trying to give the impression that she had been hit by a streetcar, yet he placed the body 237 feet away from the tracks. The streetcar could have bounced her so far only if she were made of India rubber. An autopsy later confirmed that she was hit on the head with a club or hatchet and died instantaneously. If we read between the lines of the press reports, the autopsy confirmed that the woman was the only victim who conclusively had been sexually assaulted. This discovery had a chilling effect on the accident theory.

A bloody trail in the grass and on the sidewalk made it clear she was attacked at the elevated embankment by the sidewalk.

The murderer carried her to a thicket and from there dragged her by the heels to the dump site. A large pool of blood showed where he'd briefly stopped and rested before completing his gruesome chore. Mysteriously, the woman's stockings were full of burrs of a type that did not grow on that side of the city. Some thought the killer had collected them elsewhere and scattered them on her stockings to make it seem as if she were killed in some other location. The burrs, and possibly the streetcar transfer, may have meant that the perpetrator planted false clues at his murder scenes to confuse detectives. Another possibly false clue was a pair of canvas shoes wrapped in a newspaper and left near the victim's hat, about 150 feet from the body. Among the accumulating gawkers was the same small bearded man who made a memorable spectacle of himself at the discovery of Lulu's corpse. He seemed as agitated as before, but by the time the police realized who he was, he had disappeared. His identity was never discovered.

Also among the crowd was Millie B., who was walking down Winton Road when she heard that another murder victim had been found. Out of curiosity, she joined the throng and realized to her horror that she recognized the dead woman's blue hat. Thus the victim was identified as Millie's eighteen-year-old sister, Alma S. She was a member of the choir at Winton Place Episcopal Church and made her living as what was then called a "hello girl"—that is, a telephone operator for the Park Telephone Exchange in Cumminsville, a division of Cincinnati Bell, which offered a $1,000 reward for information leading to the arrest and conviction of its employee's murderer. She worked the night shift and was on her way home when the killer attacked. On November 5, her white casket was borne by six female telephone operators to her grave in the German Protestant Cemetery near Fairmount. Buried with the rest of the battered remains were three of her teeth and part of her jawbone, all of which had been knocked out by the force of the fatal blow. The coroner presented these fragments of Alma to her brother Edward.

Alma's many admirers were checked out by the police. They concluded that her murderer was a stranger, and obviously the same man who killed Mary and Lulu. A streetcar conductor named Frank L. told the police that on the night of Monday, October 31, Alma got on his car accompanied by a short, stout man roughly forty years old wearing a slouch hat and sporting about a week's worth of stubble. They rode together to Winton Road and got off together there along with other passengers. The short man did not ask for a transfer ticket, and Frank idly wondered why he'd taken a streetcar for such a short distance. The same thing occurred on Tuesday night, then again on Wednesday night, November 2. But on that third night, Alma and the little man were the only two passengers who got off at that stop. Frank now suspected that the man was the killer, and that he rode three nights waiting for a chance to leave the streetcar alone with Alma. Frank claimed that he could identify the man if he ever saw him again. It strained credulity that "Jack the Brainer" would have murdered a woman just moments after being seen with her in a public place. Within a few days the police tracked down everyone who had been on the streetcar that night, and the mysterious man turned out to be "a prominent citizen of Winton Place," despite his seedy appearance. The press withheld his name. That he got on and off the streetcar at the same stop as Alma was only a coincidence.

Police confidently reported on November 4 that they expected to make an arrest that afternoon. But no arrests came then or ever, and the police had to concede defeat. One of Alma's brothers vowed that he would spend the rest of life hunting down the murderer.

For several weeks no strange-looking man could tread the sidewalk without being suspected of secretly being the killer, as the pages of the *Cincinnati Enquirer* demonstrate. Within about six months of the attack on Mary, eleven women reported being accosted near the cemetery. Some reports were the product of hysteria, while others were probably legitimate. On the night of November 10, a stranger grabbed nineteen-year-old Lillie R. and tried to drag her into Spring Grove. She was so terrified that she was unable to fight back, but luckily her brother George saw the attack from the window of a nearby streetcar station. He gave the stranger a comprehensive beating and had the police not arrived in time, Lillie's attacker might well have been lynched by the gathering mob. The man was Henry S., a florist's employee. The police thought they caught the Spring Grove killer for sure this time, but records showed that Henry had been hospitalized during the attacks on Lulu and Alma.

Even the daughter of the former mayor of Winton Place did not consider herself safe with the fiend lurking about. Dorothy H. reported that as she waited for a streetcar on the cemetery side of Spring Grove Avenue on November 2, she suddenly had an uncomfortable feeling. Turning, she saw a shadowy man in dark clothes and a black hat sitting like a ghost on the picket fence surrounding the cemetery: "He startled me, and I wondered how he managed to keep perched up there. He was looking at me steadily and I began to feel uneasy as if something was wrong." The man continued his bizarre balancing act but did nothing overtly menacing, possibly because a young man across the street was waiting for a streetcar. Dorothy was very grateful when her car arrived. Considering that Alma was murdered only a couple of hours later near the spot where Dorothy had her disquieting experience, it is likely that she escaped a horrible death that night.

Another woman who may have actually met the Spring Grove killer was Josephine H. of Cumminsville, who was attacked in late November by a man near the area where the three victims were fatally injured. Josephine was not prepared to submit meekly, however. When the man seized her throat, she punched him in the left eye and then drew a revolver. The attacker ran away into the darkness, Josephine firing at him until all chambers were empty. She called the police, but detectives could find no trace of the stranger. Josephine did not get a good look at him and could say only that he was "rough looking" and appeared to have emerged from Spring Grove Cemetery. If her assailant was in fact the killer, it's a safe bet he kept a low profile until his eye healed.

In November 1904, the *American Magazine* offered opinions about the series of crimes that seem curiously ahead of their time. The writer believed the Spring Grove killer was a sadist, "one whose natural love for the opposite sex is substituted by an uncontrollable desire to torture. Sadists usually begin by torturing animals and hurting a human being only when they think it won't end in murder. This is as far as they usually get. It is only the sadist with brains and courage who becomes a murderer. The impulse comes on gradually and lasts several days, giving plenty of time to plan crimes. . . . Whoever the man is the police will probably not catch him by the ordinary methods. Some accident will reveal him if he is caught at all, it is thought, or he may accidentally be caught in the act of another crime."

The writer had a good grasp of the mental workings of serial killers many decades before such monsters became common. FBI profilers John Douglas and Robert Ressler have noted that serial killers feel the urge to tempt fate (and prove their perceived superiority) by placing themselves in the police's investigation, perhaps by calling in tips or by joining neighborhood watch groups. The *American Magazine*'s writer noted over one hundred years ago: "Doubtless [the Cincinnati murderer] is one of the men who are contributing to the reward and is one of the men who now carry revolvers at night patrolling the town and looking for the murderer."

At this point the murderous attacks in Cumminsville came to a halt. Perhaps the Spring Grove killer was scared off by the patrols; perhaps he had second thoughts after potential victim Josephine H. fired shots at him. Perhaps he simply could no longer find victims near the cemetery, his favorite hiding place, since by mid-November 1904 the area had such a bad reputation few lone women dared to go anywhere near it. (The *American Magazine*'s writer observed that "not a girl within miles would stir from her house after dark these days.") Or perhaps the police unwittingly put the killer in jail for some other, less serious crime. Perhaps he temporarily moved away from the area when scrutiny became too intense. Whatever the reason for the cessation of his attacks, the citizens living near Spring Grove gradually relaxed, thinking the worst was over. A little over five years passed with no further Cumminsville atrocities.

Then on New Year's Eve 1910, thirty-six-year-old Anna L., a secretary for the Wiborg-Hanna Lumber Company, was found dead and mutilated in the snow. Like Mary, Lulu, and Alma, she was bludgeoned and found near railroad tracks, which led panicked citizens to believe the Spring Grove killer was back. But there were key differences: Anna was gagged and, unlike previous victims, her throat was slashed. The snow around her body was bloody and disturbed for several yards, indicating that she struggled with her attacker. The gagging and the trampled snow suggested the assailant spent some time with his victim, while the Spring Grove killer's method was a lightning-fast attack. Another significant disparity was that her body was found in North Fairmount rather than in Cumminsville proper.

On October 25, 1910, thirty-six-year-old Mary H. was murdered in the sitting room of her Canal Ridge house near the railroad tracks at Dane Street. Like the Brainer's three certain victims, she was bludgeoned; unlike them, she had also been slashed. Her skull was fractured in eleven places with a carpenter's hatchet and her throat so deeply cut that she was nearly decapitated. The killer left the bloody hatchet on the rear porch. Mary's purse containing $8.75 was found nearby, so the motive was not robbery. The coroner found undigested coffee in her stomach. Her chickens had not been released from their coops, and she had not yet done her morning washing. These signs indicated that she was murdered very early in the morning. Police had three prime suspects: the victim's husband, Harley, an ex-soldier from Williamsburg, Kentucky; a boarder who called himself Charles E., but who was later revealed to be a runaway named Charles N.; and milkman Herman S., who called on the house early on the day of the murder.

Charles and Herman were arrested, questioned, and released for lack of evidence, but things looked mighty warm for Harley for a time. He was suspected because his late wife had confiscated all of his pay except for one quarter per week, which she generously let him keep for his own personal use. Also, Charles claimed that a few days before the murder, Harley told him that he wished he could be rid of his wife so he could rejoin the army. Investigators were puzzled by Harley's callous attitude concerning the murder. When a man expressed interest in buying his chickens, the less-than-bereaved widower joked: "We'll kill them with the same hatchet [used to demolish Mary's head]. No, we won't. The coroner has that." On the subject of his wife's insurance money, Harley told a *Cincinnati Enquirer* reporter: "It won't take all that money to bury her, and you can bet I am going to be on hand and see that I get what is left over." The coroner believed the murderer was left-handed, as was Harley.

Despite these intriguing facts—and the *Enquirer*'s policy of reprinting for public consumption every rumor and innuendo obtainable from nosy neighbors—Harley was able to prove that he was at work when his wife met her killer. Bloody fingerprints were found in the house on a portion of a rear door casing; the police cut it out and took it to headquarters. The prints did not match Harley, Charles, or Herman.

The *Enquirer* stated on October 28: "The police are watching a man who is said to have acted suspiciously after the murders of Lulu and Alma some years ago. He is said to have disappeared immediately after the murders for some days, and it is said that he was working within a short distance of the . . . [Mary] home when the woman was killed." The man was never identified in print and nothing came of the clue.

A year after Mary's murder, on October 11, 1911, seventeen-year-old Edna H. was found lying in a backyard on Agnes Street, Cumminsville. She was bound, gagged, and unconscious, but alive. The press stated that her injuries were believed to be fatal but appear not to have run any follow-up stories. A note written in a barely literate scrawl was pinned to her dress: "Sorry we did not have acid to throw on her, too. From the one you did not like." (Did "you" refer to the authorities or to Edna? If the latter, it suggests that the attacker and his victim were acquainted.) After this incident all was quiet in Cumminsville and the Spring Grove killer terrified people only in local legend and in their nightmares. Gradually he was forgotten. Perhaps his dust now nourishes the worms in the same cemetery from whence he once spied on his victims.

After so many years and so few clues, all we can do is speculate. It is clear that the same man killed Mary M., Lulu M., and Alma S. in 1904, while the attacks after the six-year respite have significant differences from the earlier slayings: Anna L. and Edna H. were gagged, Anna and Mary H. were slashed as well as beaten, Mary H. was murdered indoors rather than near Spring Grove Cemetery, and Edna was left with a written message from her assailant. The three later attacks cannot safely be attributed to the Spring Grove killer. The same man (though not necessarily the Spring Grove killer) may indeed have murdered Anna and Mary H., as the doctor who did an autopsy on Hackney reported that the two women suffered nearly identical injuries. On the other hand, there had been an attempted sexual assault upon Anna but not upon Mary H.

Almost three years after the death of Alma, another man was apprehended on suspicion of being the killer: Christ K., a painter by trade. Not long after the murders, Christ moved to Portsmouth. His coworkers noticed that he refused to discuss the murders and that he wore white shoes and a brown coat, which they thought matched one description of the Spring Grove killer. When this was pointed out to him, Christ quickly disposed of the clothes. When his suspicious fellow painters asked him about his past, he offered a vague reply and then abruptly took off for Columbus on the excuse that he had received a telegram stating that his mother was dying. Allegedly, after Christ fled Portsmouth a bloody hammer was found in his room.

Christ's coworkers informed the Columbus police about him, and over the next year the authorities narrowly missed catching him once or twice. At last Christ, age twenty-two, was arrested on West Broad Street on September 14, 1907. Christ protested that he had lived at 3006 Bendville Avenue, New Orleans, all his life until June 8, when he went to Louisville, Kentucky, for three weeks. Then, he said, he moved to Columbus, where he got a job as a mechanic. He claimed that the only time he had ever been in Cincinnati was when he was en route from Louisville to Columbus.

Whatever evidence there was against Christ—and it seems pretty thin—it was not enough to impress the authorities in Cincinnati, one of whom sent a letter to Columbus noting that no good description of the murderer had ever been released. It was true that the police were given a pair of white shoes that allegedly belonged to the killer, but the Cincinnati detectives had "traced the ownership and proved conclusively that he was not the man." The hapless painter's coworkers were mistaken, in other words. Soon afterward, Christ K. was set free due to lack of evidence.

What information can we deduce about the Spring Grove killer after all these years? The perpetrator of the 1904 killings probably lived very close to Spring Grove Cemetery. Though the area near the cemetery was not well lit, it was full of activity: a streetcar stop was located nearby, people went to and came from work, and sweethearts strolled down the lovers' lane. After the second or third murder, the killer must have known the area would be under constant scrutiny. Likely he lived in a house or apartment near the cemetery, to where he could escape quickly after committing a crime. Possibly he had a job that gave him an excuse to be out in the cemetery after hours, such as night watchman or gravedigger.

The Spring Grove Cemetery Association kept a small shelter house in a corner of the cemetery—which, I am informed, recently was torn down—and it was theorized that the killer might have hidden there before and after his murders. Detectives found that the rear door of the house was blocked only with a light wooden bench, so the murderer could easily have traveled in and out of Spring Grove that way rather than by scaling the fence. One man, who ran an automobile shop, stated that he saw a man pacing inside the building around 8:00 on the night Alma was slain. The man did not get a good look at him but thought he was carrying a club and nervously snapping his fingers. A streetcar driver saw a man of the same general description at 8:40, leaning against the fence behind the cemetery's shelter house. He was standing in the same position when the driver made the return trip at 9:02, only a few feet from the spot where Alma was murdered around 9:30. The streetcar's headlight illuminated the stranger for mere seconds, but the driver saw that he was a stoutly built man of medium size who wore dark clothes. His face was not visible, since his coat collar was turned up and his slouch hat was pulled down low. More details were added by a third witness, Frank C., who saw the man as he ventured past Frank on the sidewalk around 7:50 p.m. Frank claimed the man was about 5'8", weighed about 150 pounds, was clean-shaven and in his midthirties. Frank also noticed that the stranger wore new shoes. The heel prints of new shoes were found at Alma's crime scene, and an old pair of badly worn canvas shoes wrapped in a newspaper was left behind. (The shelter house was used in the daytime by a florist. It will be remembered that the suspect Henry S. worked for a florist. I have been unable to determine if the florist was his employer. Perhaps the police, who often showed staggering incompetence when investigating the murders, dismissed Henry as a suspect too soon. He does not turn up in the 1910 Ohio census, so it could be inferred that he abandoned the state when the heat was on.)

A viable alternate theory is that the murderer might have been a railroad man since the three canonical victims were found dead near railroad tracks. Or perhaps the killer was a hobo who regularly rode into Cumminsville on the train, went to his hiding spot, murdered his victims, and then rode the rails out of town afterward. Since trains run on fixed schedules, it might not be coincidence that the murders of Mary, Lulu, and Alma each took place around the beginning of the month. Finally, assuming the later murders were the work of copycats, the researcher looking for the serial killer's identity must seek someone who went to jail, died, fled town, or was otherwise incapacitated after November 1904.

A Case of Hydrocephalus

James M. of Avondale was described as being "unusually bright" and "further advanced . . . than most boys his age." But the thirteen-year-old's head was enormous—it was thirty and a half inches in circumference. James's massive head killed him on June 10, 1900.

Physicians were greeted with only mysteries when they opened James's head at the autopsy. His skull contained five and a half quarts of "a fluid as clear as crystal." His brain was not solid, but rather hollow with a fluid center. And his skull was wafer thin, measuring only a sixteenth of an inch thick.

Closing Remarks, Ohio

Alexander S. shot himself in a Cincinnati government building on September 21, 1908. He left a suicide note reading: "To Whom It May Concern.—Why? Old age, sickness, threatened insanity—enough to make the tired soul seek the immortal dawn."

⊱─━─◇─◈─┤─

After making meticulous plans—including paying off his debts, writing letters disposing of his property, saying farewell to his friends, and selecting his burial clothes, pallbearers, and the hymns to be sung at his funeral—Forrest B. of Columbus killed his wife, Lena, and daughter, Annabelle, with a hatchet on February 19, 1918. Then he went to the residence of his mother-in-law and, after cutting the telephone wires, killed her and his sister-in-law. Upon returning home, Forrest shot himself. He left a final message tacked on the front porch: "Stop the newspaper."

⊱─━─◇─◈─┤─

At 11:15 p.m. on April 22, 1937, William L. of Cincinnati wrote a note: "I am going to hell at 11:45." Exactly thirty minutes later he began his journey to the sultry regions by shooting himself in the head.

When Nightmares Become Real, Part Two

Marie H., age sixteen, lived at 626 Burns Street, Cincinnati. She had a nightmare in which her mother was beheaded early in the morning of September 3, 1911. The dream bothered Marie so greatly that she died the next day of heart failure. "She died of fright," her mother explained.

There was a tragic sequel. Marie's funeral was held at her home. As her distraught eighteen-year-old boyfriend, Harry H., looked through the front window at her coffin, he drank wood alcohol, saying, "I want to go to Marie."

Suicide Prevention

Charles V. of Lima wanted to cease his own existence but he also desired to make a spectacle of himself. So on July 23, 1923, he stood on the streetcar tracks on South Pine Street and awaited the inevitable. The cars ran every twelve minutes, but much to Charles's disgust, they were late on this day. In the meantime, he attracted a large and admiring crowd who dearly wished to see a man run over by a streetcar. Finally someone called the cops, who removed the father of six from the track before slow-motion death arrived.

Charles was charged with public intoxication. The unsympathetic judge passed a unique sentence: since Charles wanted so badly to be dead, he must spend the night in the morgue rather than the drunk tank. The wannabe cadaver had to use a cooling slab for a bed and paid a fifteen-dollar fine.

Dentistry Made Easy

Sam A., a waiter on the riverboat *City of Cincinnati*, was troubled by a toothache on July 21, 1924. For a home remedy, he tied the offending molar to the boat's anchor and threw it overboard. The tooth came out, all right—and so did a piece of Sam's jaw. He bled to death in his sleep that night.

━┼━●━┼━

William S., a farmer of Monroeville, spent September 14, 1933, nursing a toothache. A man of experimental outlook, William fired a revolver into his jaw "to shoot out the ache." The doctors said his prognosis for survival was not heartening.

Come Sweat Death

Ralph M. of Cincinnati was using a power drill on September 13, 1938, when he died of an electric shock. Best the coroner could figure was that Ralph short-circuited the drill with his excessively perspiring hands.

Modern Mummy

Sixty-one-year-old Johannas P. told people that she didn't want to be buried when she died; in fact, she fully intended to return from the dead. She died in her Cincinnati home in August 2003 and got her wish: her demise went unreported until January 2006, by which time she had mummified thanks to her air conditioner running nonstop. When the machine stopped running, passersby became aware of a smell that was the reverse of pleasant. Investigators opened the house and found a mummified Johannas sitting in a chair before her television. Neither her family, who lived downstairs, nor her live-in caregiver bothered to tell authorities about her passing.

A Prisoner Gets a Visitor Who Needs No Pass

Edward H., charged with grand larceny, occupied a jail cell in Canton. He received an unauthorized visitor on the night of January 17, 1884, whose appearance alarmed him so greatly that he awoke the other prisoners and jail officials with screams of "Murder! Help!"

Jailers rushed to Edward's cell and found him so terrified that he couldn't speak for some time. When he finally did, he described a ghost who'd entered his cell. His glassy-eyed caller raised his right hand as though swearing an oath. He appeared to have a broken neck, as his head lolled about at an unnatural angle.

Jail officials were impressed by Edward's story, since he described perfectly a man named George McMillan, down to the clothes he wore, although Edward never had the pleasure of meeting him. George was the former occupant of the cell—but why he had returned for a walk down memory lane was anyone's guess, as he had been hanged in Canton on July 20, 1883, for murdering his wife. Jail officials kindly permitted Edward to spend the rest of the night in a different cell.

A Skeptic Sees Something

Frank L., a fresco painter, lived in an apartment on Prospect Street in Cleveland. Between two and three o'clock on the morning of January 8, 1886, Frank awoke to see a woman sitting on a lounge a scant four feet from his bed. "What do you want?" he asked.

The woman raised her right hand and said, "Hush, hush!" She then vanished.

Frank was a disbeliever in ghosts, so he got up to seek a rational explanation. The woman was nowhere to be seen and the door was locked. Puzzled, he got back in bed and lay there for ten minutes, pondering the strangeness of it all. Then his sheets were yanked off by an unseen force, which also tumbled Frank onto the floor. He dusted himself off, recovered his dignity, searched the apartment again, and still found no solution.

When he opened his apartment door, his next door neighbor cried, "My sister is dead!" Her visiting sister Emily, of Hamilton, Ontario, died of heart disease in her apartment within the same hour during which Frank had his outlandish experience.

Dry Goods Ghost

Weatherby's was one of the finest dry goods stores in mid- to late-nineteenth-century Cincinnati. Located on the northwest corner of Fifth and Vine Streets, the emporium rose a majestic (for the time) four stories. But there may have been more in the building than clerks and fabrics: a man once hanged himself in a third-floor room, and the place was said to be haunted.

A squad of seamstresses worked the night shift on the second floor, and they were so troubled by unnatural noises that several declared they would never return to the building after dark even if the refusal should cost them their jobs.

Their grim determination was the aftermath of an incident that took place on the night of November 8, 1888, when the store was closed and locked tight except for the women working on the second floor and their foreman. Around eight o'clock, the workers heard the sound of heavy footsteps on the floor above them, which they knew was unoccupied. It wasn't experienced by merely one imaginative person; they all heard it and stopped sewing.

"That's queer," said one. "Who can be up there?"

The seamstresses' surprise turned into nervousness when the steps slowly came down the stairs leading to the room that was their work station. Then the footsteps stopped, and only a closed door separated the women from whatever made the noise.

Their nervousness turned into mounting panic when the doorknob rattled violently, as though an impatient person on the other side demanded entrance. The foreman swung the door open. No one was there. He closed it—and then everyone heard the heavy footsteps *ascending* the stairs. The foreman opened the door again but could see no one walking up into the darkness of the third floor.

The foreman—who certainly earned his wages that night— got a light and investigated the third floor. He found nothing unusual, but as soon as he returned to the sewing room the performance was repeated: something crossed the floor overhead, walked deliberately down the stairs, and shook the doorknob. But then that something added an extra attraction: from behind the closed door came the sound of gurgling, gasping, strangling. The foreman yanked the door open, but no one stood in the doorway.

That was all the working girls would take; they would take no more! Their natural fear of the numinous overcame them. They tumbled over each other and practically levitated downstairs to the safety of the first floor, leaving behind unfinished work and the poor foreman, who had no one to comfort him as he extinguished the gas lights all by himself. His duties done, he too wasted no time getting downstairs.

A Cincinnati correspondent for the *St. Louis Republic* asked the foreman the next day if he thought he had encountered an actual revenant of the dead in the mundane setting of a dry goods store. "It is certain that there was nothing human but myself in that [third floor] room last night after six o'clock," he replied. "I opened the door both times while the knob was yet turning. If it wasn't a ghost, what was it?"

Good question!

Ghosts Have No Respect for the Working Man

Considering all the disgusting things that occurred in nineteenth-century medical schools (see sections on grave robbing and my book *Forgotten Tales of Indiana* for further edification on the topic), it was only a matter of time before someone reported that one of these establishments of dubious reputation was haunted.

John M. was the janitor at Pulte Medical College in Cincinnati—a job that required nerves of steel as well as a cast iron stomach. So it's doubtful that he was a coward. He was described as unsuperstitious and a disbeliever in the spirit world.

He and his family lived in an apartment in the medical building. His job description included tidying up after a dissection. Students were required to leave the building by ten o'clock so he and his assistant John C. could do their work. All rooms were locked and only John M. and the faculty had the key to the building's outer door.

One Tuesday night circa December 1888, both men were mopping up blood and dusting off the occasional stray pancreas, or whatever they did at work, when they both heard slamming doors and the sound of people walking around upstairs. Ghosts were the last thing on the custodians' minds: they assumed thieves or trespassers had broken in. They went upstairs to investigate. As soon as they got there the noise ceased—and commenced in a different section of the building. They went to that section and again the cacophony stopped. The two men searched every part of the college and found neither human nor shade of former human. After a half hour the strange antics ended.

But it happened again Friday night. Then the inexplicable noises occurred like clockwork between one and two o'clock every Tuesday and Friday night.

The nervous custodian asked the dean of the faculty whether he should ask the police for advice. The dean urged him not to, for if word got out, it might make the school look like rather a silly place. But John M. did consult with the police and the story got out anyway.

At last report, John M. was so unnerved by the regular, uncanny noises that he wandered the halls of the school with a loaded gun, fully prepared to increase the school's stock of corpses by one if he found a practical joker on the premises.

A Revenant's Request

Thomas S., a black painter who lived on Franklin Avenue in Columbus, was in a deep depression after the death of his wife. "I have been thinking about her all the time, day and night," he told a *Columbus Herald* reporter. "It has preyed on my mind all the time and affected my sleep, so much so that I have had one dream after another about her."

One night around May 1889 he dreamed he saw her lying in a coffin, looking about as she did in life. But something was bothering her. "Thomas," she said, "get me out of water. I'm all wet."

Thomas awoke troubled by the dream. He went back to sleep and dreamed it again—several times. Then he had the same disturbing nightmare the next three nights.

Enough was enough, and Thomas headed for Green Lawn Cemetery with several friends armed with shovels. Said the bereaved widower:

> When we reached the coffin the meaning of the dream was revealed to us. The ground about it was wet and soggy and beneath the box was a bed of water. On opening the lid we found the coffin full of water and the body of my wife floating on the same. We at once remedied the trouble and returned home, and from that time on I have experienced no further visitations at night.

Thomas's friends attested to the truth of his tale. Not really a ghost story, but close enough!

Not in Cleveland: Possible Earlier Victims of the Mad Butcher of Kingsbury Run

Author's note: An earlier, slightly different version of this story was published on my website in September 2012.

One of the most fascinating unsolved murder cases in American history is the series of gruesome crimes committed in Cleveland during the Great Depression by an unidentified criminal whom the press variously called the Torso Murderer, the Cleveland Headhunter, and the Mad Butcher of Kingsbury Run. The Butcher is famous now as an early serial killer, as well as for having escaped detection despite the best efforts of such legendary lawmen as Eliot Ness and Peter Merylo.

Interestingly, while looking through old newspapers in the course of researching true crime stories from the past, I have found possible evidence—though not solid proof—that the same anonymous killer who terrorized Cleveland from 1934 to 1938 (and perhaps later) may have claimed earlier victims in Pittsburgh in 1923 and in New York City in 1927–28 and in 1930–31.

Before looking at the earlier cases, it will be instructive to review basic facts in the dozen or so Cleveland murders attributed to the Butcher:

Victim no. 0: Unidentified white woman, probably murdered in March 1934. In mid-August 1934, vertebrae and ribs from a human body washed ashore at North Perry; the lower half of the female victim's legless torso washed ashore on the beach at Bratenahl on September 5. Part of an arm was found later. (Investigators referred to the victim as "number zero" because it is not certain that she fell prey to the Butcher.)

Victim no. 1: Edward Andrassy, white. Found September 23, 1935, at the foot of Jackass Hill in Kingsbury Run. The body was headless and emasculated but not otherwise dismembered. The killer partially buried Edward's head near his corpse, leaving hair visible on the surface so it would be found. An autopsy revealed that Edward was alive when beheaded.

Victim no. 2: Unidentified white man, also found on September 23, 1935, thirty feet from Andrassy. His remains were slightly burned. Like Andrassy, victim no. 2 was headless and emasculated, and his head was perfunctorily buried at the scene. Bloody clothing that fit the victim was found nearby, as well as lengths of rope, a railroad torch, and a bucket containing, oil, blood, and hair. The coroner estimated that he had been murdered two or three weeks before Edward—so the killer must have kept victim no. 2's body in storage and chose to dispose of it and Edward's remains at the same time. The cause of death, as with Edward, was decapitation.

Victim no. 3: Flo Polillo, white. Found January 26, 1936, behind the Hart Manufacturing building. The killer displayed his bleak sense of humor by placing the lower half of her torso, both thighs, and her right arm and hand in two half-bushel produce baskets. The pieces were wrapped in newspapers and the baskets were covered with burlap sacks. Underwear wrapped in a newspaper was placed nearby. On February 7, the upper half of Flo's torso, her legs, and left arm were discovered behind an abandoned house on Orange Avenue. These pieces were simply dumped and not elaborately wrapped. Her head was never found. Official cause of death: decapitation.

Victim no. 4: Unidentified white man, notable for his sailor-like tattoos. Found June 5, 1936, in Kingsbury Run. Shorts, shoes, socks, a cap, and two bloody shirts were left at the scene; the victim's head was wrapped inside a pair of pants. The rest of the body was found June 6 near the East 55th Street Bridge, a few hundred feet from the spot where Edward Andrassy and victim no. 2 were found. The body was neither dismembered nor emasculated. Cause of death: decapitation.

Victim no. 5: Unidentified white man, found in the woods in the suburb of Brooklyn on July 22, 1936. He was naked and headless, but neither dismembered nor emasculated. The head was found partially hidden on a pile of bloodstained clothing. He had been dead about two months; cause of death was impossible to determine. Victims no. 4 and no. 5 were murdered onsite unlike the earlier victims, who were killed elsewhere and then transported to their dump sites.

Victim no. 6: Unidentified white man, found in a creek in Kingsbury Run on September 10, 1936. His bisected torso was missing the head, arms, and legs. The victim had been emasculated. Searchers found the lower parts of both legs and both thighs in the water. Clothing was found at the scene, including a bloody shirt wrapped in a newspaper. Probable cause of death: decapitation.

Victim no. 7: Unidentified white woman. The upper half of her bisected torso, lacking head and arms, was found on the shore of Lake Erie on February 23, 1937. Cause of death was unknown, but the coroner determined that she died before decapitation. The lower half of the torso was found in the lake on May 5, but the head was never recovered.

Victim no. 8: Unidentified black woman, possibly Rose Wallace. Her skull was found partially buried under the Lorain-Carnegie Bridge on June 6, 1937. When police dug under the skull, they found a burlap sack containing skeletal remains (minus the arms and legs) and also a piece of newspaper. She had been dead nearly a year. Cause of death: unknown, but cut marks on the bones indicated that she was decapitated.

Victim no. 9: Unidentified white man. On July 6, 1937, the Cuyahoga River yielded the free-floating lower half of his legless torso and a burlap bag containing the armless, headless upper half (wrapped in a newspaper) and a woman's silk stocking. A search of the river turned up his left thigh, both lower legs, and both upper arms with hands. The man was not emasculated; his head was never found. Cause of death: undetermined.

Victim no. 10: Unidentified white woman. Her left leg was caught in a storm drain on April 8, 1938. Her headless torso, a thigh, and left foot were found in a burlap sack recovered from the Cuyahoga on May 2. The other thigh surfaced later. Probable cause of death: decapitation.

Victim no. 11: Unidentified white woman, found in a garbage dump on August 16, 1938. The torso was buried under a small pile of rocks and concrete chunks and wrapped in brown paper (like butcher paper, as author James Jessen Badal has noted), a man's coat, and a homemade quilt. Under the torso were thighs wrapped in the brown paper and secured with a rubber band. Searchers found the head five feet away, wrapped in brown paper. A cardboard box held the arms and lower legs; nearby were two empty burlap sacks and a page torn from a magazine. Cause of death: unknown, but cut marks proved beheading. She had been dead several months before her discovery, and the Butcher presumably stored her body a long time before disposing of it. (Some investigators thought the body might have been embalmed, possibly indicating a ghastly practical joke played by the Butcher or someone else.)

Victim no. 12: Unidentified white man, found in the dump near victim no. 11 on August 16, 1938. Part of his skeleton was found in a shallow hole; other bones—the pelvis, ribs, and some vertebrae—were visible on the surface nearby. The skull was found scarcely hidden in a large plum butter tin can. Several pieces of newspaper were with the body. Cause of death: unknown, but as with victim 11, cut marks indicated decapitation.

Some investigators believe that in addition to these twelve (or thirteen) victims, after 1938 the Butcher got in his work elsewhere and then returned to Cleveland for a final macabre swan song.

On May 3, 1940, three murdered men—two forever unknown, one identified as James Nicholson—were found in abandoned railroad boxcars at McKees Rocks, Pennsylvania. Two of the men were dismembered and headless, their removed sections wrapped in burlap sacks; the third was beheaded but otherwise intact. Newspapers were with the bodies, but it was thought that they had been brought by the victims themselves. The murders were so similar to the Butcher's atrocities that they attracted the immediate interest of Cleveland detectives. Peter Merylo, the lead investigator on the Butcher case for years, felt certain the three were murdered by the same hand that had claimed so many lives in Cleveland.

The Butcher may have taken his last Cleveland victim as late as the summer of 1950. On July 22 the body of Robert Robertson was found under loosely piled steel girders at the Norris Brothers' lot on Davenport Avenue. He was naked, dismembered, and headless. Robertson's clothing was nearby and newspaper pages were under the body. His head was found in a lumber pile twenty feet from the girders.

A few further points: In every case, with the exceptions of victims 7 and 10, investigators were impressed by the Butcher's obvious skill at dissecting bodies. They repeatedly noted his "anatomical knowledge" and doctors became favorite suspects among the police, the press, and the public. Most serial killers target people of a certain gender, age, and appearance, while the Butcher was unique in that he murdered both men and women without regard to age, race, or body type.

Now that we are familiar with the Cleveland Butcher's crimes and the strange calling cards he left at his dump sites, let's examine earlier unsolved murders in Pittsburgh and New York in which he may have been involved. The possibility that the Butcher murdered in locations other than Cleveland is not a new idea; even at the time, investigators noted that murders similar to the Butcher's took place at New Castle, Pennsylvania, between 1921 and 1934, and then after a respite, continued between 1939 and 1942. In his book *In the Wake of the Butcher* (2001), James Jessen Badal argues persuasively that these were the work of the Butcher. However, recently Badal has come to conclude that a different person was responsible for those murders, as detailed in his 2013 book *Hell's Wasteland: The Pennsylvania Torso Murders*.

‹‹‹•—○—•›››

At ten in the morning on October 3, 1923, Stephen K. was walking by Pittsburgh's Number 11 swimming pool at the foot of South Nineteenth Street. He was not feeling well and thought a walk might improve his health. As he passed by a doorless, windowless shed where women changed into their bathing suits, he glanced in. Instead of the bathing beauty in a state of undress that Stephen probably hoped to glimpse, he saw a headless white man in a dark blue suit lying on the floor.

(The corpse was beheaded but not otherwise mutilated, which may seem at first to disqualify him as a possible Butcher victim. However, while the Butcher always decapitated and sometimes emasculated men, he did not always cut their remains to pieces. Among his male dead in Cleveland, he dissected only victims nos. 6 and 9. He reserved most of his dismembering fury for women.)

The man was unclean and his clothing was cheap, suggesting that he was a tramp. He was small, at an estimated height of 5'7" and a weight of 125 pounds. He appeared to have been murdered in the dressing room. Bloody fingerprints were on a banister leading to the shed. There was a difference of professional opinion as to whether he had been dead for only a few hours or an entire day.

Dr. DeWayne Richey performed the autopsy. According to a newspaper report, "He said that an attempt apparently had been made to sever the head from the front and later it had been hacked off from the back." The head had been removed with "an unusually large knife," according to a separate press account. An abrasion on the body's left shoulder suggested it had been dragged.

There were plenty of leads for police to follow to determine the victim's identity. A laundry mark on the dead man's shirt read "P. Mc." He had a dagger tattooed on his right arm, and his left arm bore tattoos of a dagger, a woman's head, and some phrase in Arabic that a Syrian policeman interpreted to be "Howsan Hezer" (according to another account, "Hassan Mahmod"). Police theorized that if this were the man's name, he possibly was Turkish. His coat pocket held two photographs, one depicting three young women wearing what appeared to be student nurses' uniforms. An inscription on the front read, "Marion—Me—Bella B." On the back was written: "To Chick from Inda—my chums and I. Aren't they sweet looking?" The other photo showed one of the women alone. It was captioned "Thinking of you." A search of local hospitals failed to turn up any nurses named Inda. Some investigators thought the three women might be waitresses or factory workers.

Detectives thought at first that the killer tossed the victim's head into the Monongahela River but several hours after Stephen K. found the body, three boys found the discarded head while playing on the riverbank between South Eighteenth and Nineteenth Streets, close to the crime scene. The boys found it buried in the sand with three small rocks on top—but the killer left noticeable wisps of hair on the surface as if he wanted to make sure it would be discovered, exactly as the Cleveland Butcher did years later with Edward Andrassy and victim no. 2. (In fact, the Butcher also made lackadaisical, almost comical attempts to partially "hide" the heads of victims 4, 5, 8, 11, 12, and Robert Robertson.) The Associated Press wrote: "That no apparent effort was made to hide the head . . . was shown by the fact that a blood-soaked undergarment was found nearby and that a few wisps of hair appearing above the sand first attracted a group of boys to the scene." (In the future, the Cleveland Butcher would customarily leave clothing behind at his crime scenes.)

Once they saw the victim's face, police opined that he was "exceptionally good looking" and had an air of refinement despite his slovenly clothes. Thousands of people came to the morgue to see the body, but despite the victim's distinctive tattoos and his reattached head no one could identify him, leading police to believe that he was not from Pittsburgh.

October 5 saw the emergence of the mysterious Inda, who had inscribed the photographs in the victim's coat. Inda W. was, in fact, a nurse at Jefferson Hospital in Philadelphia. She told authorities that she gave the photos to Charles Munroe McGregor from Kittanning. Five additional persons who saw the body in the morgue declared that it was McGregor. Others thought the victim might be William Boland, an orderly at Pittsburgh's South Side Hospital who had been fired on September 30 "because he did not do his work properly." Intriguingly, Boland's fellow orderlies believed his home was in Cleveland and stated that his "habits . . . were always shrouded in mystery"—so more investigation of William Boland may be in order.

The matter was settled on October 7, when James McGregor of Homestead, Pennsylvania, saw the body and stated unequivocally that it was his son Charles, age twenty-one, who last lived on Jefferson Street in Kittanning but had not contacted his parents for the past year. Charles was a baker by trade, but he had a "roving disposition," according to his father. Just recently, for example, Charles took a trip to Detroit on a whim.

Pittsburgh detectives may have felt that the solution to the mystery was at hand once they identified the body—but at that juncture the investigation stalled forever, although some of the more imaginative detectives thought the murder was the result of "oriental vengeance" because the victim was decapitated and his head buried in the sand, and because he had an Arabic tattoo. Charles's killer was never found.

Disembodied pieces of male and female murder victims were found sporadically in New York City between 1927 and 1931. A woman's torso was fished out of the Hudson River off West 200th Street on the night of July 21, 1927. News articles don't mention whether the head was attached. The *New York Times* described the torso, which had been in the river for several weeks, as having the legs "cut off above the knees, the left arm below the shoulder and the right arm at the shoulder joint." A couple of days later, a barge captain saw human body parts floating in the Hudson near the Jersey shore opposite Weehawken. A woman's left arm was recovered, as well as a floating trunk bearing the initials "J. C." It was thought the woman's body may originally have been stored in the trunk but its inside was clean.

On August 26, 1927, a man in Whitestone, Long Island, in the borough of Queens, went into an isolated thicket "in the sandy flatlands north of Flushing" to pick cherries. There he discovered a nude man with his head cut off close to the shoulders in a shallow gully a few feet from the corner of 24th Road and 157th Street. The body was hidden in sumac bushes. Bloody sand near tire tracks indicated that the man had been murdered elsewhere and transported to the gully by car. Two or three separate sets of shoeprints were at the site—some apparently made by a woman's high heels, but it was impossible to say when they were made. No clothing was found; a number of burlap sacks were, but police acknowledged that they possibly were trash thrown into the gully by someone other than the murderer.

Investigators found an object that appeared to be a human tongue in a tree stump about fifty feet from the body. This grisly clue suggested a revenge murder or a Mafia-related slaying until the acting chief medical examiner determined that it was only a fungus. A stolen car was abandoned three blocks from the scene and a muddy coat was found a block from the site, but their connection to the murder, if any, was not uncovered.

An autopsy showed traces of neither poison nor alcohol in the man's system. He had been beheaded with a heavy knife. He was well built and "in remarkably fine physical trim." His soft hands indicated that he had been well-to-do and not a physical laborer.

Another dead man was found in Glendale, Queens, on the night of August 27, but his murder did not seem related to the earlier killing. The second man was shot twice, lying openly in a gutter, and not mutilated in any way—but his death led police to theorize briefly that both men were victims of a gang war. The Glendale victim had opium in his pockets and was quickly identified as Michael Felco, an ex-convict and narcotics dealer, and likely target of a drug hit. No connection was ever found between the murders of Felco and the headless man—who was never identified although the police scoured the vicinity for clues and placed the body on public display at the Bellevue morgue.

On May 1, 1928, police recovered the nude torso of a woman floating at the southwest end of Governors Island. The head, arms, and one leg were neatly severed, but the other leg appeared to have been violently ripped off the body. The autopsy revealed that she had been in the water several weeks and bore no knife or bullet wounds, and the dismemberments apparently were done with a cleaver. The murder was never solved nor was the woman identified.

Portions of a disarticulated, recently deceased muscular young man turned up several miles apart in Manhattan on the morning on November 24, 1930. The legs were wrapped in sheets, stuffed in a suitcase, and placed on a sidewalk close to the East River. (It will be remembered that the Cleveland Butcher occasionally "packaged" pieces of his victims by wrapping them in butcher paper, newspapers, quilts, or burlap bags—also, that his two favorite means of disposing of his victims were leaving them out in the open where they would shortly be found or tossing them into bodies of water.) A trunk retrieved from the Hudson River contained the man's torso and arms wrapped in oilcloth. A pair of pants was neatly folded atop the torso. The chief medical examiner who performed the autopsy found that the victim had been drinking heavily before death. Noting the skillful dismemberments, the doctor remarked that the slayer was "a man who knew how to use a knife." One news account states: "The body had been severed so cleanly that authorities were inclined to suspect the slayer of some surgical knowledge."

Both the trunk and the suitcase contained articles of seedy clothing. (A few years later, the Butcher would enigmatically leave clothing with five Cleveland victims; clothes were also left at the New Castle, Pennsylvania, and Robertson murder sites, which many criminologists consider the Butcher's handiwork.) Although his uncalloused, well-manicured hands bore no traces of having performed manual labor, the victim evidently was a hobo since a claim check for the Mills Hotel—a notorious flophouse—was found in one of his pants pockets. Investigators went to the hotel and claimed the satchel, which contained an alarm clock, a gray suit, a gray cap, three work shirts, and the Bridgeport, Connecticut, *Post* of September 2. (The reader will recall the Butcher's curious habit of leaving pages from newspapers or magazines at crime scenes, which he did in six of the Cleveland cases; this idiosyncrasy was also represented at the Robertson and New Castle murders.) The *New York Times* described the clothing as "apparently belonging to a laborer," but whether it belonged to the victim, the murderer, or neither could not be ascertained.

On December 3, Mrs. James C. of Jamaica, Queens, tentatively claimed the body as that of her husband. But the victim appears never to have been positively identified despite the best efforts of fifteen detectives who dredged the river in search of the head, tried to find the store where the oilcloth had been purchased, and attempted to track the laundry marks on every scrap of clothing found with the body.

John D., a Queens salesman, was driving on the Williamsburg Bridge from Manhattan to Brooklyn on the night of March 27, 1931, when he saw a left thigh lying in the roadway. The deputy medical examiner declared that the thigh came from a woman in her early twenties who had been dead fewer than forty-eight hours. "The dissection, he said, showed the work of a professional hand," according to the *Times*.

On March 30, workmen in a lumberyard in the vicinity of the Williamsburg Bridge found a portion of a torso—only, the medical examiner thought this portion came from the right side of a "powerfully-built man" who died more recently than the woman from whom the thigh had been removed. Was a maniac killing and butchering both men and women? This would be a rare circumstance among serial killers, who generally select victims of a particular appearance and gender—though the Butcher who terrorized Cleveland a few years later had no such inhibitions.

On March 31, the upper left and right arms, a left thigh, and a lower left leg minus the foot were found in the water at the foot of Grand Street in Brooklyn. (The news account does not mention if these parts came from a man or a woman.)

On April 12, a "mutilated pelvic section," wrapped in a towel and a Brooklyn newspaper dated March 27, was found in Glendale, Queens. It was left near a cemetery by someone who appears to have shared the Butcher's Stygian sense of humor. Medical examiners could not determine the gender of the victim, but the portion was taken to the Kings County morgue and placed with all the other recently discovered human fragments.

On May 31, a Brooklyn patrolman spotted three suspicious packages in a vacant lot near Ten Eyck Street and Morgan Avenue. One contained the head, forearms, feet, and hands of a man about thirty-five years old with manicured fingernails and curly brown hair, who seemed to have been "fastidious in personal appearance." Another package held several garments with faded laundry marks. Because he had been dead two months, detectives thought he was the man whose scraps had been turning up all over the city since March 30. (On the other hand, the corpse might have been female—the medical examiner couldn't be certain because of its less-than-mint condition. But he believed it to be male.)

The press gingerly described the corpse's injuries, but if we read between the lines, it appears to have been emasculated (assuming the body was male). The *Louisville Courier-Journal* of June 1 states: "Extreme brutality of the butcher was apparent, police said, 'from the manner in which certain parts of the body were cut and hacked, as though with a meat cleaver or ax, leading to the conclusion the killing was a sex murder of the most vicious type.'"

Other aspects of the dump site were notably Butcheresque. One package was wrapped in the April 16 edition of the New York *Daily News*, and another in the March 26 *Brooklyn Daily Eagle*. The third package contained a silk shirt, several pieces of men's silk underwear, and a pair of women's panties.

The persons whose parts had littered the city for the past two months were never identified, but the four-year string of unsolved murder cases involving disembodied humans ceased in New York after this final onslaught against social decorum and good taste. Three years later, pieces of people started turning up in Cleveland's vacant lots, gullies, and waterways.

That's a lot of disembodied murder victims—but are any (or all) of the cases related? In the course of my research in historical true crime, I have found many accounts of headless bodies. Decapitation in murder cases is not all that rare: removing the victim's head is a way of ensuring that identifying him or her will be difficult. If the bodies found in Pittsburgh in 1923 and in New York City between 1927 and 1931 were merely headless, there would be little reason to suspect they were early victims of the Cleveland Butcher. However, one must consider the prospect because these cases share several elements—some of them ritualistic and unique—with the Cleveland murders. None of the earlier murders has *all* of these bizarre elements, but they all have *some* of them: decapitation, dismemberment, the head puckishly hidden in such a manner that it must be found, clothing and/or newspapers left at the murder scene, severed body parts carefully wrapped or packaged, victims either displayed brazenly or disposed of in water.

While we will probably never know the Butcher's true identity, there are plenty of intriguing suppositions. One of the Cleveland detectives' leading theories was that the Butcher was a hobo or a railroad employee; either circumstance would have kept him constantly on the move. Perhaps the Butcher performed his dismemberments in one location, went elsewhere to kill again, and then returned to old haunts when the heat was off, coming back to the same locations over and over like a murderous circuit rider. As a tramp or a trainman always on the go, he could have committed murder almost anywhere in the nation with little chance of getting caught.

As a final note, other pet theories of Clevelanders in the 1930s held that the murderer was a doctor, a medical student, a hunter, a mortician, a mad scientist, or a professional butcher. After all, the killer's anatomical knowledge and skill with a knife had to be explained somehow. However, *if* the same man killed in New Castle, Pittsburgh, and New York City between 1921 and 1931—and *if* that man happened to be the Butcher—it raises the possibility that investigators who pursued these theories were wasting their time. It may be that the Butcher had had no medical training whatsoever, but rather had dismembered so many people over the years that by the time he got to Cleveland it only *seemed* as if he had surgical skill.

Murder Will Out (One of These Days)

On January 12, 1889, cattlemen chased a pair of horse thieves to their hiding place, a dugout on the banks of the Canadian River in Indian Territory (Oklahoma). Rather than surrender, the thieves fought it out until both were shot to death.

While inspecting their hideout, one cattleman found a largely illegible diary under some rocks, hidden by one of the anonymous criminals. In an entry, the writer confessed to the October 17, 1863, ax murder of an elderly man named Jacob B., who lived by himself eleven miles from Zanesville, Ohio. The writer confessed that he and two other men were paid $1,000 to do the deed.

The nephew of the murdered man confirmed that evidence at the crime scene corroborated statements made in the diary. None of the murderers was ever found—at least, it appears, not until January 12, 1889.

Death Row Dramas: Ohio

Most old-time executions went without a hitch (so to speak). But accidents could happen and occasionally did. When Cincinnati murderer Patrick Hartnet was hanged at the Ohio State Penitentiary on September 30, 1885, a miscalculation resulted in his being nearly decapitated by the rope. "The scene was a most sickening one," wrote a reporter, "and it was with difficulty that the executioners could summon courage to take the body down." But Patrick's hanging seems hardly grosser than the brutal crime that led to it: in January 1884 he forced his wife to say her prayers and kiss the bedroom floor as he hit her twice with an ax in full view of their five children. When police arrived, Patrick was dancing a sprightly jig around his wife's body and twanging away on the musical instrument known then as the Jew's harp.

Harry Glick was a real hard case. He had already served two sentences in a workhouse and three in the Ohio State Penitentiary—twice for assault with a knife and once for arson. During his third stay in the pen, Harry helped build the prison's electric chair. After his parole he got in serious trouble again for shooting an officer at Wooster on June 23, 1912. The policeman died ten days later. Harry was pronounced guilty in August but because he was intoxicated at the time of the shooting, he was given life imprisonment rather than a death sentence. He barely escaped the irony of having to sit in the chair he constructed.

Ernest Frederick arrived home after receiving treatment in a sanitarium for a "nervous ailment" and was displeased by rumors that a man named Walter Holcomb had been courting his wife while he was away. On February 28, 1927, Ernest confronted his rival at the post office in Warren, and—thanks to Ernest's having brought two guns with him—more was perforated at the post office that day than merely stamps. The coroner counted eight bullets in Holcomb's body. Clearly, Ernest should have spent more time soothing his jangled nerves in the sanitarium.

A legal problem arose: the murder occurred on government property, and federal law ruled that the trial therefore must be held in the US district court—also, anyone convicted there of first degree murder must be "hanged by the United States marshal on the same premises where he is convicted." A marshal's interpretation of the law meant that if convicted and given the death penalty, Ernest would have to be hanged right there in the courtroom.

It would have been an interesting situation. Instead, in July Ernest was sentenced to life in prison at the Atlanta federal prison.

⊳─┼─◈─○─◈─┼─◅

On October 28, 1928, John Sabo, nicknamed "The Kid," turned twenty-one. He also happened to be an inmate in Columbus, who was scheduled to go to the electric chair soon. He celebrated with a party to which seven other death row convicts were invited. John did the best he could with his ten-dollar budget—though the cons had to eat their cake with cardboard knives and forks, since they were not permitted metal cutlery. On June 28, 1929, the governor commuted the young prisoner's sentence to life in prison. Perhaps that's what John wished for when he blew out his candles.

⊳─┼─◈─○─◈─┼─◅

As Bert Walker sat in the electric chair at the Ohio State Penitentiary on November 10, 1930, he said to the witnesses: "A rather shocking evening." Some might argue that he deserved the death penalty for that pun if for no other reason.

⊳─┼─◈─○─◈─┼─◅

Everett Jones, a death row inmate from Springfield, who shot a poolroom owner during a holdup on July 4, 1937, admitted that he "never had the courage to live decently." Yet he must have felt the need to shift the blame for his failings onto someone else, because before his execution on March 26, 1938, he wasted five minutes of everyone else's time—though not his own—by reading a lengthy statement in which he blamed his downfall on *society*, especially the Ohio prison system. "The robberies I committed outside were moral protests," he insisted. When he finished his oration, Everett sat in the electric chair, seemingly unaware of the contradiction in his statements. In his insistence that society forced him to commit crimes, Everett was a man far ahead of his time

>-+-•-0-•-+-<

When Harvey Roush sat in the electric chair at Columbus on April 26, 1939, onlookers heard him mutter, "I shall not kill."

>-+-•-0-•-+-<

Twenty-year-old Rex Bush of Mentone, Indiana, killed the town marshal of Clyde, Ohio, over seventy-three cents. At his trial in February 1939, Rex bet a companion twelve cents—all the money he had—that he (Rex) would be sentenced to the electric chair. The jury gave him a life sentence, but on the other hand he lost twelve cents.

>-+-•-0-•-+-<

On the other end of the gambling spectrum, when Oliver Dressler, a.k.a. Jack Russell, went on trial for kidnapping and murder in Chicago in November of the same year, he wagered fifteen cents he would "get the chair." He won the bet.

Toledo Terror

Within a few months three women in Toledo were clubbed to death by an unknown assailant. Lydia Baumgardner was murdered on August 21, 1925; Emma Hatfield on September 8, 1925;

and Mary Hundley on January 19, 1926. Almost a dozen additional women were attacked but survived. The police arrested a number of degenerates, many of whom were sent to asylums. The assaults stopped and people breathed easier, thinking that the "clubber"—although unidentified—must have been committed or frightened away.

Then came proof that the fiend had gone nowhere.

On the night of October 25, 1926, someone raped and murdered a schoolteacher, Lily Dale Croy, as she walked from a night class at Toledo University. She was clubbed three times on the head in the yard of Washington School, only two blocks from her house. The next morning the janitor found her mutilated body crammed under a fire escape.

On October 26, George Alden came home from his factory job to find his forty-seven-year-old wife, Mary, dead on the dining room floor. She was shot several times.

Two Toledo women were brutally murdered within twenty-four hours. The term "serial killer" was still a half-century in the future, but citizens were only too aware of those three other unsolved murders that had occurred in the city within the last fourteen months. Could they all have been perpetrated by the same killer? The three earlier victims were attacked at night in isolated areas and bludgeoned with clubs or iron instruments, but Mary Alden was shot in the morning in her own home. On the other hand, all five murders took place within a few blocks.

The city's women stayed home at night. The Toledo Teachers' Association offered a reward of $1,000 for the arrest and conviction of Lily's murderer; a newspaper offered an additional $500 and the Toledo Automobile Club chipped in $100. No one was arrested, but also there were no new murders, and with the passage of time citizens relaxed their guard.

⊷⊶⊷◦⊷⊶⊷

Early in the morning of May 29, 1928, an intruder let himself into Alex Sielagowski's house with a skeleton key and abducted his seven-year-old daughter, Dorothy, from her bedroom. The home invader was foolhardy, since the child shared a bed with three sisters and her father and brother slept in an adjoining room. The stranger drove away with Dorothy and strangled and raped her. Then, further proving his recklessness by returning to the scene of the abduction, he placed her body on the porch of her uncle Joseph, who lived across the street.

The abandoned car was found a half mile from the victim's house. A child-sized handprint was on one window and fresh blood soaked the back seat. The car was stolen the night before, and police theorized that the killer took it for the express purpose of committing the crime against Dorothy.

In his frenzy, the killer left a damning clue: the child's body bore bite marks indicating that her slayer had a missing front tooth.

Suspicion fell quickly upon twenty-six-year-old taxi driver Charles Hoppe, father of a year-old child. Charles and his wife were former boarders of the family—in fact, his wife was the victim's cousin. And Charles was minus a front tooth. His wife was suspicious when her husband came home soaked in blood at four thirty on the morning of the murder claiming he had been in a fight.

On May 30 police dug up a fresh mound in their backyard and uncovered bloody clothes. A dentist made an impression of the suspect's teeth and found that they perfectly matched the bite marks on Dorothy's body. In the face of this evidence, the spiritless Charles confessed. The only excuse he could offer was that he had been drunk at the time.

The police wanted to get a full confession from Charles, but once he was in custody they received a confession that was even fuller than they hoped for. Not only had he killed Dorothy, he admitted he also murdered Lily and committed "other attacks" on Toledo women. He didn't admit murdering Lydia, Emma, Mary H., and Mary A., but it is almost certain that he did.

Hoppe's defense attorneys tried to make a case for his insanity, but the jury didn't buy it. On November 30, 1928, Hoppe took his punishment in the electric chair in the Ohio State Penitentiary at Columbus, the full extent of his crimes probably never to be known. The folks in Toledo weren't exactly sorry to see him go.

It's Hammer Time

Back in the era of the bobbed hairdo, the cloche hat, and the flapper dress, an attractive twenty-one-year-old blonde in Perry got miffed at her husband one night. His name was Thomas Edward West, her name was Velma, the date was December 6, 1927, and the cause of their quarrel was—

Well, Velma wanted to go to a friend's house in Cleveland to play bridge. Her husband said no. He went upstairs to the bedroom. Seething, Velma followed. When Thomas sat on the bed to remove his shoes, his bride of less than a year struck him on the head with a handy claw hammer. Then she hit him thrice more. After thus stunning him, she tied his hands and feet and beat him to death with the hammer, transforming his head and face into "a shapeless mass."

Then Velma burned her bloody clothes, changed into clean ones, wiped up the blood in the bathroom, and went to Cleveland to play that all-important game of bridge. She stayed overnight at her friends' house. While there, she danced and played songs on the piano, including "Just Like a Butterfly," "Caught in the Rain," and—irony alert!—"I'm Tired and Lonely for Home" and "Missing You Dear."

She was arrested in Cleveland the next day as she visited her mother, Catherine Van Woert. The two had just gone Christmas shopping; Velma purchased handkerchiefs for her husband.

Reporters seemed to be as much interested in Velma's admirable good looks and fashion sense as in the fact that she'd beaten her husband to death after a trivial argument. Journalist Marguerite Mooers Marshall described Velma's "thick, permanently waved golden hair fluffing about the long oval of her face, her blue eyes cloudless . . . Velma West is about five feet inches in height and weighs 107 pounds. She is slender to emaciation."

At first Velma said that her husband cranked up the car for her and that she had no idea what befell him after she left for the bridge party. No one believed her. Then she told the sheriff that she struck Thomas in self-defense. She impressed everyone with her composure and utter lack of outward emotion. Even her mother had had no clue that anything was out of the ordinary during her daughter's visit. Said the sheriff, "I never in all my days saw or heard of a woman like her."

One old fuddy-duddy who needed to get with the times said at her arraignment: "Her husband wanted her to stay at home. That's where she should have been! That's where wives belong— they shouldn't gallivant around to bridge parties. Her husband wanted her to stay home—so he got murdered for it."

Velma fainted in the courtroom on December 12 when the judge ordered her held without bond. She had been under the impression that pounding her betrothed's head to a jelly with a hammer was a bailable offense. She also expressed naive surprise when, on January 12, 1928, she was indicted for first-degree murder. That meant she was a candidate for the electric chair if found guilty.

Defense attorney Francis Poulson refused to reveal in advance what his strategy would be, but it did not take a legal genius to guess it would be either self-defense or insanity. At first, Francis and fellow attorney Richard Bostwick opted for self-defense. But they surprised everyone when they suggested that she be allowed to plead guilty to the lesser charge of second-degree murder and thus go straight to prison without a trial. Under these circumstances, she would get a life sentence. Court watchers were surprised again when the prosecutor agreed to the compromise. Most likely no one wanted to put a woman in the electric chair, especially a young and pretty one.

In addition, one of Velma's friends, Mabel Y. of Cleveland, told the sheriff and attorney Poulson what she considered the *real* motive for the murder, and the court agreed it was best to strike a deal and not give it publicity. Since Velma did not go to trial, we will never know the big secret. It appears, however, that she had more motives in addition to the secret one: one was that she *really* wanted to go play bridge, and another was that she wanted to be sure her husband stayed home while she was gone and she thought the best way to guarantee his fidelity was to caress his head repeatedly with a blunt object.

Velma was sent to the women's reformatory at Marysville on March 7. (I bet she wasn't assigned a job in the prison tool shop.) She took comfort in two things: at least she would be eligible for parole in ten years, and she wouldn't be confined in solitary.

Those two bright spots in her otherwise gloomy predicament were destined to flicker and go out. In 1938 the parole board denied Velma freedom although she was considered an "honor prisoner." On June 19, 1939, Velma—thirty-three and suffering from a heart ailment—escaped with three other inmates. The Associated Press news syndicate unfeelingly referred to Velma as a "flapper era husband slayer," as if she were some sort of historical relic. She left behind a three-page note stating she had lost hope of parole and that, convinced her remaining time on Earth was short, she wanted to have "one last good time" before she died. She apologized for escaping to the reformatory head, Marguerite Reilley, stating that she would return if her departure "hurt Mrs. Reilley too much."

After a five-week spree, Velma and one of the other escapees, Mary R., surrendered in Dallas. Velma regretted her actions: "I found the world changed. I had never been outside Ohio until I escaped. . . . I wouldn't call my last three weeks exactly a good time, and I wouldn't escape again if I had the chance. It isn't worth it." Velma and Mary agreed that the folks at the prison had "always treated us swell."

But those lenient days were over. Reformatory superintendent Reilley said: "Velma better get her publicity now because when she gets back it'll all be over. She's going out of circulation." Velma was to spend a week in a dark solitary cell on bread and water, followed by three more weeks in a solitary cell with the same bill of fare, after which she would get "some assignment where she won't be heard of." Reilley added: "There'll be no inhumanity, of course." Like hitting someone with a hammer.

Velma died in prison on October 24, 1959.

Mad Medics, Part Three

Dr. William R. Dabney opened his practice in Marietta around 1898. He specialized in complaints of the eye, ear, and throat, and performed complicated operations every day. No one suspected Dr. Dabney had gone insane until a farmer named Jacob Schaad came to have a tumor removed from his upper jaw. Jacob was taken to the operating table and put under anesthetic on May 23, 1912.

When Dr. Dabney got to work, two other surgeons realized something was not quite right with Dabney's manner and remonstrated with him. The doctor angrily ordered them to leave the room. After they departed, Dabney dissected the face and throat of his unconscious patient. The nurse ran screaming from the operating room and brought back the two other surgeons, who parted the raving Dabney from his scalpel with considerable trouble. Jacob died two days later.

Dr. Dabney was committed to the Longview Asylum in Cincinnati on August 13, 1913. More than twenty years later he was considered a possible suspect in the notorious dissection-murders committed by Cleveland's Mad Butcher of Kingsbury Run, but by that time Dabney presumably was deceased or still committed.

A Stubborn Cuss

Three unmarried Glenn siblings—two sisters and a brother named John —all lived together in Urbana.

Originally there were three Glenn brothers. Once their father, a wealthy Urbana settler who owned a tanyard, bought new coats for two of them but ran out of money before he procured one for John. Father explained the situation to son and said he'd buy him a fine coat later. John angrily said he would never wear a coat again as long as his father lived. John went to his room and remained there the next fourteen years, coming out at last to attend his father's funeral—while wearing a coat, which he perhaps regarded as a symbolic victory.

After the paterfamilias expired, the siblings hired an artist to fresco the entire house. A reporter writing in 1889 said, "The walls and ceilings are filled with grotesque figures, serpents and animals." The sitting room was decorated to resemble a forest, complete with vines climbing the walls and the little critters of nature peeping through holes in the trees. John didn't like the decorations and again confined himself to his room—this time for four years, coming out to attend the funeral of a brother who had provoked him.

John died in October 1900. A cousin of his father, Edward Glenn, was the founder of Cincinnati's suburb Glendale.

Hard to Swallow

Somebody should write a learned dissertation on the weird things that have been found in Ohio women's stomachs. A Toledo madwoman with a mania for swallowing foreign objects died in November 1898; when she was dissected at a medical college, students found these items in her: a quart of hairpins, needles, brass pins, pumpkin and melon seeds, small nails, pieces of glass ranging from one to three inches long, and "other indigestible substances." The hairpins were bent at right angles and over five hundred in number; there were as many brass pins and almost as many needles. Among all this junk and scrap metal was a ring set with a fine stone. The autopsy revealed that her diet resulted in a three-inch-wide hole in her stomach.

Elizabeth D., a sixty-year-old Marion native, died of peritonitis at Columbus State Hospital on August 16, 1899. When doctors peeped into her digestive organs during the autopsy, they found the handles of five silver spoons and fifty cambric needles in her stomach. Her bowels yielded fifty more needles. A year before, Elizabeth told an attendant that she swallowed the spoon handles but no one believed her.

>─<*>─<0>─<*>─<

In 1898 Elizabeth G. of Napoleon drank well water and complained afterward that she swallowed a snake, which was causing her discomfort. Everyone thought she was just nuts, but in September 1899 a doctor gave her an emetic, probably to humor her. The physician felt a trifle foolish when she vomited forth a number of creatures with heads shaped like a fish's but with bodies and tails like a snake's. Elizabeth insisted her bowels were not free of serpents, so surgeons performed an operation. They pulled nine snakes from her intestines. The runt of the litter measured one foot, seven inches; the largest was two feet, three inches long. The obvious objection is that they were common tapeworms, but the doctor preserved one of the beasts in a jar of alcohol and told a reporter: "Yes, we removed nine snakes, or something that resembled snakes, from [Elizabeth's] stomach. These things are something new to me and I am unable to give you a name for them. They have eyes like those of a fish, but a regular snake body. We placed two or three of them on the floor and they ran around and wiggled like an ordinary snake until they became chilled through and then died. There is nothing about these reptiles resembling tapeworms."

Faithful until Death, Part Three

Charles F. lost a shootout with Prohibition officers in July 1924 and was buried in a lonesome graveyard near Lancaster. His dog Nero followed the hearse to his master's resting place, and there he stayed until his own death on March 14, 1925. Nero would leave the grave only for brief food breaks.

Clark's Secret

Clark H. was a clerk and delivery boy for Crossroads Grocery in Summersville. He was only twenty-eight and his childhood sweetheart was Oletha M. of York Center. They were scheduled to marry on January 5, 1939, but Clark disappeared the day before. He was found at the bottom of a quarry pool bound with copper wire and tied to a five-gallon milk can loaded with rocks. The coroner said Clark was alive when cast into the icy water.

Outraged residents of Summersville and York Center swore they'd lynch Clark's murderer if they got their farmwork-strengthened hands on him. Oletha cried, "How could anybody kill my man?"

Clark's delivery truck, which was found near the death site, held $147 in cash and an additional $5 was in the dead man's pocket. Police reasoned that there must have been a motive other than robbery.

A mysterious news announcement came on January 7: Clark had committed suicide. The copper wire binding his body was traced to the store where he worked and the shoe prints leading from his truck to the quarry matched his shoes. The authorities were not ready to reveal the reason for the suicide: "The verdict, authorities said, would be based on newly-discovered evidence, the nature of which was not revealed. . . . [The police sergeant] declined to discuss the new developments but asserted a solution was imminent."

The truth, as revealed the next day, was that poor Clark was a hermaphrodite and felt he could not go through with the marriage. The prosecutor explained:

> He was as much woman as man and he realized marriage would be unthought of. He had a horror about anyone finding out about his condition. Only his mother knew. He had postponed marriage several times. When he saw there was no way of postponing

marriage this time and that to reveal the fact of his physical condition was out of the question, he weighted himself down with rocks in a milk can in hope that his body would be so decomposed when it was found that his physical condition would not be known.

But evidently someone knew Clark's secret, because that unknown someone tried to break into the morgue and steal his body.

4

CREEPY KANSAS

Not So Sharp as His Name Suggests

DAVE SHARP, A GAMBLER, TOOK A REAL GAMBLE WHEN HE unearthed the coffin of George W., a Wellington dance hall proprietor, and filched George's $250 diamond pin. Dave gave the bauble to a woman he fancied and was so foolish as to tell her exactly how he'd procured it. Once he seemed interested in another woman, his vindictive girlfriend told the authorities and Dave was arrested at Caldwell on May 17, 1882.

Buried Alive: Kansas

The following story was told at a meeting of the Board of Governors of the National Soldiers' Homes in April 1901. A soldier named Clark sank into a coma at the Kansas Soldiers' Home. He woke up in a four-dollar coffin, wearing his old uniform. He rocked the coffin back and forth until it broke—fortunately, he had not yet been buried. He popped up out of the casket and found himself in a church in the dark of night. The "dead man" ran down the aisle, the sight of which nearly caused the night watchman to go into a coma himself. While recuperating in the hospital, Clark told the governor of the Kansas Soldiers' Home that when he awoke in the coffin, he knew he wasn't dead because he was hungry and his feet were cold: "If I had been in Heaven I would not be hungry, and if I had been in Hell my feet would not be cold."

><+>-0-<+><

The five-year-old daughter of a couple seemed to die at Hanston on August 11, 1901. On the way to the cemetery next day, a bolt of lightning allegedly hit the metallic casket and opened it, whereupon the child sat up and asked for her mama.

Creativity in Suicide: Kansas

A farmer who lived near Larned craved to take his own life in a particularly nasty way. On October 14, 1922, he tied a rope to the collar of his unruliest horse and tied the other end to his own neck. The spirited steed took off at a trot, and when it finally returned to the barn, it dragged what remained of the farmer behind it.

><+>-0-<+><

Florence M. was visiting her parents in Pittsburg. Her father came home on July 3, 1939, and found a note: "I've gone fishing. Just reel in the line when you want me. Love, Flo." Everyone wondered what that meant. When they found her rod and reel anchored under a stone, they pulled up the line and landed Florence, drowned, with the hook attached to her pajamas.

The Hateful Dead

Something was persecuting Fred K., a farmer who lived near Great Bend, and that something did not seem human. It bothered Fred so much that in July 1927 he announced he would soon abandon his ancestral home. He described the ghost's antics to reporters—phenomena that ranged from faintly amusing to vaguely disturbing.

Faintly amusing: "He hangs pictures backward on the wall, blacks my hired man's eye, opens the family Bible and changed the Virgin Mary [statue] in different places," said Fred.

Vaguely disturbing: "Last winter we all saw him peeping in the windows but we could never find any trace of him in the snow." On one occasion, five heavily armed farmers waited for Fred's supernatural pest to materialize. When it did, they fired upon it with many a round of buckshot. The form "flitted away" unperturbed and unbleeding. According to a reporter's description, "The five farmers are willing to make affidavits that the 'spook' rose high in the air and floated soundlessly over a six-foot wire fence like a slow-motion picture of a pole vaulter."

"I believe this fellow wants me to leave," said Fred. "He's got something on his mind and maybe that's it. He wouldn't keep up his pestering me if it wasn't."

∫

NIGHTMARISH NEBRASKA

Libel on a Tombstone

JAMES P. OF LINCOLN CAME HOME EARLY ONE DAY IN February 1893 and found his wife "in the company of a male friend." During the ensuing fracas, his wife burned to death when her clothes became saturated with lamp oil and ignited after she tried to warm herself by a stove fire. James was arrested but proved in court that her immolation was accidental. Nevertheless, his wife's father, George G., erected a magnificent six-foot monument over her grave on which he stated that her husband had murdered her. James sued his father-in-law for $5,000, alleging that the inscription was libelous. The lawsuit generated considerable talk in its time, but I have been unable to discover its outcome.

Getting in the Last Word: Bizarre Epitaphs, Nebraska

A story making the rounds in 1912 alleged that an unnamed Nebraskan buried his three wives in the same plot but was too stingy to give each an elaborate monument. His ingenious solution was to make all three share the same epitaph by giving each spouse a small monument with her name engraved on it—"Mary," "Elizabeth," "Matilda"—along with a carving of a hand pointing to a larger stone in the center of the plot. Each of the three individual stones bore the inscription "For epitaph see large stone."

Timely Ends, Part Three

As Michael S.'s father lay dying of consumption, he told his son that he (Michael) would not live to see his thirtieth birthday. Several years later, as his son worked as chief electrician at Armour's packing plant in South Omaha, he was electrocuted when he touched live wires. The date was November 29, 1902; he would have turned thirty if he had lived until the following Sunday.

Creativity in Suicide: Nebraska

Wilson W., a farmer who lived three miles north of Brock, cut his wife Mary's throat a little after midnight on February 27, 1900. After performing this atrocity he placed a handkerchief on her neck, put pennies on her eyes, and wrote a note stating, "You will find her entirely dead." Then he walked to the cemetery and cut his own throat and shot himself on the grave of his first wife.

༄

In May 1914, a couple from Burton had a quarrel that culminated in the wife drinking poison. Her husband begged her to take an antidote. She refused, so he drank poison too. He died quickly—after which his wife took an antidote and survived, making her the kind of person who would cheat in a suicide pact.

Closing Remarks, Nebraska

Dr. Edwin Katzkee from Omaha probably did not intend to kill himself. He left a notebook with instructions on how to use a pulmotor to revive him in case his experiment went too far. Also, a note stated that suicide was not his intention: "This is just my way of contributing to medical and scientific archives." In other words, he meant to research death and use himself as a human guinea pig. On November 25, 1936, the thirty-four-year-old doctor gobbled massive doses of cocaine and, apparently lacking a notepad, wrote about his sensations on his office wall.

At first his handwriting and thoughts were clear, but the former became illegible and the latter incoherent as the evening wore on. At the onset he wrote in neat letters: "Eyes mildly dilated. Vision excellent." This was followed discursively by an opinion that carbohydrates might make a good antidote to poison. Then: "Now able to stand up." "Partial recovery. Smoked cigarette." At one point, feeling rather pleased with himself, the doctor wrote: "Results will be recorded in Rx books! Have a university and college [illegible] any findings. They better be good because I am not going to repeat the experiment."

He recorded that his vision was growing dimmer and his heart weaker. He developed "a staggering gait." He thought his voice was "apparently okay," and yet when he tried to speak, no sound came. The final legible word he scribbled was "paralysis."

But for all that, the doctor wasted his time and his life. Medical men agreed that his little experiment had no value due to early onset of delirium. All he left for posterity was a creepy story, but that's more than many have done.

Ghostwritten

William A. worked as a farmhand for a man named Bills, fourteen miles west of Nebraska City. He was an ordinary man with an extraordinary story to tell.

He married a woman named Lulu in Illinois in 1881. She died of consumption in 1884. William swore later that he personally witnessed her lying in her casket and saw the coffin closed and buried. Shortly afterward, the grieving widower moved to Kansas.

He hadn't been there long when he got a letter from Lulu, dated after her death and postmarked from the town in Illinois where they used to live. William compared the letter to notes written by Lulu before she died—the handwriting matched. In the new letter Lulu said she was lonely, missed William, needed his help, and urged him to return to her. In short, the contents were nothing out of the ordinary, but the writer added mysteriously: "You all thought I died, but I did not, and am much better than when I saw you last."

After that, William received letters irregularly from his dead Lulu—or was it his living Lulu, or someone pretending to be her? He lived in Concordia, Kansas, until March 1887, when he pulled up stakes for Nebraska; in June he got a letter postmarked Concordia in which Lulu reproached him for leaving town before she could visit him.

William logically suspected that he was the butt of an uncommonly sick practical joke. He sent a bundle of the letters to Lulu's parents in Illinois. They were baffled, stating that the penmanship was identical to hers.

He got a letter from Table Rock, Kansas, in which Lulu claimed to be ill and out of money, and requested that William come visit her. He fairly flew there to get to the bottom of the mystery. He found that a sick woman stayed in the local hotel for a week but had already left for parts unknown. The desk register included her signature—no place of residence given—and it matched the writing in the letters. The hotel staff described the guest: she looked a great deal like the late Lulu.

William was in a lather of confusion by this point. He took a trip to Illinois and had his wife's body exhumed on the chance that she had not actually died. Her remains were right where they were supposed to be.

A writer for the *Kansas City Journal* who covered the weird story wrote: "[William] is a fairly educated man, not at all superstitious, but acknowledges that the affair has worried him a great deal. His reputation here is good, his employer speaking very highly of him."

Assuming that the dead have better things to do than write letters and that ghosts don't check into hotels, what was going on? The letter asking for financial help suggests that someone was pulling a very elaborate hoax to mulct money from William—but if so, why did the perpetrator check out of the hotel before he showed up, which would rather seem to defeat the purpose of the scam? What would have happened if William arrived in time to see "Lulu" face-to-face? Is it likely that the itinerant farmhand was wealthy enough to warrant being the target of an elaborate scheme? Were the letters written by a clever forger who also just happened to bear a physical resemblance to the late Lulu? If so, how did the forger get samples of Lulu's handwriting to begin with?

It should be noted that on one occasion, William got up the nerve to send a letter back to Lulu. It was returned to him by—heh!—the Kansas City dead letter office.

Lynched

George S., held on a charge of rape, was removed from the courthouse at Omaha on October 18, 1891, by a mob determined to hang him. George expired from fright but the vengeful mob beat his corpse and hanged it from a wire anyway.

⊢•⊹•○•⊹•⊣

Barrett S., the treasurer of Holt County, embezzled every penny of the county's money and spent it or loaned it to friends. He went to prison for five years. Perhaps hoping his misdeeds had been forgiven, on December 31, 1894, he went for a carriage ride with his family near O'Neill. A mob of men forced the carriage to stop and, before Barrett's family, they blindfolded him, hanged him, and flung his body in the river.

The story has a strange aftermath. On April 4, 1895, a group of O'Neill boys were discussing the lynching. Ten-year-old Grover L. asserted that getting hanged is painless, and to prove it he fastened a hitching strap over a post, tied the other end around his neck, and stepped off a box. By the time his companions realized what was happening, little Grover had proved his point.

The Shadow Defense

One Sunday afternoon in 1910, someone placed a bomb on Omaha political boss Tom Denison's porch—a suitcase containing a dozen sticks of dynamite and a device for setting them off. The bomb did not kill him, but it was still an attempted murder punishable by life imprisonment. Jim E. was suspected since he was known to have quarreled with Tom.

When Jim went on trial in January 1911, things did not go his way. Two unimpeachable young women swore convincingly that they saw a man who resembled Jim near the crime scene at two thirty in the afternoon as they were leaving church. A photograph was entered into evidence proving they had been at church on the date of the attempted bombing. The picture clearly showed Jim's accusers standing among a group posing before the church.

It seemed like Jim's goose was thoroughly cooked but his attorney John Yeiser, a native of Danville, Kentucky, looked at the picture and noticed something, the significance of which had escaped everyone else: the steeple cast a shadow on the horizontal planks of the church wall. John showed the photo to an astronomer at Creighton University, who calculated the time of day the photo was taken based on the angle of the shadows. His conclusion was that it was snapped at exactly 3:21:29 in the afternoon—an hour later than the time when the mistaken witnesses swore they saw Jim at the crime scene.

Jim was acquitted based on the craftiness of his attorney, the expert knowledge of the astronomer, and the reliability of the sun.

Midwestern Monster

Who tried to break into their cabin? That's what woodcutters Lon M. and John H. wanted to know. They came home from work on the night of November 26, 1887, only to find the door had been tampered with. There were fresh tracks in the ground. Lon stayed at the cabin, located near Nebraska City, while John took off in pursuit.

After an hour's fruitless searching John was ready to go home when he stumbled over a terrifying creature shaped like a man "but so frightfully deformed as to leave only a faint resemblance" to a human. It was naked, had pop eyes and fangs, and seemed to be handless. It ran bent over: "The monstrosity in locomotion used its feet and what were undoubtedly its arms, from the elbows to where the hands should have been, as forefeet."

That sighting was plenty for John, who briskly hurried back to the cabin. Next day the woodsmen and their neighbors followed the creature's tracks but gave up at sunset. At some point during the posse's searches Lon found the monster in the brush, tried to capture it, and was severely bitten in the arm. On November 29, a posse of twenty resumed the hunt across a snowy landscape. The tracks stopped at the river, and the men assumed the critter had drowned while crossing—they hoped so, anyway.

6

UNUSUAL IOWA

Suing the Snatchers

A UNIQUE CASE OF BODY SNATCHING CAME TO LIGHT IN December 1902, when Eleanor and Homer L. sued the Rex Embalming Company and the undertaking and embalming firms of W. F. Pettis & Co. and W. C. Harbach. The couple accused the defendants of swiping their relative John A. from the grave in 1896, embalming him, and exhibiting his shell as a "petrified man" in Des Moines and all over Iowa. The couple demanded $10,000 to soothe their hurt feelings and, presumably, also requested the return of John.

Getting in the Last Word: Bizarre Epitaphs, Iowa

On George Taylor, in Oak Hill Cemetery, Tama: "Assassinated July 19, 1913, by a dirty coward whose name is not worthy to be mentioned here."

On Nancy Walker Smith (1785–1853), in Wiscotta Cemetery, Redfield: "Connecticut gave her life; New York her husband, Humphrey; Missouri a home and eight children; Iowa a grave."

Eccentric Interments, Iowa

John M. of Guthrie Center was an old-fashioned kind of fellow who really hated those newfangled automobiles. He loathed them so much that he refused to ride in them and would sometimes defiantly walk right in front of their paths. He was struck twice—the first time he was lucky. The second not-so-lucky occasion was in mid-December 1934. Before he succumbed to his injuries on December 27, his final request was that there be no cars in his funeral procession. Accordingly, the streets of Guthrie Center were cleared of all autos on December 31 as the old merchant was carried to his final resting place in a horse-drawn hearse followed by a line of antiquated buggies.

Strange Wills, Iowa

From the will of Oscar L. of Des Moines, who died on October 18, 1931: "In case of death, dress me in warm underclothes and in my dress suit, turn my body slightly to the right side, face in the same direction."

Dottie Pawns Herself

Dottie of Des Moines was hard up for money on that January day in 1907, so she went to a pawnshop and sold the rights to her corpse to the proprietor. The bill of sale read:

> I, Miss Dottie M., of my own free will and without coercion of any kind, do hereby sell to Mose L. my body after death, to do with as he sees fit, for the consideration of ten dollars. The said Mose L. shall not take possession of my body until after I am dead and if at any time during my life I wish to cause this bill of sale [to become] null and void [I] shall pay to Mose L. or his assignees $10 in good and lawful money of the United States, [and] his interest in my body shall cease.

Mose's business failed and in April 1915 he filed a petition in bankruptcy court to determine whether Dottie's future body could be counted as an asset. (Dottie was still alive and living in Denver.) The court ruled that her body would be of no value after death and should be considered neither an asset nor a liability.

Creativity in Suicide: Iowa

A man from Dubuque went to the outhouse on May 30, 1878—nothing newsworthy about that. But his family thought he had stayed in there an unconscionably long time. They called his name repeatedly; he answered each time. But when curiosity finally got the better of them, they opened the door and found the man disemboweling himself with a knife and tossing pieces of his intestines to hogs. "It was a most sad and disgusting affair," correctly lamented the press.

⊷━◦━⊷

John M. was a stonecutter in Dubuque whose job consisted of laboriously lettering inscriptions on tombstones with long chisels. On the night of December 16, 1885, an expressman stopped by John's shop en route to the cemetery to pick up a gravestone. He likely emitted a shrill shriek when he found that the proprietor had driven two chisels crosswise into his head. One, seven inches long, was embedded horizontally through his head in front of his ears; the other one went through the center of his forehead to a depth of two inches. He was still able to speak and asked the delivery man if he would kindly drive the chisels in deeper. The press called John's demise "a case unparalleled in the history of suicides."

⊷━◦━⊷

Jacob B. of Iowa City killed himself on March 16, 1903, by placing a three-corner file in a gun barrel and heating the barrel of the weapon in a stove. The gun fired when it got hot, sending the file through Jacob's heart.

><·<>·o·<>·<

Carl P. amazed the citizens of Webster City on August 27, 1907, by setting a pile of paper money on fire, throwing his jewelry in the sewer, and then announcing that he was about to kill himself. He crossed the street, shouted for everyone to watch, and then capped the dramatic gestures by shooting himself in the head. It will surprise no one to learn that Carl was a professional actor.

><·<>·o·<>·<

A woman who lived near Davenport poisoned herself and her family with strychnine on August 2, 1910. But first she sewed everyone a burial robe.

><·<>·o·<>·<

Maria (or Marie) M. threw her six-year-old stepson Nicholas into the Cedar River at Waterloo on August 7, 1924. She explained that she wanted to commit suicide and thought being hanged for murder was as good a way as any.

><·<>·o·<>·<

Egnat T., a midget and grocer in Waterloo, was four feet, ten inches tall. He hanged himself in his store on September 15, 1934, by jumping off a cigar box. His fatal leap totaled three inches.

Bitter Ironies, Part Four

James H. was testifying in a Des Moines courthouse on May 9, 1907. When asked the standard question about his age, he replied: "I am sixty-five, but sound as a dollar and good for at least eighty-five." After which he gasped and died almost instantaneously of heart disease.

Closing Remarks, Iowa

George B., a fifteen-year-old Cedar Rapids high school student, rode his bicycle into the countryside during a thunderstorm on the night of April 1, 1920, and blew out his brains with a revolver. A note on his body read: "I am killing myself because I am too lazy to keep on living and take the responsibility of life. I don't believe in religion of any kind."

A woman from Norwalk went crazy on Halloween 1937 and shot five of her seven children and then herself. She left a note to her two surviving sons: "You will find us dead this morning. Don't get excited." She added, "I have stood all I can take and best to take the kids along. All that saves you boys is no more shells." The woman and all five children were buried in a twenty-foot grave in Webb Cemetery.

A Most Mortifying Blunder

Hensley M., a traveling tobacco salesman from Louisville, Kentucky, stopped at Moore and Co.'s drugstore in Atlantic, Iowa, on June 7, 1910. He asked the pharmacist for a tall frosty glass of Hunyadi mineral water. The pharmacist handed him a bottle with the Hunyadi label.

A few seconds after quaffing, Hensley grimaced and asked, "What is that stuff, anyway?"

"Hunyadi water," said the clerk.

"Doesn't taste much like it."

Then Hensley turned ghost white. He shouted, "You've poisoned me!" He sank to the floor and died within ten minutes.

A careful examination of the bottle proved that despite its label, it contained formaldehyde. The drink had essentially embalmed him.

Moore and Co. apologized, but the next thing they knew attorneys representing Hensley's family were suing to the tune of $10,000.

Shooting the Sheet

In the winter of 1889 a ghost was wont to rise near Silver Lake, four miles west of Casey, and scare the fool out of everyone who beheld it. One February night the ghost scared a team of horses so badly that they panicked, tipped over the buggy, and nearly killed a farmer's wife.

The suspicious farmer thought a shotgun might make a fine ghost-repellant, and he waited in the environs of Silver Lake four nights without success. The spirit appeared on February 28 and, after receiving a load of buckshot in its hide, emitted a most unghostly cry of "My God, don't shoot any more!"

The farmer, having winged his spook, sportingly provided the wounded wraith with a doctor's care. The true identity of the "ghost" was left out of the papers, but he allegedly was a land speculator who wanted to scare people away from the area so he could buy the land near the lake at a cut-rate price.

Maynard Appreciates the Finer Things

Pearl S. and her much younger lover, Maynard L.—ages thirty and eighteen, respectively—plotted to murder Pearl's sixty-year-old husband of a week, farmer Dan S. of Elkader. One of them shotgunned the old gentleman on May 5, 1936, but when caught they blamed each other in their confessions. Pearl and Maynard were both convicted, given life sentences, and paroled in September 1952.

All in all, it was a run-of-the-mill crime of passion, but worthy of inclusion due to one delightful, bizarre detail: when young Maynard was arrested, he had five harmonicas in his pocket. "I like good music," he said.

Consumed by Rats, Part Two

A long time ago Dubuque had a sewer that extended from the corner of Main and Fourteenth Streets to the foot of Main Street; to the east stood Jackson Square Cemetery. In 1880, a writer for the *Dubuque Times* remembered an incident from his boyhood involving cesspool and cemetery.

He and other boys used to explore the manmade underground cavern on Saturdays. Part of the fun, the writer acknowledged, was the aura of constant danger. The sewer was two feet wide, five feet high, and its ceiling was made of loose arched stones that constantly threatened to wiggle free and brain some ragamuffin. A distant open hole provided scant light. Every now and then the children would find a "treasure" swept into the sewer by street cleaners, such as a silver spoon.

On one occasion, the writer reminisced, a flood "tore Seventeenth Street to pieces and washed numbers of the dead bodies of Jackson Square in all directions." Unearthed coffins and bones of Dubuque's former residents were scattered about the streets. The following Saturday the boys explored as usual, curious to see what damage the flood did to the sewer. "The old sewer never looked gloomier or more dismal," the journalist remembered, "and as the heavy wagons rolled overhead, the rumbling sound created seemed to vibrate from one aperture to the other." The floor was submerged under slush several inches deep.

The writer managed to get far ahead of his companions when his wanderings were halted by loud squeaks:

> In front of me I saw a hundred or more large mammoth rats greedily and savagely devouring something which could not be identified owing to the rats covering it completely. My call to my companions frightened [the rats] and as they left the object for a second I was horrified to see it was a skeleton partly covered with flesh. It had been washed from the old burying ground, and for days it had served as food for these disgusting objects.

The boy's shout frightened the rats away from their meal—but only for a second. Then "the hungry vermin rushed back to the body and the squealing noise as they fought for the dried and withered flesh was perfectly unendurable and would soon drive one mad."

Our hero couldn't resist shying a rock at the rodents. Big mistake: the rats swarmed in panic. The boy clubbed one with a stick as it passed. A bigger mistake: the expiring rat unleashed a squeal that was a battle cry to the others, and the young explorer soon had all the rats he could handle heading in his direction. As he belabored them with his club, his friends finally showed up with a light and the rats scattered.

The boys got out of the sewer in one piece; the skeleton was given "a second decent burial," presumably by grown-ups; the rats enjoyed a feed; so, except for the rats that were bludgeoned, everybody won.

Losing by a Nose

Circa December 1882, a barber and a "foolish young man" were romantic rivals in Dubuque. The FYM won the girl and then committed two serious lapses in judgment. The first was to go to the loser's establishment for a shave. The second was to tease the former rival about his loss once ensconced in the chair. The tonsorial artist retorted by slicing off the winner's nose with a deft sweep of the razor. As the *Virginia City Chronicle* remarked: "Human nature, armed with a razor, is a dangerous thing."

Silent Types: Iowa

Because he was jilted at the altar in 1889, "Silent Bill" P. of Audubon took a strange revenge on the world by never speaking again. He even refused offers to appear on radio shows.

Silent Bill's self-imposed silence ended with his death on May 23, 1939, at age eighty-six. But afterward his relative Frank C. revealed that Silent Bill's fifty-year silence had been marred once and only once. After Frank asked him a barrage of questions, Silent Bill said, "Confound it, can't you give me a chance to think it over?" Annoyance succeeded where the temptation of radio celebrity had not.

Carnival Collateral

When the traveling freak show came to Webster City in June 1902, the proprietors boarded at the Park Hotel. They abandoned the hotel on June 6, leaving a bill for thirty-two dollars. But as a show of good faith, the absconding managers left as collateral one of their star attractions: a girl who weighed 612 pounds and presumably had an appetite to match. They never returned.

7

MACABRE MINNESOTA

Snatched a Long, Long Way from Home

"SCIENCE MUST DO HER WORK OF COURSE, BUT SCIENCE must be decent in doing that work," commented the *Louisville Courier-Journal* on page 1, August 9, 1878. The indignant editorial was occasioned by this incident: a deceased young man, identity unknown, was found floating in the river with a bullet in his head, indicating murder or suicide. He was buried in the city potter's field—the burial site for the anonymous and/or impoverished. Investigation proved that he was John W., son of the Episcopal bishop of Minnesota. Louisville authorities took shovels in hand to exhume John so he could be sent to his family in the Midwest. The dead man was still in his grave, but the coffin lid had been tampered with by grave robbers who left the graveyard without their prize. Very likely John—whose remains spent considerable time in the water—was in too much disrepair to suit their purposes. He would have made a very poor medical specimen indeed: a reporter described him as being "in a frightful condition, the face black and without shape"; his body was "a ghastly mass of almost shapeless putrescence"; and the meat dropped from his bones when the undertaker touched him. The authorities held their noses, packed young John in ice and charcoal, and a day later his brother freighted him home to Faribault.

The attempted snatching of John inspired a *Courier-Journal* reporter to check into the topic of grave robbing. He found that because laws against the same were strict in Ohio, medical colleges in that state got their cadavers from resurrectionists working in Indiana and Kentucky. One of them spilled the beans to the journalist about the favored method for snatching bodies.

The only necessary tools were a spade, a keyhole saw, and a rope. (A bottle of whisky to fight off the chill and stoke one's courage was also desirable.) In the movies, stealers of corpses are depicted as unearthing an entire grave, but in real life this would have been considered unnecessary labor since the thieves had no interest in toting away the coffin. Only half the grave—the upper half—needed to be uncovered, and a professional could manage it in eight minutes. Once the upper half of the coffin was unearthed, the robber would cut the lid with the saw. Soon enough, he would be staring down onto the waxy countenance of the fragrant dead—preferably by the light of the moon, because that was even creepier.

By grabbing the sides of the coffin and repositioning his weight, the industrious ghoul could crack the lid. Broken portions of the lid would be removed; a rope was lowered into the grave and tied around the subject's neck, and then he or she would be pulled up out of the hole. Savvy snatchers always threw the body's shroud or other clothing back in the grave. A legal loophole held that stealing the clothes was a felony, but taking the body was only a misdemeanor. Technically speaking, the corpse didn't "belong" to anyone but its raiment did.

Once smuggled to a medical school, physicians opened a vein in the cadaver's neck, pumped in arsenic as a preservative, and stored it in a pickling vat where it awaited its chance to increase the store of humankind's knowledge via dissection by students.

The talkative body snatcher regaled the *Courier-Journal* man with other tricks of the trade and ghoulish yarns. Once, he said, his team accidentally pulled the head off a woman while extricating her. He affirmed that most of their merchandise was stolen from potter's fields rather than private cemeteries, and that they received between eight and twelve dollars for a specimen, which translated into modern currency would be between roughly two and three hundred dollars. Medical students wore long gowns during dissection to keep from getting "juices" on their clothing. If the body emanated a little stink, the students smoked pipes to reduce their disgust. During winter months bodies tended to freeze too solid to dissect, and then students took turns swinging a corpse before a fireplace until it thawed sufficiently. But God help them all if they kept the body at the fire too long, because then "the fat melts and runs down into the floor, producing a queer and sickening odor."

Sometimes undertakers worked in collusion with grave robbers by "marking" the fresh bodies that were worth stealing. That saved resurrectionists the trouble of working hard to snatch a body only to find it riddled with some loathsome communicable disease or in a state of unusable rottenness. Obviously, the grave of young John from Minnesota had not been so "marked."

(A final disgusting note: the *Courier-Journal* reporter visited the potter's field a few days after the authorities removed John W. from his grave, and found that pieces of his broken coffin were *still there*. The journalist wrote: "A stench most horrible arose from the coffin yesterday and could be noticed a quarter of a mile to the windward side, though only deep, dark, clotted blood spots remain to tell the tale of its occupancy.")

Ghouls Just Want to Have Fun: Minnesota

Some folks living in Winona—and that includes the constabulary—in the early 1920s had some strange ideas concerning the dead. Thomas B.'s daughter Frances died on November 15, 1916, and over the next five years her five brothers died one by one, culminating in the passing of Frank on December

31, 1921. The only surviving children were four married daughters. The father wondered—as is only natural—if Frances's spirit somehow had been responsible for the deaths of his five sons. So he and a neighbor rang in the New Year by going to St. Mary's Catholic Cemetery and exhuming Frances and his son Joseph to "confirm certain signs."

Rumor spread that he decapitated his daughter's corpse and placed her head at the foot of the coffin in the superstitious belief that it would end the deaths in his family. Thomas didn't deny opening the graves, but said the bodies were skeletal and that he didn't mutilate them.

But of course the police simply couldn't take his word for it— plus, the public wanted to know. The authorities announced that they would open the graves of Frances and Joseph to see whether their heads were missing or atop their necks where God intended them to be. Even if they weren't, Thomas could not be punished since he would have committed no crime under Minnesota law. The graves were opened to satisfy morbid curiosity rather than for legal reasons.

On January 8, 1922, the lids creaked open and the siblings were found to be intact.

Buried Alive: Minnesota

Medical science in the time of our ancestors was not up to snuff when it came to determining the difference between a coma and death. The result was that many persons woke up in their graves or came within a hairbreadth of doing so. Consider the bizarre fate of Cora S., age nineteen, of Saint Paul. She can be considered one of the lucky ones—depending on one's definition of "lucky"—because instead of being hastily planted, her doctors were conscientious enough to admit they were not certain she had entered the Void. She became ill with some strange, thoroughly nineteenth-century-sounding malady called "consumption of the blood," which made blood gush from her nose and drip from her pores. Cora seemed to die on December 1, 1886, having no pulse and no discernible breath, but just to be on the safe side her mother, Anna, placed Cora in an aboveground vault at Lakewood Cemetery. One imagines that if she were not dead, spending a couple of months in a chilly crypt during a Minnesota winter was not exactly a health tonic. Anna believed in faith healing, and with help from some fellow practitioners she removed the body from the vault on February 1, 1887, and took it to her house at 420 Northeast Fifth Street. There it remained in a nice cozy bed until the middle of the month—an action that excited the interest of the city health officer. A noted Minneapolis physician wrote a lengthy piece on the puzzling case for the newspapers, in which he noted: "Notwithstanding that the body had been kept in that warm room for two weeks, there were no traces of decomposition whatsoever." There matters rested until February 18, when Cora's attendants heard a noise issuing from her throat, after which—as the doctor diplomatically phrased it—"the body began to change rapidly." In other words, she commenced decomposing with a vengeance. The doctor told Cora's mother it was now safe to bury her. Let's hope he was correct!

><+<0<+<

In March 1900, Lizzie W., age eighteen, slipped into a trance at her home on Rider Avenue in Saint Paul. Her deathlike symptoms were so convincing that her parents called in the mortician. But before the professional could get to work, Lizzie stood up, tore off her shroud, and asked bystanders what all the commotion was about.

><+<0<+<

On December 12, 1910, John R. of Westbrook drank carbolic acid while in a suicidal humor. Next day, as the undertaker prepared to inject embalming fluid into his artery, the "corpse" sat up and said, "Hello, Bill!" There were two very surprised men in the funeral home *that* day.

John recovered though his face was permanently scarred by the carbolic acid. He said that he was plumb tickled to be alive.

Had the embalming fluid entered his body, of course, he would have "eaten dandelions by the root," as the French say.

Eccentric Interments, Minnesota

John R., of Saint Paul, went to fight with the British in the Boer War. His mother made an English pudding—his favorite dish— and preserved it for him to eat when he returned. But after getting a postcard from John in 1899, his parents never heard from him again and had no idea as to his fate. His name did not appear on the rosters of the dead or wounded. Nevertheless, his mother kept the pudding stored away in a bureau awaiting the day of his return. In January 1916 his mother went to Saint Paul City Hospital with a broken leg. She died on January 26 and was buried with the pudding at her request.

Strange Wills, Minnesota

Some families pass down valuable secret recipes from generation to generation. When "Fisherman" John J. died in Stillwater on November 9, 1926, his twelve-year-old nephew, George L., inherited a strange legacy indeed: the family's secret method for locating the corpses of the drowned, a lost art for which John had achieved a national reputation. John used the secret to recover five hundred bodies, and his father employed the same method to find a thousand.

Clubs You Wouldn't Have Wanted to Join: Minnesota

On July 21, 1885, thirty-four former soldiers from Company B of the First Minnesota Regiment—all veterans of the First Battle of Bull Run—formed a tontine called the Last Man Club. It met at Stillwater every July 21, the anniversary of the battle, and at each meeting a bottle of rare Burgundy wine was present but not opened. The idea was that the last surviving veteran would drink a toast in memory of his comrades in arms.

By 1923 only four members were left: Peter Hall of Atwater; John Goff of Minneapolis; Charles Morey Lockwood of

Chamberlain, South Dakota; and Emil Graff of Saint Cloud, Florida.

The July 1929 meeting was held at the Minnesota Club in Saint Paul. Only Peter, John, and Charles remained. John died a month later.

Peter died on April 18, 1930. The Last Man proved to be Charles Lockwood, age eighty-seven. On the forty-fifth anniversary of Bull Run, Charles held the final ceremony in Stillwater's Lowell Inn, which stood on the site of the old Sawyer House—where the club had been formed in a spirit of humor. The room held thirty-three empty chairs, each decorated with a black bow. The sole survivor read the names of his departed fellow soldiers and drank a toast from the old bottle. Then he disbanded the club.

But Charles wasn't quite ready to say the final good-bye to his companions. In May 1931 he toured Washington, DC, on behalf of his regiment, which had camped behind the Capitol in 1861. He told reporters of having seen President Lincoln:

> I remember the first time I saw Abe Lincoln. It was on Arlington Heights—a grand review. He sat on a fine black horse, with his plug hat set back, like this—and that plug of hair of his was hanging down like this. I thought he was about the homeliest man I ever saw in my life. . . . I saw him three or four times while we were camped around here before and after the Battle of Bull Run. Once I called on him and shook hands with him—that was after Bull Run. He was always kind to all the soldiers and glad to see them.

Charles gave the wine bottle to a historical society. He answered the final bugle call on October 4, 1935.

Don't Mess with Nels

Because attorney Nels Q. of Lakefield and his wife, Anna, were both subject to cataleptic spells, they feared that they might be embalmed while alive. In Nels's words, both "had had very narrow escapes from death by the hands of the man known as the undertaker."

So great was their phobia that they made a pact. According to Nels, "My wife and I agreed that in [the] event either of us should apparently die, the other would not call an undertaker for three days, but would watch over the body, keep the room temperature at 85 degrees and now and then speak sympathetic words of encouragement to the departed one."

(The reader is invited to pause for a moment and imagine this scene.)

But Anna died in March 1934 while visiting cousins in Mason City, Iowa, and her unthinking relatives had her embalmed. They became the target of a $60,000 damage suit filed by Nels in March 1936.

Succinct Obituaries, Part Three

From June 1919: "Rochester, Minn., June 21.—Harry R., quarryman, attempted to open a twenty-five pound keg of powder with an ax. The family requests no flowers."

Creativity in Suicide: Minnesota

A court clerk of Watonwan County found it expedient to commit suicide in Saint James in this fashion on July 8, 1895: first he beat his head to a pulp with the blunt end of a claw hammer; then he used the claw end to mangle his dome still further. He recently had been released from an insane asylum. Also, he was described as "prominent in state politics."

⊳─⊷─○─⊶─⊲

Emir O. of Duluth wanted to commit suicide in Detroit on September 4, 1911; he also wanted to write a farewell note to his sweetheart. He combined both goals in a time-saving way by cutting his throat with a razor and using his blood as ink. Employing a toothpick as a pen, he wrote, "Elda, good bye. Emir."

⊳─⊷─○─⊶─⊲

An unnamed well-dressed Minneapolis woman committed suicide in late December 1913 by leaping off a bridge. She landed feet first on a block of river ice and froze in a standing position, and thus made a depressing yuletide spectacle to citizens who saw her while on their way to and from the community Christmas tree a half block away.

><+><>+<

Miner Charles M. blew himself to atoms with dynamite at Chisholm on October 12, 1916. The reason: people teased him over his striking resemblance to a character in the Sunday comics pages.

><+><>+<

Gus N. hanged himself in the lobby of a Duluth hotel on Christmas Day 1916. He used a cord from a Christmas package.

><+><>+<

George W. permitted a train to run over him at Lake City on August 7, 1930. But because he wanted to go out in comfort, he dragged a chair to the tracks and sat on it till the end came.

Impressing Their Congregations: Minnesota

A reverend spoke to the Oak Park Congregational Church in Minneapolis on February 1, 1891. His text was "Is Life Worth Living?" He died of apoplexy after finishing the sermon.

Concussive Candy

On July 5, 1934, Louis R. of Hobart took a bite of something that he assumed was a piece of candy. It was actually a "torpedo," a kind of firework. Spectators had an unpleasant sight when the smoke cleared, and Louis's mistake ended fatally two days later.

Cabin Fever

Harry M. and Joseph B. were trappers who shared a cabin in the forest near Virginia, Minnesota. The pair got snowbound and, inevitably, cabin fever set in. Tempers grew shorter and shorter until Harry and Joseph got into a drunken argument on January 19, 1935, that ended in Harry stabbing his partner to death with a hunting knife and then mutilating the remains.

But because of the heavy snow, Harry had to spend more than two weeks sharing his living quarters with his slowly decomposing friend and thinking about the ramifications of his actions.

Boy Genius with a Shotgun

"Few of the great tragedies of history were created by the village idiot, and many by the village genius."—Thomas Sowell

On August 4, 1938, Harlan H., a seventeen-year-old farm youth who lived near Pine City, shot to death his father, Walter, his invalid mother, and his younger brother. He set fire to the house and fled but was captured after wrecking the family car.

Why did Harlan—described by teachers as "a brilliant lad"—murder his family? He had grand aspirations of starting a magazine on "social and political questions," which he was certain would be for "the greater good of society," and he felt his dreary family would only hold him back: "They were better than average parents, but I couldn't have worked out plans for the magazine while they were alive. . . . For as long as they lived I would be more or less obligated to stay at this farm."

The jury was not impressed with young Harlan's idealism and his idea that the untimely deaths of a few were justified if the masses could be enlightened. On November 5, Harlan was sentenced to life in prison, where he could benefit humankind by breaking rocks and making license plates.

A Good Sport

A Saint Paul detective fatally wounded a man while arresting him on a minor charge in June 1911. The man was rushed to a hospital, where he made a two-hundred-word recording before he died. The detective went on trial on June 24, and history was made when the victim became the first man to testify at his own inquest via phonograph. "I have no grudge against any man or woman," said the Voice of the Dead. "I am suffering for my folly."

Because he was such a good sport about it, the detective was acquitted.

8

WEIRD WISCONSIN

Death's Embrace

IN SEPTEMBER 1873, LUCIUS C. OF MENASHA TOOK A SIP OF what he supposed to be brandy. He supposed wrong: it was carbolic acid. He had enough time to shout, "My God, I have been poisoned!" and embrace his wife. He died in midhug and passed away in such a muscular spasm that rescuers had to use a lever to remove his arms from his wife's neck.

Exhuming Maggie

An unusual case of grave robbery—legally speaking—occurred in Port Washington. When young Maggie R. died in September 1885, wild rumor held that her death was caused by a botched abortion. Four officials opened her grave on September 26 and removed her body to see for themselves. They were the district attorney, the sheriff, a local doctor, and the county superintendent of schools. (I have no idea why the county superintendent of schools was asked to help. Maybe he was handy with a shovel.) An autopsy showed no evidence of abortion and Maggie was reinterred. Problem was, the investigators had not cleared the exhumation with her mother first, and out of retaliation she had them tried on charges of grave robbery. In November all four indefatigable seekers of the truth were found not guilty.

Buried Alive: Wisconsin

A case of premature burial was, er, unearthed late in 1889. In November a "prominent family" in Madison was stricken with diphtheria. One of their servants wanted to flee for her home in the country, but the doctor ordered her to stay put. A child in the family died of the disease, and the frightened domestic took to her bed and died—so it seemed—within a few hours. She was immediately buried, as was standard procedure for anyone who died after being exposed to contagious diseases such as diphtheria, which can even be spread by laughing. It was reported on December 13 that the servant's parents exhumed her body for removal to her hometown, *and* "upon opening the casket they were horrified to discover that the body was lying on its face, the hair wrenched from the head, and the flesh literally torn from the face and hands." The names of the parties involved were not released.

‹‹‹•○•›››

Eli and Bessie W. of West Superior were Jewish and therefore had religious objections to grave desecration. But after Bessie passed away and was buried in Duluth, Minnesota, two rumors came to the fore: one was that her husband poisoned her, and the other was that she had been buried alive. Her family wanted to know the truth and insisted that the coroner open her grave although if a gentile did so, it would violate Jewish custom. The coroner obtained permission from the district attorney, but when he arrived at the cemetery in Duluth on January 15, 1899, he was confronted by an angry mob who agreed with her husband that the grave should not be opened. The coroner wisely desisted—for the moment, that is. By nightfall he had gained permission from Jewish authorities to exhume Bessie, and he did so accompanied by ten Jews, who performed the appropriate ceremony. Then the coroner took her body to his morgue in West Superior for an examination. Though Bessie had lain in her grave four days, the coroner came to two ironclad conclusions: she had been neither buried alive nor murdered. Cause of death was "congesting of the fallopius." Vindicated, her husband threatened to sue his late wife's family—especially his brother-in-law, who had punched him in the head at a synagogue.

According to Jewish law, once Bessie's grave was opened it could never be used again. Jewish authorities filled in the hole with psalm books and dirt and said they would erect a monument on the grave explaining why it was empty. She was buried in a new grave almost alongside the old one.

⊱─⊱─◯─⊰─⊰

Pardeeville was the scene of a horrifying discovery at the end of March 1898. Julia Sarah S., who died in 1885, was exhumed in Rosedale Cemetery for removal to another plot. When the coffin lid was opened, onlookers found her lying on her side. She woke up at some point and gnawed the fingers on her right hand.

⊱─⊱─◯─⊰─⊰

In the third week of January 1899, young Jacob G. died at his home in Nasewaupee. It came as no surprise since he had been sickly for some time. His father Charles went to Sturgeon Bay and telegraphed the child's relatives. They brought a coffin and held a wake. Jacob's family placed his body on an undertaker's cooling board and was in the midst of washing him when he jumped up and tried to escape the house. When the family caught Jacob, he explained that he had been in a trance for the last forty-eight hours, during which he could hear everything going on around him but was powerless to speak or move. Within a few hours he would have been dressed, coffined, and buried. The good news was that he was not prematurely buried; the bad news was that on January 20 he had to be confined in an insane asylum.

Mike S., a stranger, died while passing through Sullivan on Election Day 1912. A coroner's jury determined heart disease to be the cause. The body was kept three days; no family members claimed it, so Mike was prepared for burial at the county's expense.

On November 9, the coffin was loaded into a horse-drawn hearse. En route to the graveyard, the horses were spooked by a train and ran away, throwing off the driver and dumping the casket into a ditch. The injured driver was assisted by none other than the man he was about to bury; the shock of the fall evidently snapped him out of a cataleptic state. A Sullivan news correspondent wrote: "But for a runaway of the horses drawing the hearse in which he was being carried to the grave, [Mike] would today be buried alive beneath the customary six feet of earth."

Thrifty but Squeamish

Horace B. of Oak Creek was a whopping six feet, seven inches tall. When he died on May 14, 1884, he was too long to easily fit in the coffin his family had purchased. An ingenious nephew cut off part of one of the corpse's legs with a handsaw. While performing this carpentry, the nephew fancied he saw the body move and he fainted. Another relative had to finish the chore and lop off part of the other leg besides. When word got out, the nephew was nearly lynched before cooler heads prevailed.

Getting in the Last Word: Bizarre Epitaphs, Wisconsin

A gravestone in Catholic Cemetery, La Pointe, has inspired comment due to its well-intended but poorly worded sentiments:

> *To the memory of Abraham Beaulieu*
> *Born 15 September 1822*
> *Accidentally shot 4th April 1844*
> *As a mark of affection from his brother.*

Remains to Be Seen: Wisconsin

Around 1891, a man died at Oshkosh and was buried in Riverside Cemetery without an embalming. But the ground itself embalmed him through natural processes, as workers discovered when they exhumed him in August 1901. They found him "in an excellent state of preservation, not petrified but mummified, the same condition . . . as that of the Egyptian mummies."

Eccentric Interments, Wisconsin

In 1899, an unnamed woman in Frankfort lay on her deathbed. As astonished neighbors watched, she asked her husband to go upstairs and bring back the skeleton of a certain loved one. He left the room and returned with an armload of bones, including a skull that still had some hair attached. The dying woman embraced the bones and wept and made a fuss over them until she went to the Plantation of Past People herself.

This was unseemly enough, but then the widower buried his wife and the skeleton in the same coffin. An also-unidentified Frankfort farmer went to the coroner and demanded an exhumation and an investigation. Whose skeleton was it? Why did the woman wish to share her coffin with it? Why did the Frankfort farmer think the situation any of his business? It was all so mysterious!

Timely Ends, Part Four

In early December 1902, it was reported that Hartwell W., a brakeman on the Chicago, Burlington and Quincy Railroad, had been killed when he fell off the train and was cut in half. It was a false report—for a week, anyway, when Hartwell died in exactly that manner south of La Crosse on December 10.

Creativity in Suicide: Wisconsin

Anna S. was traipsing across the golf course at Washington Park, Milwaukee, on June 22, 1903. Instead of the lost golf ball she sought, she found the body of a man named Otto N. nestled among the trees at the fifth hole. Otto had downed a bottle of poison—but not before drawing a cartoon of himself drinking poison.

On September 30, 1910, a woman of Neenah hanged herself by using her wedding dress as a noose. She was despondent over her husband's suicide the previous April.

Arthur M. stripped nude and hanged himself from a blue and red painted cross in the parlor of his home in Superior on July 20, 1921. A few days before, he took photos of himself "in a posture of death." Hundreds of sightseers trooped through the house and glimpsed Arthur before the coroner removed the body. Arthur's friends said that his fondest wish was to be "the savior of the IWW" (Industrial Workers of the World).

Cassel N., a twenty-year-old medical student at the University of Wisconsin in Madison, became obsessed with death, suicide, and the hereafter when his friend Joseph M., a University of Chicago student, killed himself on January 2, 1927. Cassel spent the next few weeks defending Joseph's actions.

On January 23, Cassel shot himself in the head. He left a note explaining that he had formed a pact with fellow student Robert H. of Oak Park, Illinois, in which Cassel would kill himself to find out "how things are over there" in the afterlife. The note informed Robert to keep on the alert for a message from beyond. But if Cassel solved the "riddle of life and death," it appears that he kept the punchline to himself.

Wisconsin Death Trip

The chief statistician for the Wisconsin Board of Health collected quaint notations made on death certificates filled out by the state's doctors. Here are choice ones listed in an article from October 1913:

- A mother "died in infancy."
- "Went to bed feeling well but woke up dead."
- "Died suddenly at the age of 103. Up to this time he bid fair to reach a ripe old age."
- "Deceased had never been fatally sick."
- "Died suddenly. Nothing serious."
- "Pulmonary hemorrhage—sudden death. (Duration, four years.)"
- "Kick by horse shod on left kidney."
- "Deceased died from blood poison, caused by a broken ankle, which is remarkable as the automobile struck him between the lamp and the radiator."

"Hypnotized to Death"

Nineteenth-century newspapers employed vagueness and euphemism to spare their readers' sensibilities, but existing details indicate that Samuel Buxton pulled off one weird murder. The following is what the national press reported; the reader can speculate on what actually happened and how it was accomplished.

Samuel, age fifty-five and originally from Ohio, lived with his wife and three children at Viroqua, Wisconsin, not far from Sparta. Their neighbor was a woman named Mary A. Jones, who lived alone in her farmhouse; one newspaper described her as a "young woman," another deemed her "elderly," and a third said she was forty. All accounts agree she was a "maiden" (journalistic euphemism for an unmarried virgin). Or at least, for a while she was.

Something about Mary must have ruffled Samuel's feathers, because in 1891 he commenced sending her obscene letters "purporting to come from a witch." These tawdry missives, we are told, somehow "hypnotized" Mary and "caused her ruin." (That is, she started sleeping clandestinely with Samuel.)

After three years of this, Mary was infatuated with Samuel, but the cad wanted shed of her. He figured that if his magic letters convinced Jones her "chaste treasure [to] open" (to hijack Shakespeare's words), he could talk her into *killing herself* the same way. She got a letter from the "witch" informing her that if she would merely hang herself just a little bit, she would survive the experience—but Samuel's wife would die, leaving him open for marriage.

The miraculously gullible woman tried to do exactly that and failed on her first attempt. The second try, performed two weeks later on October 21, 1894, was successful. Samuel himself kicked away the chair on which she stood and, as she died, robbed her dwelling of every cent he could find.

Samuel's role in the suicide was uncovered almost immediately because the dead woman's brother had grave suspicions about him and told the authorities. He was arrested on October 27 and hustled off to Sparta to avoid a lynching. His preliminary hearing was held in the wee hours of the morning of October 29; he pled guilty on October 30 and was sentenced to the prison at Waupun for life.

Jean-Paul Dutch Ovens His Wife

Jean-Paul Soquet, a farmer who lived seven miles from Green Bay, murdered his four-year-old son by throwing him down a flight of stairs. He sewed the child's body in a canvas sack, and during the funeral would allow no one to inspect it. Could anything be more suspicious? Yet nothing was done about it. Mrs. Soquet Number One died under suspicious circumstances not long afterward. Nothing was done about that either.

He remarried. In 1873 the ill-tempered husband, Mrs. Soquet Number Two, and their children had neighbors named Mr. and Mrs. M. One day Mr. M. died two hours after consuming pancakes. After his burial it was deemed wise to exhume and examine him. The autopsy revealed eight grains of arsenic in his stomach. Again, nothing was done.

Two weeks after Mr. M. died, Soquet's Wife Number Two also died with identical symptoms. Jean-Paul married the widowed Mrs. M. The convenience of the situation aroused suspicion, and the second Mrs. Soquet's grave was opened—but her body was gone!

Wife Number Three did not get along with her husband and filed for divorce several years after they married. She threatened to tell the authorities that he murdered her first husband by adding arsenic to the flapjacks. On December 31, 1886, Jean-Paul visited his estranged wife with a gun in his hand. Neighbors heard shrieks in the night; next day the house bore signs of a struggle, including bloodstains and human hair on the furniture. The tracks of a sled led from her house to his. But there was no trace of Wife Number Three.

Number Three was never seen alive after her husband came calling. Their grandchildren said, "Grandpa baked two whole nights in the oven, but he did not bake any bread." They meant that Jean-Paul cremated his troublesome wife's remains a piece at a time in a large Dutch oven. A letter allegedly written by the missing woman turned up later, breezily stating that she was still alive and dwelling elsewhere. Yet she did not take any of her jewelry or money when she "moved away." By and large, nothing was done about these astonishingly suspicious circumstances.

Wife Number Two may have disappeared from her grave, but she turned up again in an unexpected place. Her son was plowing on the farm one day when he unearthed a human arm wearing a gold band that he recognized as his mother's wedding ring. The world would learn later that Jean-Paul had stolen his wife's body and reburied it on his property. The terrified young man vanished, and it was suggested in some circles that Jean-Paul had something to do with it.

In 1887, Jean-Paul was arrested on a charge of having murdered Wife Number Two fourteen years before. He was found guilty on May 21, 1890—after a trial that cost Brown County a then-astronomical $10,000—and given a life sentence in the state penitentiary at Waupun. He swore that he would escape and take a life for every day he spent in the cooler.

Jean-Paul did break out of prison on September 27, 1890, by the simple expedient of nicely asking the guards at the prison's potato farm if he might go for a stroll beyond the fence. Officials kept the escape of this dangerous man a secret until October 1 because they *hoped* they could recapture him and avoid bad publicity. Once the news got out, there was mass panic among the forty persons who had testified against him.

I could find no evidence that Jean-Paul was ever recaptured. He was credited with six murders, and if he changed his name and moved away from Wisconsin, he might have committed many more.

Wisconsin Whoppers

Eight-foot skeletons were unearthed at Montello in November 1881. On August 31, 1905, two skeletons—each more than seven feet long—were found in a gravel pit at Forest, near Fond du Lac. "The skulls are as large as those of two ordinary persons and the thigh bones are almost six inches longer than those of a six-foot man," said a press account.

She Thinks He's People

Edith W. of Waukesha was engaged to Edward H. Tragedy struck when Edward died of typhoid just before the wedding date.

Comedy struck when a Maltese cat turned up at Edith's house soon after Edward died. She believed in transmigration of the soul, and on his deathbed her fiancé told her that he would always be near her in some form.

Could Edward's soul be residing in that Maltese? Edith thought *yes*, and she did what anyone in her circumstances would do: she took the cat to Binghamton, New York, and married it on March 6, 1901. Several ministers refused to help the couple tie the knot, but out in the country she found a justice of the peace "who performed some sort of a marriage rite," according to a vague newspaper account, leaving us to wonder what "some sort" of a ceremony entailed.

Presumably Edith spent the honeymoon flicking the ticks off her husband's hairballs.

Getting His Hand In

A Wisconsin Representative picked up his mail at the House post office in Washington, DC, on December 19, 1902; he had a package that he *thought* might be a Christmas gift from a constituent. He opened it to find not a diamond-studded watch fob but a decomposing human hand packed in cotton.

After the representative recovered from the shock, he read the accompanying letter, which explained everything. Adam G. lost his hand after being shot while serving in the military. Adam had affectionately kept it preserved in a jar of alcohol for years and thought he should mail it in as proof of his injury when applying for a pension.

9

MYSTERIOUS MICHIGAN

Ghouls Just Want to Have Fun: Michigan

WHEN WELLINGTON B. DIED IN SAGINAW ON MARCH 2, 1919, he was one of the ten wealthiest men in America. His will was notable for unceremoniously shafting his children and grandchildren. It ordered that his vast fortune would not be dispersed until twenty-one years after his last grandchild died. Twelve of his descendants received Wellington's $100 million estate in 2011, twenty-two years after the death of his last surviving grandchild.

Wellington appears to have made a postmortem habit of dashing the hopes of those who wished to get rich quick at his expense. On March 13, 1922, someone in search of jewelry broke into his mausoleum. The ghoul got so far as to place the coffin on the floor and open the lid. There were no valuables to be had, but at least he got to meet Wellington.

A Collector of Heads, and Worse

A couple were so proud when they moved into their new home in Royal Oak! And there were rooms for their children to explore, which is precisely what the kids were doing in the attic on February 11, 1927. When they opened an old trunk, they found objects wrapped in newspapers. They unwrapped the paper and four skulls stared back at them with empty eye sockets.

The police took the children's new playthings away. The skulls were female; two braids of hair—one bloody and blond—were also packed in the trunk, as were a number of clippings from Pittsburgh newspapers, all referring to society women. The clippings had telephone numbers written on them. The trunk also yielded a notebook containing the names and numbers of socially prominent women from Pittsburgh, Cleveland, and Detroit. The police refused to release the names in the notebook—many of which were followed by the penciled word "White"—but details got out all the same. One skull was wrapped in a 1921 issue of the *Pittsburgh Post* and on the newspaper scrap the names of four women were underlined: one with the notation "Hazel 4142"; one with the notation "March 5, 1925"; one marked "The Barrington"; and one with the notation "Hazel 2542." Two names in the notebook also were leaked: Mrs. Harold W. and Mrs. Horace E., both of Detroit. All of the women mentioned in the notebook and the clippings were alive and well. Police theorized that they might have been "marked for harm." None of the women could shed any light on the mystery, but Mrs. W. said "Hazel 2542" was her phone number.

Investigation proved that the trunk had been the property of James Coyner, aliases Ed Crayton and Alonzo Robinson, a black former tenant of the house and presently a convict in the prison at Michigan City, Indiana. James admitted that the trunk was his but said he had no idea how skulls came to be stashed in it. His claim was not believable, considering that in November 1926 he was convicted of robbing a woman's grave in Oak Hill Cemetery in Hammond, Indiana, and was serving a three-to-ten-year sentence. He hid the body in an abandoned house, where it was found by playing boys the day after the grave robbery. The police kept the house under surveillance and arrested James when he returned. The ghoul admitted he had planned to take the cadaver to Bernice, Illinois, but would not say why.

Another circumstance casting doubt upon James's innocence was that he wrote a number of incriminating letters to his sister Emma R. in Chicago. In one, dated November 1926, he asked her to smuggle some hacksaw blades to him, adding: "You all do not know my trouble. I have not had a chance to tell you. This may not amount to anything here, but there is something else. If that comes against me, I am through forever."

In another letter, James used similar language when beseeching his sister to somehow get his acquaintance George R. to claim the trunk: "They may find something else on me, and if they do I am through forever. Don't let George be too slow or it may cause me to lose my freedom forever." Nothing suspicious about that!

James was once employed at Bernice and investigators thought he might have robbed graves there. He attracted the interest of police in Toledo since he had lived there in 1926, right around the time several women were clubbed—some fatally—by an unknown assailant. (James was innocent of those crimes, at least; see the "Toledo Terror" section in the "Odd Ohio" chapter.)

The police grilled James relentlessly, but he refused to answer questions regarding how he came to have four skulls in his trunk and whose heads originally contained them. The prosecuting attorney and chief of police even forced him to look at the skulls face-to-face—as it were—but the tactic failed to shake him. He said only that if he chose to, he could tell them "about a lot of murders and murderers," especially in the Detroit area, "but I'll die first." That tantalizing hint was all he would give.

The authorities couldn't make the prisoner talk, so the mystery of the trunkful of skulls remained unsolved. The grave robber served his sentence, was paroled in June 1934, moved down

South, and faded into obscurity. But if people thought they had heard the last of James Coyner, they were sadly mistaken.

On December 8, 1934, someone tried to murder the entire family of Aurelius Turner in Cleveland, Mississippi. Aurelius was beaten with a hatchet and shot through the back of the head; his pregnant wife, Louella, was slashed and also beaten with a small hammer found beneath her body. The heads of both adults were crushed; both were dismembered and the pieces strewn about their bedroom. Parts of Louella's body were missing—cut off and carried away by her killer. Two children survived the attack but the elder, age six, also was badly beaten.

Police suspected James was the murderer and mutilator of the couple. He went into hiding for a month but was caught thanks to his habit of writing obscene letters to anyone he thought might appreciate one. The law caught him on January 12, 1935, after a pitched battle in the post office. James was carrying Aurelius's watch as well as bits of Louella's hair. When the authorities searched his house, they found three pieces of a human body preserved in salt.

What were anatomical specimens doing in James's house? Though at first he exhibited the same sullen refusal to talk he had exhibited when asked years before about the trunkful of skulls, on January 16 James finally confessed to cannibalism. When asked why he had cut off pieces of Louella, he replied, "Oh, I took the skin to see how it felt."

"Did you bite this piece of flesh?" asked the district attorney, pointing at a portion of human remains retrieved from James's house.

"Yes," said the prisoner. He also admitted at last that he stole the four trunk skulls from graves because he "wanted the bones."

Bolivar County authorities filed a request for permission to exhume Louella to see if the missing portions from her anatomy matched the chunks found in James's residence. Presumably everything checked out.

James was found guilty on February 4 after a one-day trial and sentenced to hang on March 5. Soldiers with bayonets sat in the courtroom, the courthouse was surrounded by barbed wire and machine guns, and two hundred soldiers from the National Guard took James to a "lynch-proof" jail at Jackson. Despite (or maybe because of) these precautions, the trial attendees displayed "no evidence of disorder" according to a reporter.

Before dawn on his last day, James walked to the scaffold. The weather was appropriate for the occasion: it was still dark and rain soaked the prisoner and his guards. He laughed as the black hood was placed over his head and the noose tightened. He was hanged a few hours ahead of schedule to thwart possible mobs.

James was buried in the potter's field at the county poorhouse. Midwestern America would not be set agog by the activities of such a murderous, ghoulish, grave-robbing cannibal until the saga of Ed Gein unfolded in Plainfield, Wisconsin, in 1957.

Buried Alive: Michigan

A prostitute known as "Canada Em" died in jail at Bay City on September 2, 1875. Her friends had her exhumed on September 3. According to a news dispatch, when the lid was opened, ten witnesses saw that the "corpse had turned on the side. One hand was clenched, the hair was over the face, and there was every indication that she had been buried alive."

⊷•◦•⊶

Around the end of May 1884 an Irish immigrant named Hugh M. died in Detroit. He was coffined and temporarily placed in a vault. Eight days later his uncle opened the vault so Hugh could receive a proper burial. The uncle was horrified to find the glass window of the casket broken and Hugh sitting up! He cut his hands while breaking out of the coffin and was weak and pale from hunger, but he was alive. His family attempted to conceal the story but admitted it was true after it leaked out.

⊷•◦•⊶

Dwight H., a young man in Alamo, prided himself on his skills as a hypnotist. On January 9, 1888, he gave a demonstration in which he put a woman named Annette G. under his influence and made her smoke an unladylike cigar.

This was such a success that he hypnotized a woman named Kittie R. and ordered her to feign death. The spectators—a small circle of friends—were amazed by her highly realistic imitation. It was so convincing, in fact, that her respiration ceased. The village doctor, unaware of the hypnotism, examined Kittie and said she died of heart disease.

On the night of January 12, Dwight thought it wise to skip town on the sly, but before he left he made Annette swear not to tell on him. But at Kittie's funeral the next day, Annette went hysterical at the graveside.

When she recuperated, she told about the hypnotism. There was a mad rush to unearth Kittie's freshly buried coffin in case she was only in a mesmeric trance. A doctor from Paw Paw touched one of her tendons "with a sharp-pointed rod [and] a slight contraction was noticed." He pronounced her alive, but just barely. Had Annette's conscience not gotten the better of her, Kittie would have suffocated underground.

Officials begged hypnotists to come to Alamo and try to snap Kittie out of her trance. Many tried; all failed, and it was assumed that only Dwight could bring her around. But he was in hiding, probably in fear of being charged with manslaughter.

What happened next? The national press didn't say, so let's hope Kittie isn't still under a trance in some Michigan attic.

Fear of Slow Suffocation Is the Mother of Invention

As the above examples show, premature burial—while rare— was a legitimate concern. Fortunately American know-how was up to the challenge, and inventors came up with all sorts of devices to combat the problem, ranging from the practical to the demented. For example, in 1888, a patent attorney reminisced to a *Washington* [DC] *Star* reporter about the time a man in Grand

Rapids sent him a package containing what appeared to be a dollhouse with a miniature coffin attached by rubber tubes. It was a model of the inventor's device for rescuing the prematurely buried. His idea: bury the coffin containing the dearly (but not actually) departed; build the house-like structure over the grave; when the occupant awoke after a good nap, he could get oxygen from the rubber tubes and climb a ladder that connected coffin to house via an underground chamber. Once inside, he would find a key so he could unlock the structure and go home and give his family the surprise of their lives. The house over the grave would even contain a fresh suit of clothes so the undead could reemerge in style. The inventor was miffed when the patent attorney told him his idea was not practical.

Work Smart, Not Hard

This unseemly yarn begins in November 1888, when the son of a Detroit patrolman went sailing on Lake Erie. A few days later the capsized boat was found, but no trace of the boy. His body finally washed ashore at Brest in June 1889. On the twenty-seventh, his father traveled to the town to reclaim the remains, which he found in a mutilated condition.

The grieving father was told that the coroner, after removing any items of value from the body, ordered it buried on the beach. The grave diggers dug a hole and then found it was too small. They could have made the hole bigger, of course, but their logic dictated that it was easier to make the corpse smaller. So they beat the boy's arms and legs with sticks until they were sufficiently broken enough to wedge him into the grave. They even jumped up and down on what was left of the body to pack him in that much more efficiently.

Eccentric Interments, Michigan

The S. S. *Alpena* sank on October 15, 1880, during a ferocious storm—called the "worst gale in Lake Michigan recorded history"—with the loss of everyone on board, including a doctor.

His widow, Eliza P., died on January 15, 1909; in accordance with her wishes, her body was cremated and her ashes scattered in Lake Michigan on August 8, so she could rejoin her husband.

Strange Wills, Michigan

A doctor died at Sparta on August 2, 1910. His only heirs were two pet monkeys, to whom the physician willed his farm. His housekeeper was permitted to live at the farm if she took care of the privileged primates, who were known to have attacked and bitten at least one pesky neighborhood boy.

Infidel Inscriptions, Michigan

When neighbors of stonemason Herman M. passed his house at 308 Stanton Avenue, Detroit, on November 10, 1905, they found that he had expressed his contempt for religion by erecting a monument to Satan, complete with horns and a pitchfork. The statue was fourteen feet high and depicted Old Scratch stooping behind a pulpit. Obviously a garden gnome wasn't good enough for Herman!

He explained his unique taste in lawn decoration: "Isn't it as good as anything else in the way of an ornament? Would you have me put the statue of a saint up there? He is my friend. He spoke the first and last truth. I do not believe a word of the Bible. It is a pack of lies from beginning to end, but Old Nick tells the truth." Apparently Herman thought the Bible "a pack of lies" *except* for the parts about Satan, but his thinking on this point was unclear.

DIY Sermon

The justice of the peace of Muskegon took no chances on having a lackluster funeral oration. It was reported in 1914 that he recorded a sermon of his own composition, including "a brief history of his life . . . together with something of his hopes for the hereafter." The phonograph was to be played before mourners when the evil day came.

Getting Stiffed, Part Two

A Detroit undertaker went to the residence of Vincent D. on September 20, 1921, seeking a payment of five hundred dollars for the funeral expenses of Vincent's wife, whose coffin was in the house. Instead, the widower grabbed a gun and chased the undertaker away. The mortician had the law on his side, however, and two constables went to the house and repossessed the coffin. They left Vincent's wife lying on a couch and the irate husband was free to dispose of her as best he could.

Never Say Die

Willard H. of Burlington was so certain he would cross the bar in 1934 that he had his gravestone made in 1919 bearing the dates 1854–1934. But the year came and went and still Willard thrived. He was still alive as late as June 1939, when he reportedly spent a portion of every day in New Burlington Cemetery polishing his erroneously dated tombstone.

Arthur's Practical Joke Backfires Somewhat

Arthur T., age sixteen, deemed it the height of humor to dance the Charleston in a rowboat full of teens sailing in Saint Mary's River at Sault Ste. Marie. Arthur performed his exhibition dance on June 20, 1926—as the boat neared the rapids, yet. Only one of the seven passengers survived, and it wasn't Arthur.

Creativity in Suicide: Michigan

It would seem an impossibility to commit suicide by holding one's breath; when the attemptee lost consciousness, he or she would automatically start breathing, right? But at least one person is on record as having done so: On January 18, 1916, Mary T., a patient at the State Psychopathic Hospital in Ann Arbor, held her breath till she expired. Even the use of a pulmotor could not bring her back from the brink.

Only a few weeks after her marriage, eighteen-year-old bride Neva F. of Kalamazoo held a party for some friends on the night of April 5, 1921. She danced to "Till We Meet Again," explaining that the song was played at the dance where she'd met her husband. Her friends noticed that by the end of the song she was having convulsions. Then she toppled over dead. The partygoers later found that Neva had swallowed poison in her bedroom just before cranking up the phonograph.

William M., a professional gambler, often remarked that a man should not live past age sixty-five. In September 1921, William himself turned sixty-five. On September 18, a few days after his birthday, William locked himself in his Detroit boardinghouse room and let the cards decide if he should live or die. If the first card he drew was red, he would live; if black, he would commit suicide.

When his landlady forced the door open later, she found William dead on the floor with a cut throat. The top card on the table was an eight of spades. All the gambler had to his name was seventy-two cents and his clothes, which suggests that he should have gone into some other line of work.

Albert R. disappeared from his Crump farm in the middle of the night on May 4, 1932. His family searched for him the next day and found that he had dug his own grave, climbed in, and buried himself except for his head and arms. He used his free hands to shoot himself in the head with a shotgun.

Burt W. of Flint made a general announcement that he wished to kill himself. His family dissembled his shotgun and hid all the pieces. Burt found all the parts one by one, reassembled them, and shot himself on May 12, 1936.

Back to the Old Drawing Board

Twenty-two-year-old boy genius George W. of Dundee was certain he had come up with the greatest invention of the age: it was nothing less than a potion that would revive the dead! Of course, there was only one way to test it, and rather than sensibly get a volunteer, young George was determined to try it out on himself. He wrote a lengthy note to his skeptical friends, informing them that they would soon rue their jeers and raillery:

> To My Benighted Friends. It is now 2:20 a.m. on Saturday, March 3, 1877, and my mind is fully made up to pass the ordeal of which I am to be a sacrifice. The mysteries that lie unfolded in the physical part of man will, in a short time, be given to the world. Having failed in my efforts to satisfy scientific men of the truth, soundness, and utility of this grand discovery by experiments in the animal world, and knowing that such an invaluable secret is held only by myself, I shall, before six hours have passed, give the world sufficient proof of my reasonings. The Almighty Being gave man faculties, and placed before him powers, leaving him to penetrate their apparent mysteries. But to me who has brought to light these hidden powers, everything is plain, and when we notice our actions to harmonize with our occult qualities, we have no fear of a change to our constitutional elements.

And so on in that vein. George ended with the request that his remains be taken to a professor of the State Normal School and that he take some of George's chemical creation, which the inventor modestly called his "creative, all-changeful material assistant," pour it on the corpse, and then apply electricity. If his calculations were correct, George would once again tread the earth.

After writing the note, the young inventor set his plans in motion. But George's genius didn't end with merely bringing the dead back to life; he also created an ingenious homemade suicide machine to transform the living into the dead. The contraption had a wooden frame that supported a spinning wheel, attached to which were knives, bits of scythes, and a fearsome ax head. George started the machine with a complex set of pulleys and then put his head in position to receive maximum punishment from all those whirling blunt and sharp objects. "His head . . . was slashed and cut beyond recognition," said a correspondent from the *Detroit Tribune*. "When found, his brains were oozing out of a deep cut in the back part of his skull."

Nearby were the letter quoted above and a beaker of fluid labeled "creative, all-changeful material assistant," just like in an episode of *Batman*.

Somnambulistic Slayings, Part Three

Despite Chester K.'s having a history of sleepwalking and domestic harmony, on September 26, 1928, a Detroit jury found him guilty of manslaughter after he shot his wife while asleep, as he claimed. The prosecutor argued successfully that the April 1928 shooting sprang from inebriation rather than somnambulism. "If you let this man get away with this kind of story, you open the door for every disgruntled husband and wife in this state to a safe avenue of disposing of each other," said the prosecutor. "Did you ever hear of a family containing a sleepwalker which permitted such a person to keep a loaded shotgun within ten feet of his bed?" The jury—while finding Chester guilty— recommended mercy just to be on the safe side. The *Louisville Courier-Journal* predicted an outbreak of insomnia among Michigan housewives.

Spanking Surprise

On September 1, 1907, a woman gave her seven-year-old son a spanking for some infraction at their home in Bear Point, near Cheboygan. The woman enhanced the corporal punishment by brandishing a shingle. Little did she know that he had a dynamite cap in his pocket.

Closing Remarks, Michigan

Henry J. hanged and shot himself in a shed on his farm at Otter Lake on April 1, 1912. He left a note containing tender advice for his widow: "Now you have a chance to get a third husband; for God's sake don't talk him to death."

⊢•◦•○•◦•⊣

On June 17, 1938, an unnamed official at the Michigan Hospital for the Criminal Insane committed suicide by burning himself in a car on the highway near Ionia. The man left a note explaining that if he had not killed himself, he would have killed two others: "This is a deliberate act of suicide chosen as the alternative to two murders I had planned to commit. The intended victims will know who I mean."

Killer Cure

People thought Edna L. of Au Gres had committed suicide, but when her autopsy was held on November 1, 1913, the truth proved far stranger. She had carried a bottle of carbolic acid in a breast pocket, which she used in diluted form to treat a sore throat. The cork came out of the bottle and the acid ate into her chest and heart.

Theatrical Realism

Amateur actors rehearsing a play in Bad Axe on March 25, 1936, were surprised when Edward P. hit the floor after being "shot" with a prop gun. But remove those quotation marks: the actor was hit with a real bullet accidentally left in the weapon. Edward P. died on March 29. The same fate befell high school student Edward M. of Blencoe, Iowa, who was killed on January 25, 1938, during a rehearsal when a fellow actor mistakenly substituted a real pistol for the toy prop used before.

The Devil and His Works

Reverend John Haviland Carmichael of Wellsburg, West Virginia, came to an end that starkly contrasted with his calling. He was ordained a Methodist minister in 1880, and after several years' success in the South, he was transferred to Benkelman, Nebraska. He went to the Detroit Conference in 1897 and moved to Saint Clair County, Michigan, in 1899. Over the next decade he rose so highly in the eyes of the community that by 1906 he had become the pastor at three Methodist churches located in the rural towns of Rattle Run (near Columbus), Adair, and China. The reverend lived his life as blamelessly as a reverend ought and made his home in Adair with his wife and three children.

On the morning of January 5, 1909, the fifty-six-year-old reverend told his wife that he had to go to the church at Rattle Run to arrange revival meetings. She last saw him waving at neighborhood children as he rode away on a horse and buggy.

Hours later, Myron B. was standing at a crossroads near the Rattle Run church, waiting to keep an appointment. The freezing winter air forced him to the unlocked church for shelter. When he stepped inside, he saw evidence of a murder both atrocious and recent. Blood was splattered over the floor, the pews, and the communion table. Shreds of blood-soaked clothing were strewn about and a wicked-looking dirk lay in plain sight. There was no trace of the minister. Myron summoned the Port Huron sheriff.

The police noticed a rank smell coming from the church's front and rear furnaces, each of which turned out to contain part of a dismembered human body. The flames were doused and the body parts recovered. The corpse had been almost consumed by fire, but part of the torso, a jawbone, and false teeth remained. Coins were found in the ashes, indicating that robbery was not the motive. Police also found a hatchet head in one furnace, its handle burned away. Only one of the victim's legs was found in the furnace; both feet were missing. Baffled detectives assumed that the killer took these anatomical specimens with him.

On January 6, the day after the murder, the reverend's horse was found tied to a tree in Pine River, twenty miles from the Rattle Run church. His overcoat was in the carriage. These clues, along with the fact that Pine River was located on the Grand Trunk Railroad line, made it evident that a fiend cruelly butchered the beloved reverend for reasons unknown and fled by train.

But then further clues surfaced and all bets were off.

Residents of Adair noticed that *two* men were missing: the reverend and Gideon Browning, a carpenter and part-time sailor. Police discovered that the reverend visited Gideon the morning of the day before the murder. Gideon's nephew reported overhearing a conversation between the two, during which the reverend had promised the carpenter a job where he would have to do nothing but "stand around and smoke cigars." What he meant by this, the reverend's daughter claimed, was that he had written a manuscript called *The Devil and His Works* and he intended to make Gideon his book agent. Despite its title and the occupation of its author, the work was secular and lurid. The reverend's wife complained that he wrote a couple of "trashy novels." She stated: "I saw some of [his manuscript] once, a few sheets. I don't remember what they said, but I felt called on to tell him he should not write such things. But he persisted."

Witnesses saw Reverend Carmichael and Browning conversing at the train depot at Adair on the morning of the murder; Gideon boarded the train to Port Huron, a trip paid for by the reverend, and soon afterward the preacher rode off to the Rattle Run church. Later that day Gideon took the train back from Port Huron. Oddly, he did not ride all the way home to Adair, but instead got off at Hickey, where he inquired of two men the way to the Rattle Run church, telling each of them that he had an appointment to meet someone there. It looked as though the reverend sent Gideon to Port Huron on an errand, after which he met Gideon at the church, where one of them ended up dead, dismembered, and stuffed into two furnaces.

Although at first it was universally believed that the preacher met a foul end, the belief was soon replaced by an even more unthinkable conclusion: the reverend, pillar of the community, was himself the murderer of Gideon. False teeth and a stickpin found in one furnace were proved to have belonged to the missing carpenter. The reverend's flock even faced the disheartening possibility that their former shepherd had inherited a streak of insanity; the reverend's wife revealed to the press that her husband's sister was an inmate in a West Virginia asylum.

Whenever a notorious fugitive is on the loose, the power of suggestion forces well-meaning souls to imagine seeing him tramping down the sidewalk in their faraway towns. Not surprisingly, people in several states thought they encountered the crazy preacher on the lam. Within hours of the murder a "highly nervous" stranger offered Frank C. of Saint Clair, Michigan, two dollars if he would give him a boat ride across the river to Canada. Frank managed to turn down the tempting offer. In Cedarburg, Wisconsin, a man resembling the reverend made himself conspicuous on Thursday, January 7, by refusing lodging at several hotels because their storm windows would make a quick and surreptitious exit too difficult. The ubiquitous madman was also spotted in Indiana, Chicago, and Toronto, Ontario; all of these latter sightings took place within hours of each other.

The Carmichael-spotters in Chicago were correct. He stopped there on his way to Carthage, Illinois, where he arrived on January 8. There he hid out at a boardinghouse under the assumed name John Elder—probably a weird pun, since he was an elder in his church and often was addressed as such by his parishioners. He appeared upbeat and hinted that he was a Catholic, possibly to throw the curious off the ecclesiastical scent. He spoke with enthusiasm about building a woodworking factory in town.

Early in the morning of January 11, after writing a letter to his wife and a lengthy confession to the Port Huron sheriff, Carmichael went to a wooden shack behind the boardinghouse and slashed his throat with a pocket knife. The cut was not sufficient to cause a quick death, and after several hours the reverend died of exposure to the cold. The search for the missing reverend was over, but those left devastated by his actions wondered why he'd murdered Gideon, dissected the body, crammed the pieces in the church furnaces, and then fled. The true answer was found in the letter he wrote to the sheriff, which dripped with raging delusional paranoia: "The man [Gideon] had such a hypnotic influence over me that I felt that something must be done. I felt greatly ashamed that a man said to be short-minded could be able to compel me to yield to his will, but I said nothing about it."

The reverend ascribed superpowers to his victim. Gideon, it seemed to the reverend, had the ability to appear at will in unexpected places: "Three times he came to the rear of my barn and talked to me through the manure hole; twice he was at the river when I went to water my stock, and each time I felt that he was doing something that he was proud of." On one occasion, Gideon hypnotically persuaded the reverend to give him a buggy ride to Port Huron; there Gideon asked the reverend to buy a toy hatchet for his son. "I began to tell him to go and do his own buying," wrote the preacher, "when he set his eyes upon me in the queerest sort of a look, something like the look of a snake's eyes. Then I felt his influence tightening his grip on my mind." The reverend lost the battle of wills and purchased the toy. Another time, at the Adair train depot, Gideon used his mental powers to influence the reverend to walk on the rails. The reverend poignantly described the humiliating experience: "All the while I felt as small as a bantam chicken."

At last came January 5, 1909, the day when the hapless minister could take no more. According to the reverend's final letter, Gideon told him that he wanted to get married that day at the Rattle Run church, although he already had a wife from whom he was separated. When the two met at the church, Gideon encouraged the reverend to stoke the furnaces hotter and hotter. Meanwhile, the preacher kept looking out the window, anticipating the arrival of the wedding party. At length, the carpenter laughed and confessed it was a practical joke: "There ain't no use looking, for there ain't going to be no wedding. Well, elder, I wanted just to have a little fun. Consider yourself an educated man and look down on a poor ignorant fellow like me. And I just thought I would show [you] what I could do. I knowed if I could handle you I could handle other men, too, and make a big thing out of it."

After making a fool of the reverend, Gideon further demonstrated his powers of hypnosis by forcing the reverend to raise and lower his arm against his will. Then the reverend noticed that Gideon was holding a hatchet. The reverend grabbed the weapon, but then Gideon drew two knives from his pockets and started chasing the minister. In a state of panic, the reverend threw the hatchet and slew his tormentor—or so he thought, for he came back to life as the infuriated reverend stabbed him with one of the knives. A few more blows from the hatchet solved his Gideon problem forever. The reverend then exchanged clothes with the corpse, cut the body into pieces, tossed them in the church furnaces, and made his escape.

Three days after the reverend's suicide, four Detroit physicians performed an autopsy and found that the preacher had suffered from several brain abnormalities. Gideon's widow, who lived in Auburn, New York, stated for the record that her husband had no occult powers and had not been studying hypnotism. The *New York Times* found the case interesting enough to note editorially that it is impossible to hypnotize someone against his will and also impossible to make a hypnotized person do something that he would not ordinarily do. Carmichael mistook his own symptoms of insanity for hypnotism and turned on the man he fancied to be his persecutor.

A Very Clean Murder

Robert C. of Detroit was angry when he lost his job at a laundry. He took revenge on his coworker Edwin M. by pushing him into a laundry vat and turning on the motor to 300 RPM. Robert was sentenced to life in prison on March 13, 1936.

Consumed by Rats, Part Three

Villagers found a male body on the road between Pere Cheney and Fletcher on July 10, 1887—a body so mangled that its identity was not discernible. It was scooped up and carted away.

It is only human nature to want to see places where murders occurred or where bodies have been found, so a young man named Davis returned to the spot in the road where the corpse had lain to drink in the atmosphere.

Not long afterward, the courtroom doors burst open while an inquest was being held on the corpse. The frantic intruder was Davis, blood-spattered, wearing tattered clothing, and brandishing a bloody club! He said he had the solution to the mystery: when he got to the death scene, he was jumped upon by starveling rats coming from all directions. He clubbed as many as he could, but they chased him almost all the way to the courthouse, and even so some of the rodents clung to his clothes and nipped him. The unknown dead man, said Davis, must have been attacked and mutilated by rats.

In Which Benny Gazes Up at Himself

Some of the most interesting murders seem like a horror film come to life. This thought probably did not occur to the detectives called in to inspect the house at 3587 Saint Aubin Avenue in Detroit, on July 3, 1929, for in their day horror films contained little more terrifying than Lon Chaney's latest astonishing makeup job. No vision on celluloid could equal what the police found in the house.

Earlier on that summer morning, around ten o'clock, a real estate dealer named Vincent E. dropped by to make a business call. Could you go back in time to witness this moment, you would see Vincent knocking on the unlocked front door and waiting a little while after receiving no answer and then cautiously entering. All would be silence for a few moments; perhaps you would hear faint footsteps. Then you would see Vincent running back outside and screaming for help.

Detectives were there within a half hour. Unfortunately, so were squads of reporters who received a tip that some nameless horror was waiting for them in the house. Investigators found Santina Evangelista, age thirty-eight, in bed. She was nearly decapitated; her attacker attempted to amputate her arms. Her eighteen-month-old son, Mario, lay dead beside her. In another bedroom were the mutilated bodies of three other children: Angelina, age seven; Matthew, age five (this victim may actually have been a girl named Margaret: accounts differ); and Eugenis, also known as Jean, age four. They were all killed by blows to the head with a sharp object; one child's limbs were severed. Angelina's body was found on the floor near the bedroom door. Apparently she woke up during the carnage and tried to escape.

The greatest horror of all was discovered when the police opened the door to a first-floor room used as an office by the master of the house, Benjamino (Benny) Evangelista. Among the clutter were two swords—neither was used in the commission of the massacre—a wig, and a false beard, the purpose of which was never discovered; on the floor were three large photos of a child lying in a coffin. Benny was almost fully dressed and sitting at his desk, but his head was missing. The police found it on the floor, eyes looking heavenward. On the wall overlooking the grotesque tableau were a crucifix, a wooden cross, and a print of da Vinci's *The Last Supper*.

Benny had had some singular notions about interior decorating. His house was filled with religious icons, pictures, and other objects representing the Christian faith. Yet in the basement was a séance room containing a homemade altar over which hung papier-mâché and wax effigies, "hideous and grotesque in the extreme," in the words of the local press. The figures symbolized "the ten celestial planets" (including the sun and the moon: Benny had no use for astronomical accuracy). They were "painted revolting colors and covered with hair clipped from dogs." The centerpiece was a large object resembling an eye that was electrically lit from the inside. Journalists theorized that the eye was supposed to represent the sun—if so, in Benny's imagination the sun could be both an effigy and an illuminated eyeball at the same time. A reporter noted that the walls and ceiling of this room were lined with puffy light green cloth, making it resemble a padded cell in an insane asylum.

The police may not have been familiar with forty-four-year-old Benny, but he was well-known to Italian immigrants in Detroit in the days just before the Great Depression. He was born in Naples around 1885. Benny joined his older brother Anthony in Philadelphia in 1903. They lived together for six years but had a falling out concerning Benny's increasingly unorthodox religious beliefs. Although a Catholic, Benny started a cult in 1906. The brothers and their families moved to Detroit in the early 1920s, but Benny and Anthony remained estranged and rarely spoke.

Benny became a real estate broker and landlord. He attended the local Church of San Francisco. Although his devotion to Catholicism was such that some called him a fanatic, he reestablished his cult in Detroit. This secondary source of income led to prosperity and possibly to the murder of his family. He became, as crime writer Jay Robert Nash stated, a kind of Henry Ford of the supernatural. The cult bore the grand title Union Federation of America, which seems a name more appropriate for an organization of truck drivers. After the cultist's death his priest told the *Detroit Free Press*: "[Benny], no doubt, was insane. Of that I am sure, although he was shrewd and seemed to have quite a lot of intelligence in other matters. . . . I do not believe [Benny] was sincere in practicing the creed he had established. Rather, I believe he founded the mysterious cult with all of its weird props and practices, with the sole idea of making money." Benny and his wife bothered the priest so often with reports of their mystical visions and claims that they could conjure up devils that he finally ordered his assistant to stay away from them for fear of a scandal.

Benny ambitiously wrote (or rather dictated, since his command of English was poor) and copyrighted his own bible in 1926: *The Oldest History of the World, Discovered by Occult Science in Detroit, Mich.*, a book that he claimed took exactly twenty years to write. At the time of his death Benny was scheming to create a movie depicting the history of humankind as related in this weird little volume. I own a rare, fragile first edition of this unreadable crackpot classic and reproduce a couple of lines from the preface to provide an example of Benny's style: "By the willingness of God, my respect to this nation, I shall do my best to tell you of the Old World. I shall tell about the world before

God was created up until this last generation, and I shall explain to you your descendants." It is a violent tome populated by Adam and Eve, witches, a male warrior named Rowena, and a prophet called Miel of the Ape, among many other figures. The book ends with a promise of three more volumes, which the author did not survive to write. The upshot of Benny's book seems to be that he is a prophet and that he has nightly visions between midnight and three. Since he and his family were murdered late at night, perhaps Benny was having visions in his office when he met his gruesome fate.

Benny told his fellow immigrants' fortunes at ten dollars per session. He sold hexes and charms and performed faith healing. He sold a love potion and according to the local department of health, "he had a permit to practice medicine so long as he did not use drugs or prescribe medicine." These restrictions did not prohibit him from the lucrative sale of herbs. Benny even poked pins in a voodoo doll when necessary. His friends were long embarrassed by his habit of giving "frequent religious demonstrations on the street," staring upward and waving his arms at the sky. By 1929 Benny was rich enough to afford a two-story frame house. The Fates smiled upon the enterprising con artist until the night of July 2, when he and his family became so shockingly truncated.

A crime scene must be kept in pristine condition; this was as true in 1929 as it is today. Unfortunately, by the time detectives arrived at the household, policemen, coroner's deputies, reporters, and citizens afflicted with morbid curiosity had ransacked the place. The only viable clues left for detectives were footprints left about the house and the killer's bloody fingerprints on the front door's latch. However, the real estate dealer, Vincent E., might accidentally have left the bloody footprints as he ran through the house in panic, since they matched his shoe size.

Investigators wrestled with the problem of figuring out how the murderer, who was probably drenched with blood, managed to escape from the house and into a suburban neighborhood without attracting attention. They also were stumped as to motive, since the killer appeared not to have taken valuables. Sixty officers assigned to the case painstakingly searched through numerous boxes in the home. Hundreds of papers, trinkets, and pieces of clothing were examined, all to no avail. One peculiar but initially promising find was a box full of women's underwear, each bearing the name of its former wearer. Police theorized that a jealous husband remonstrated with Benny, but they discovered that the underwear had been used in a voodoo ritual intended to find missing persons.

The difficulty of the case led the frustrated police to try some unconventional—not to say absurd—methods. Within a few days of the murders they heard from an astrologer who claimed that according to the stars, the killer would surrender soon. The stars were honestly mistaken. Officers arrested a harmless curiosity seeker who attended the funerals and questioned employees of a company Benny had commissioned to create the ghastly effigies that dangled from the ceiling in his basement séance room. A police lieutenant theorized that the killer "was a degenerate or a mentally deficient person scared into killing the family through fear of his basement idols."

The police's thirst to catch the criminal resulted in a surreal incident. A month after Benny was buried, it occurred to some detectives that he might have murdered his own family and then committed suicide. They thought Benny "managed to chop up his family, behead himself, *and then* hide the murder weapons," in the words of crime writer Nash. They went to Mount Olivet Cemetery in the middle of the night, exhumed Benny's body and took fingerprints. They did not match the ones on the door latch. (This entertaining account may be a garbled version of an event that occurred in March 1930—see below.)

Over the years the police would interrogate more than five hundred persons to solve the mystery. As often happens in real-life murder mysteries, the case yielded many intriguing suspects, some of whom were nearly as bizarre as Benny himself. On July 3, 1929, Detroit police arrested thirty-four-year-old

Angelo Depoli and his four Italian roommates. Angelo lived near Evangelista, and in his barn detectives found a wicked curved knife "of the type commonly used in cutting bananas from the stalk" that appeared to be stained with blood, a short ax, and a pair of recently washed shoes. (Later tests indicated that the stains on the ax and knife were not blood.) Angelo admitted that he knew the family but denied killing them. Three of his fellow Italians were released after a thorough grilling by the police. Angelo, an illegal immigrant, refused to talk to the police about the fifth remaining roommate, and in retaliation the authorities had Angelo deported to Italy so quickly he didn't even have time to return to his rooming house.

Despite his denials, Angelo might have had some connection to the crime. His last roommate—the one he didn't want to talk about—is called Umberto Pecchio, age forty-two, in the *Detroit Free Press* of July 5. This was a typo; one of the major emerging suspects in the slaying was Umberto Tecchio, a tenant of Benny's who took his wife to Benny for medical treatment several times. None of the roommates questioned along with Umberto could swear that he had been in his room all night, and in addition, he had a documented violent streak. Allegedly he was an extortionist for the Black Hand. On April 19, 1929, three months before the murders, Umberto had stabbed to death Bartolomeo M., brother of Umberto's wife, Theresa, over an unpaid debt. It was ruled self-defense and the killer was not even tried. Theresa divorced him three weeks later.

Umberto was one of the last people to see his landlord, Benny, alive. He went to Benny's house on the night of July 2, 1929, to make the final payment on his house. Police lost interest in the suspect when his friend Camillo Treas insisted that he accompanied Umberto on his errand and that when they left the residence around eight o'clock, Benny's head was still attached. He admitted that Umberto talked to Benny "in a loud voice," but this was not significant since he "always spoke in a high, excited voice and even in normal conversation seemed to be angry and quarrelsome." The alibi seemed airtight, and Umberto was turned loose. He died of a cerebral hemorrhage on November 26, 1934, following a drinking binge.

In August 1935, several months after Umberto's death, police again became interested in him. Witnesses came forward who had been afraid to speak while he was alive. As we have seen, Camillo Treas provided Umberto's alibi by claiming to have accompanied him to the family house on a mundane errand on the night of July 2, 1929. But now Camillo added that Umberto entered their rooming house by the back door early on the morning of July 4, carrying a canvas mason's tool bag three feet long—just the right size for concealing a machete or two. No one had seen the canvas bag since.

By 1935, Umberto's ex-wife—now known as Theresa M.— had married twice more. She told police that after the divorce from Umberto, she married a man named Louis Peruzzi. To add domestic insult to matrimonial injury, the new couple lived at 2675 Scott Street in the house Umberto bought from Benny on the last night of Benny's life. The loss of his residence did not sit well with Umberto, and according to his ex-wife in early 1932 he threatened to blow up the house. This he did not do, but on November 9, 1932, someone shot Louis through the heart as he enjoyed a smoke on his porch. The police ruled it a suicide, even though (presumably) no gun was found at the scene.

Theresa claimed that Umberto murdered the family with a couple of Spanish machetes that Benny himself used to behead chickens during his cult rituals. Benny kept the blades mounted to the wall over his desk, and they were the only items known to be missing from the house after the murders. (Early reports state that an ax was the murder weapon, but detectives later claimed the wounds were "too long and too deep" to have been made by an ax. Possibly the killer brought an ax to the crime scene and inflicted some wounds with it and then, seeing the machetes, decided to use those as well.) Theresa insisted that she saw the machetes in a bag owned by Umberto. Police searched the dead man's personal effects but never found them. Perhaps he disposed of the weapons some time during the five years between the murders and his death.

Twenty-year-old Frank C. was another witness. In 1929 he was a paperboy, and he claimed that around five o'clock on the morning in question, as he delivered papers on his bicycle, he saw Umberto standing on the Evangelista family's front porch. Frank recognized Umberto and shouted a greeting. In return he received a grunt. When later in the day the boy heard about the butchery at the house, he realized Umberto might have done it. Word of what he saw got back to the police, but they stopped investigating the promising lead when a detective received erroneous information that Frank was dead.

In light of this new information, the late Umberto was again briefly considered the major suspect. But there were problems. The police assumed the killer must have been soaked in blood, but former newsboy Frank admitted that the man he took to be Umberto did not appear to be bloodstained. More importantly, Umberto's fingerprints did not match the ones left by the killer.

The police entertained other theories. At the time of his picturesque demise Benny was involved in lawsuits concerning his real estate business. Perhaps a disgruntled client took revenge? Some detectives thought that the killer was the same unknown individual who murdered Mrs. Henry Cipinski and her three children at River Rouge, Michigan, in June 1929, only two weeks before the massacre. In both cases the dead were similarly mutilated. Rumor held that Benny acted as a "go-between" for the Black Hand, leading to the possibility that a crime lord had ordered his execution. Perhaps a lunatic brought to Benny for treatment killed the family. This theory received support, albeit secondhand, from George P., a Lansing tailor who told police of a woman he knew in Detroit who went to Benny for medical advice. Benny told her that he "feared death from some person who had come to him as a patient." The woman was questioned but the identity of the mysterious patient was never discovered.

Or maybe the family were wiped out by a rival cult. This theory was being explored as late as November 1932, when police interrogated Robert Harris, a mentally unbalanced Tennessean who led a hundred-member Detroit voodoo cult called "The Order of Islam." Robert had been arrested for sacrificing forty-year-old James J. Smith on an altar. Specifically, this meant that Robert crushed James's skull with a car axle and then stabbed him in the heart with an eight-inch knife. Robert readily admitted killing James, who was "some stranger—the first person I met after leaving my home," but insisted that he knew nothing of the other murders, having moved to Detroit a few months after they occurred. Authorities took Robert's palm print, but that was the last time the papers mentioned any possible connection.

According to one story—which, as we shall see, may be untrue—perhaps the best suspect was Aurelius Angelino, an old friend of Benny's who shared his interest in mysticism. They met as immigrants in Philadelphia, where both worked as railroad repairmen. In 1919 Aurelius supposedly performed a crime in Lancaster, Pennsylvania, similar to the butchery ten years later: he was said to have taken an ax and killed two of his four children. Aurelius was sent to the asylum but escaped three times. The third time, in 1923, was permanent. He was never recaptured and his fate remains a mystery.

According to this version of events, detectives wondered if the newsboy Frank C. actually saw Aurelius on the porch that fatal morning and mistook him for Umberto Tecchio, since Aurelius and Umberto resembled each other. Furthermore, while Aurelius's fingerprints were not on file, he was known to be left-handed. A left-handed man made the bloody prints on the door latch. Had Aurelius, an escapee from an asylum, tracked his old friend to Detroit and then butchered the entire family over some ancient, unknown grudge—perhaps related to the occult?

Police thought that the killer might have gotten a few twisted ideas from Benny's "bible," *The Oldest History of the World*. As a local paper noted, "Evangelista pictured one character in his bible wrenching the head of an antagonist from his shoulders and hurling it at his feet, a fate such as the author, himself, suffered. Several other characters in Evangelista's writing suffered dismembered arms, just as Mrs. Evangelista and one of the children were mutilated." Perhaps the fate of Benny points a moral to aspiring cult leaders: the money is good and the power is gratifying, but beware the follower who takes his lessons too seriously.

An alternative theory denies that Aurelius Angelino ax murdered his own children and went on to kill Benny and his family, proposing instead just the opposite: that Benny murdered Aurelius's children. It is a fact that in March 1930, the police exhumed Benny's body and found that his fingerprints resembled bloody prints left at the Angelino crime scene in 1919. Maybe the insane and missing Aurelius came out of hiding long enough to exact some tit-for-tat revenge upon the faith healer and his family.

BIBLIOGRAPHY

Arizona Republican [Phoenix]. "Rather Die Than Work." February 12, 1892, 2.
————. "Story on a Stone." September 8, 1893, 1.
Associated Press. "Mummified Body Found in Front of TV," *CNN.com*, January 10, 2006. http://www.com/2006/US/01/10/mummified .body.ap/html.
Badal, James Jessen. *Hell's Wasteland: The Pennsylvania Torso Murders.* Kent, OH: Kent State University Press, 2013.
————. *In the Wake of the Butcher.* Kent, OH: Kent State University Press, 2001.
————. *Though Murder Has No Tongue: The Lost Victim of Cleveland's Mad Butcher.* Kent, OH: Kent State University Press, 2010.
Belvidere [IL] *Daily Republican.* "Robs Grave of Wife's Corpse." May 16, 1912, 1.
————. "Robs Grave of Wife's Body." May 17, 1912, 6.
Cedar Rapids Gazette. "Two Elkader Murder Lifers Given Paroles." September 10, 1952, 10.
Chicago Daily News. "Ate Lindloff Meal; Ill." July 5, 1912, 2.
Chicago Inter-Ocean. "Superintendent Guinea, of Calvary Cemetery, Finds Himself Again in Hot Water." August 1, 1886, 8.
Chicago Tribune. "Another Murder Laid to Seeress." October 27, 1912, I, 8.
————. "Arrest Seeress as Poisoner; Five in Family Victims?" June 15, 1912, 1.
————. "Arsenic Found in More Bodies." June 28, 1912, 11.
————. "Bodies of Seeress' Husbands to Be Exhumed in Milwaukee." June 21, 1912, 11.
————. "Calls Mrs. Lindloff Wooer." June 26, 1912, 9.

———. "Death and the Stork Jostle Each Other at Graveyard." September 20, 1913.

———. "Denies Bail to Accused Seeress." June 18, 1912, 17.

———. "Examine Body of Husband of Seeress; Find No Poison." June 23, 1912, I, 8.

———. "Find Mrs. Lindloff Guilty; 25 Years." November 5, 1912, 1+.

———. "Find Poison in Two Lindloffs." June 20, 1912, 13.

———. "Finds Poison in Another." June 30, 1912, I, 5.

———. "Hint New Deaths in Lindloff Case." June 29, 1912, 4.

———. "Hunt Woman in Poison Case." June 25, 1912, 8.

———. "Lindloff Murder Trial On." October 25, 1912, 3.

———. "Lindloff Trial Tears Open Past." October 26, 1912, 3.

———. "Louisa Lindloff Tells Own Story." November 2, 1912, 3.

———. "Mrs. Lindloff Ill at Jail." November 6, 1912, 12.

———. "'No Compromise,' Lindloff Plea." November 3, 1912, II, 5.

———. "Poison Net Fails to Move Seeress." October 29, 1912, 3.

———. "Seeress at Son's Burial." June 17, 1912, 11.

———. "Seeress Invokes Help of 'Spirits.'" June 16, 1912 I, 7.

———. "Seeress May Testify Today." October 31, 1912, 3.

———. "Seeress Moved by Evidence." October 30, 1912, 3.

———. "State's Witness Helps Seeress." November 1, 1912, 3.

———. "Suicide in Aurora Would Wear Glasses in Grave." August 6, 1921, 1.

———. "Tired of Life; Drinks Acid." June 27, 1912, 13.

Cincinnati Enquirer. "Arrests Made in Murder Case." October 6, 1904, 5.

———. "Bloody Bowlder [sic]." October 9, 1904, 9.

———. "Box Contained Cocaine." October 7, 1904, 7.

———. "Clews Only Deepen Mystery." October 5, 1904.

———. "Fog Concealed Assassin . . ." November 4, 1904, 12, 4.

———. "Gazing through Window at Sweetheart's Bier . . ." September 5, 1911, 2.

———. "Husband of Mary Hackney Closely Questioned . . ." October 27, 1910, 9.

———. "In the Cemetery." November 8, 1904, 12.

———. "Indianapolis." October 22, 1877, 1.

———. "Is Fired into Geisler's Breast at Stroke of Eight . . ." September 30, 1915, 8.

———. "Man Who Claims to Have Been Receiving Letters from Dead Wife." October 30, 1887, 16.

———. "The Mueller Murder Mystery." October 4, 1904, 3.

———. "Mutilated Body of Young Wife." October 26, 1910, 8.

———. "Not Blood on Crutch." October 7, 1904, 7.

———. "Positive Proof of Foul Crime . . ." November 5, 1904, 9.

———. "Scene of Hackney Murder . . ." October 31, 1910, 12.

———. "Shoes May Furnish a Clew . . ." November 7, 1904, 10.

————. "Stoutly Built Man with Slouch Hat . . ." November 6, 1904, 9.

————. "Subpoena Served on Hackney." October 30, 1910, 9.

————. "Suspects Let Go by Police." October 28, 1910, 14.

————. "Thousands of Morbidly Curious . . ." October 3, 1904, 10.

————. "Tragic Fate of Mary Hackney Seems Near Solution . . ." October 29, 1910, 18.

————. "Using Own Blood as Ink." September 5, 1911, 1.

Circleville [OH] *Herald*. "Death Edict Is Commuted." June 28, 1929, 1.

Cleveland Plain Dealer. "Believe Engineer Died by Own Hand." August 20, 1933, 1A+.

————. "Find Engineer in Mystery Death Is Heavily Insured." August 21, 1933, 11.

————. "Seek Purchaser of Knife as Last Clew in Poison Mystery." August 22, 1933, 5.

Clinton [IA] *Mirror*. "Human Body Is His Asset." June 5, 1915, 7.

Colangelo, Drema. E-mails to author. February 1, 2006; February 2, 2006.

Columbus Evening Dispatch. "Arrested for Cincinnati Strangling Mysteries." September 14, 1907, 1.

————. "Christ Koehl Is to Soon Go Free." September 17, 1907, 3.

————. "Cincinnati Does Not Seem Anxious." September 16, 1907, 3.

————. "Suspected of Two Murders . . ." September 15, 1907, 3.

Daily Illini. "Prison Cemetery 'Ghost' Silenced." July 29, 1932, 3.

Danville [VA] *Bee*. "'Spirit Lover' of Elfrieda Knaak Is Asked to Resign." November 30, 1928, 4.

Dayton Daily Journal. "A Sad Wedding." January 10, 1884, 4.

————. "Died: Hochwalt." Obituary. January 10, 1884, 1.

Decatur [IL] *Daily Review*. "Corn Stalks on the Coffin." December 1, 1903, 7.

Decatur [IL] *Evening Herald*. "Alienists Say Young Woman Could Have Put Herself in Trance . . ." November 1, 1928, 1.

————. "Find Elfrieda Knaak's Friend." December 2, 1928, 30.

————. "Man Who Said He Killed Elfrieda Knaak Wanted to Disgrace Relatives." December 6, 1928, 1.

Detroit Free Press. "'Divine Prophet,' Wife, Four Children Hacked to Death." July 4, 1929.

————. "Kin Estranged from Prophet." July 5, 1929.

————. "Leader of Cult Admits Slaying at Home 'Altar.'" November 21, 1931.

————. "Letter Leads Police to Ax Slaying Clue." July 15, 1929.

————. "Massacre of Six in Cult Family Baffles Police." July 5, 1929.

————. "May Solve Six-Year-Old Massacre." August, 18, 1935.

————. "Seek Second Shrine in Ax Deaths." July 7, 1929.

————. "Solution of Killings Is Seen in the Stars." July 5, 1929.

Detroit News. "Evangelista Data Ordered." August, 19, 1935.

Duluth Herald. "Queer Deaths in Wisconsin." October 4, 1913, 1.

Duluth News Tribune. "Body Is Exhumed." January 16, 1899, 1.

———. "Wolfen May Now Sue." January 17, 1899, 6.

El Paso Herald. "Boy, 'Too Lazy to Keep on Living,' Commits Suicide." April 2, 1920, 1.

Elyria [OH] *Chronicle-Telegram.* "Horrible Death." November 1, 1913, 7.

———. "Reopen Furnace Death Enigma." August 15, 1929, 1.

Evangelista, Benny. *The Oldest History of the World Discovered By Occult Science in Detroit, Mich.* n.p.: 1926.

Evening Independent [St. Petersburg, FL]. "Sorority Ritual Is Performed for Margaret Praigg." October 10, 1928, 12.

Fort Wayne [IN] *News.* "Scared Him to Death." January 13, 1904, 7.

Freeport [IL] *Journal-Standard.* "Defense Claims White Pigeon Sign of Innocence." August 9, 1934, 16.

Furman, Bess. "Last Man of Last Man Club Pays Washington Visit . . ." *Louisville Courier-Journal*, May 8, 1931, 1+.

Gettysburg [PA] *Times.* "Autos Batter Girl's Body." October 24, 1922, 5.

———. "Seventh Victim of Clubber Is Found in Toledo." January 20, 1926, 3.

Goldsberry, Julie. "Lake Bluff Furnace Murder Mystery." May 9, 2001. February 6, 2006, http://courseweb.stthomas.edu/mjodonnell /coursework/j225/GOLDSBERRY/furnace.htm.

Goshen [IN] *Daily News.* "Strange Apparition." August 13, 1889, 3.

Hagelberg, Kymberli. *Wicked Akron.* Charleston, SC: History Press, 2010.

Hammond [IN] *Lake County Times.* "Dead Girl Is Initiated in Bloomington." October 9, 1928, 1.

Hammond [IN] *Times.* "Boys Drink Gin, Then Rob Hessville Grave." April 7, 1937, 1.

———. "Young Ghouls Will Be Tried on Two Charges." April 9, 1937, 61.

Hickman [KY] *Courier.* "Buried Alive." February 15, 1884, 4.

Hiertz, Jack F. "Dearth of Clues in Furnace Torture Mystery." *Decatur* [IL] *Evening Herald*, November 1, 1928, 1.

Hobart Mercury [Tasmania]. "News and Notes." February 14, 1903, 7.

Huntsville [AL] *Daily Mercury.* "Convict Escapes." October 3, 1890, 1.

Iowa Recorder [Greene, IA]. "Girl Repels the Ripper." November 23, 1904.

Ironwood [MI] *News—Record.* "Heaven Lost to Him." September 12, 1896, 13.

Lake Forester [Lake Forest, IL]. "Authorities Probe Lake Bluff Mystery." November 2, 1928, 1+.

———. "Barney Rosenhagen, Veteran Lake Bluff Marshall, Collapses." December 14, 1928, 1.

———. "Charles Hitchcock, Lake Bluff Officer, Resigns from Force." December 28, 1928, 1.

———. "Hold Knaak Inquest . . ." November 9, 1928, 1.

———. "Knaak Case Probe Being Continued." November 16, 1928, 1.

———. "Lake Bluff Now Has New Chief of Police." December 7, 1928, 3.

———. "Rosenhagen, Lake Bluff Chief, Dies." December 21, 1928, 1.

———. "Two Are Arrested in Burglary Probe." August 14, 1929, 2.

———. "Two Hitchcocks Are Held . . ." August 23, 1929, 2.

———. "Young Hitchcock Is Sentenced . . ." November 15, 1929, 6.

Lancaster [OH] Daily Eagle. "Starts Life Term Today for Murder." July 13, 1927, 1.

Lesy, Michael. Wisconsin Death Trip. New York: Anchor Books, 1991.

Lima [OH] Daily News. "Death Removes Woman Held for Many Crimes." March 16, 1914, 1.

Lincoln [NB] Evening State Journal. "Two Life Sentences." November 28, 1925, 2.

Lock Haven [PA] Express. "Six Women Pallbearers . . ." February 14 1927, 7.

Louisville Commercial. "Ghouls' Work in Ohio." October 9, 1884, 1.

Louisville Courier-Journal. "1 of 6 Awaiting Noose Develops Gruesome Wit . . ." February 5, 1927, 1.

———. "2 Boys Confess Theft of Skull. . . ." April 7, 1937, I, 1.

———. "2 of Family Slain, Child Is Beaten." December 10, 1934, 2.

———. "2 Women Slain in Toledo in Day." October 27, 1926, 1+.

———. "6 Drown as Boy Charlestons in Boat." June 21, 1926, 1.

———. "612-Pound Negro in Pawn for Board Bill." June 12, 1902, 7.

———. "$10,000 Asked for Death of Morton." August 14, 1910, IV, 1.

———. "A Burker Jerked." September 13, 1884, 2.

———. "A Chicago Mystery." March 27, 1895, 2.

———. "A Demented Doctor." August 7, 1885, 4.

———. "A Demented Mother." June 11, 1882, 2.

———. "A Father's Folly." January 13, 1879, 4.

———. "A Good Place for Wives." August 6, 1905, I, 2.

———. "A Hard Man to Kill." November 22, 1888, 1.

———. "A Haunted College." January 13, 1889, 10.

———. "A Heartless Brute." August 2, 1886, 2.

———. "A Horrible Sensation." July 26, 1878, 1.

———. "A Horrible Story." May 13, 1883, 15.

———. "A Horrible Story." June 30, 1889, 5.

———. "Insane Surgeon Attempts Vivisection Operation." August 14, 1913, 1.

———. "A Little Corpse That Kept." November 14, 1882, 4.

———. "A Man Hater's Funeral." December 8, 1897, 4.

———. "A Mesmerist's Ugly Trick." February 11, 1888, 2.

———. "A Michigan Bedtime Story." Editorial. September 28, 1928, 6.

———. "A Monster Caged." October 30, 1894, 3.

———. "A Monstrous Story." January 23, 1887, 4.

———. "A Murderer's Suicide." May 1, 1884, 1.

———. "A Mystery Solved." March 24, 1890, 7.

——. "A Novel Method of Suicide." January 7, 1886, 4.

——. "A Pet Bear Kills a Child." October 26, 1886, 4.

——. "A Remarkable Recovery." July 5, 1885, 3.

——. "A Sentence Sermon." November 2, 1925, 6.

——. "A Suicide Neatly Carried Out." September, 19, 1889, 2.

——. "A Trifle Creepy." March 24, 1900, 6.

——. "A Voice from the Grave." May 12, 1889, 14.

——. "Abused in Life and Maligned in Death." April 12, 1903, II, 4.

——. "Acid Eats into Heart." November 9, 1913, II, 13.

——. "Actress Kills Herself in a Chicago Hotel." July 30, 1903, 2.

——. "Aged Infidel Dead." September 3, 1908, 2.

——. "Aged Man Who Hated Motors . . ." January 1, 1935, I, 1.

——. "Al Hankins Dead." August 26, 1897, 5.

——. "An Early Start." September 30, 1885, 5.

——. "An Iowa Barber's Crime." December 28, 1882, 3.

——. "An Ohio Girl's Joke." March 15, 1883, 2.

——. "An Old Clown's Death." November, 19, 1888, 2.

——. "An Old Man Frightened to Death." March 7, 1883, 2.

——. "Anchor Pulls Jaw, Tooth; Man Dead." August 1, 1924, 5.

——. "Another Body Found." September 22, 1878, 1.

——. "Another Slain Man Is Found in Queens." August 28, 1927, I, 26.

——. "Another Trunk Horror." September 12, 1886, 10.

——. "Arose From His Coffin." April, 18, 1901, 7.

——. "Astrologer Killed After '5' Warning . . ." April 12, 1939, I, 1.

——. "Astrologer Killed on 'Unlucky Day.'" April 10, 1939, I, 20.

——. "At First Wife's Grave." February 27, 1900, 6.

——. "At the Grave's Brink." January 15, 1900, 5.

——. "Attempt Seen to Steal Body of Slain Man." January 7, 1939, I, 7.

——. "Awful Retribution." May 9, 1886, 5.

——. "Ax Killer Tells Police of Deed." January 17, 1939, I, 4.

——. "Back to Life." February 5, 1891, 2.

——. "Ball Strikes a Knife." October 28, 1902, 5.

——. "Betrayed by a Diary." January 13, 1889, 11.

——. "Blonde Slayer Regrets Escape . . ." July 27, 1939, I, 9.

——. "Bluebeard Soquet." May 22, 1890. 1.

——. "Boasted of Health, Gasped and Died." May 10, 1907, 1.

——. "Body Changed into Mummy." August 29, 1901, 12.

——. "The Body Claimed." March 29, 1896, I, 2.

——. "Body Was Exhibited as a Petrified Man." December 25, 1902, 2.

——. "Bonds of Last Man's Club End in Toast." July 22, 1930, 1.

——. "The Borrowed Time Club Hearkens to Dead Voices." March 3, 1912, IV, 6.

——. "Boy, 17, Kills 3 in His Family . . ." August 5, 1938, I, 4.

——. "Boy Almost Buried Alive." January 22, 1899, II, 4.

——. "Boy Chokes Out Life under Church Desk." March 11, 1907, 5.

———. "Boy Gets Secret of Finding Bodies." November 11, 1926, 1.

———. "Boy Slain Playing at William Tell." August 1, 1932, 1.

———. "Bride Gives Death Dance . . ." April 7, 1921, 5.

———. "Buried Alive." December 14, 1889, 3.

———. "Buried by Moonlight." August 26, 1880, 1.

———. "Buried in a Cask of Rum." December 28, 1885, 3.

———. "Buried with a Skeleton." May 6, 1899, 6.

———. "Burned at the Stake." October 4, 1895, 7.

———. "Bury Pudding with Her." February 11, 1916, 7.

———. "By Way of Experiment." April 5, 1895, 3.

———. "Case of Tools Switched for Urn of Husband's Ashes." June 24, 1911, 9.

———. "Changed His Mind." October 15, 1898, 4.

———. "Chicago Murder Sifted." January 14, 1928, 1.

———. "Chicago Newspaper Man in 'Chamber of Horrors.'" February 4, 1913, 1.

———. "Chided as 'Comic,' Dynamites Himself." October 13, 1916, 1.

———. "Children Find 4 Skulls in Trunk." February 12, 1927, 1.

———. "Clubbed to Death." November 4, 1904, 1.

———. "Coroner Driven Away." January 16, 1899, 2.

———. "Corpse Taken from Casket for Debt." September 21, 1921, 6.

———. "Committed Suicide on Grave of His Wife." May 24, 1911, 4.

———. "Convict Wins 15-Cent Bet He'll Get Chair." November 23, 1939, I, 12.

———. "Crack-Brained Genius." February, 19, 1888, 2.

———. "Dark, Solitary Cell Decreed for Fugitive Husband Slayer." July 28, 1939, I, 11.

———. "Daughter's Grave Opened . . ." January 7, 1922, 1.

———. "Dead and a Good Story." January 27, 1892, 1.

———. "Dead This Time." May 2, 1889, 4.

———. "Death Ends Dog's Vigil at Grave." March 15, 1925, I, 9.

———. "Death Results from Earthquake Nightmare." November 6, 1906, 1.

———. "Death Row Convict Wins Humor Contest." September 15, 1923, 3.

———. "Death-Watch Pact Told in $60,000 Suit." March 27, 1936, I, 12.

———. "Desecrating the Grave." December 31, 1878, 1.

———. "Desperate Attempts at Suicide." September 2, 1896, 9.

———. "Died, as He Promised, on Stroke of Eight." September 30, 1915, 4.

———. "Disemboweled Himself." May 31, 1878, 1.

———. "Disturbing the Dead." August 9, 1878, 4.

———. "Doctor Diagnoses Own Ills; Fills Death Blank." March 11, 1922, 1.

———. "Doctor's Awful Crime." October 8, 1896, 2.

————. "Dog Has Waited 10 Years for Man." December 5, 1934, 1.

————. "Dog's 13-Year-Long Vigil Ends in Death." December 20, 1936, I, 17.

————. "Doomed Youth Gives Birthday Party for Fellow Condemned." October 29, 1928, 1+.

————. "Dora Meek Sleeps Her Last Long Sleep." October 17, 1904, 3.

————. "Dora Meek Is Waking Up Gradually." January 28, 1903, 6.

————. "Doubter Dies of Burns." December 31, 1937, II, 5.

————. "Dramatic Suicide of Actor in Iowa." August 28, 1907, 1.

————. "Dreams Burglar in House; Kills Wife." August 14, 1917, 5.

————. "Drinks Poison and Succumbs." June 8, 1910, 1.

————. "Drowning of 6-Year-Old Boy by Stepmother . . ." August 10, 1924, I, 1.

————. "Driven to Death." March 21, 1890, 1.

————. "The Drummer Who Took Five Certain Routes to Death." July 30, 1899, III, 8.

————. "East River Dragged in Search for Head." November 26, 1930, 1.

————. "Eccentric Wills." Editorial. January 28, 1935, 4.

————. "Economy in Epitaphs." May 4, 1912, 9.

————. "Embalmed Alive." December 28, 1888, 6.

————. "Escapes Death Chair He Helped Build." August, 19, 1912, 4.

————. "Even Strangers Invited In." January 20, 1896, 3.

————. "Ex-Loves to Carry Hoosier to Grave." December 24, 1926, 1.

————. "Executed for Killing 2." April 27, 1939, I, 4.

————. "Father Electrocuted on Daughter's Plea." June 1, 1922, 1.

————. "Father of Miss Seigadelli Takes Charge of Body." July 1, 1903, 4.

————. "Fight between Grave Watchers." February 15, 1877, 1.

————. "Find Girl Unconscious in 'Murder District.'" October 12, 1911, 1.

————. "Five Silver Spoons." August, 18, 1899, 3.

————. "For the Superstitious." September 29, 1889, 12.

————. "Fourth Victim." January 2, 1910, II, 10.

————. "Frightened to Death." June 24, 1888, 4.

————. "Fulfilled Father's Tragic Prophecy." November 30, 1902, III, 3.

————. "Gambler, Staking Own Life, Loses." September, 19, 1921, 9.

————. "Ghoul Hanged for Killing Two." March 6, 1935, 3.

————. "Ghoulish Work." November 1, 1885, 12.

————. "Ghouls Hunt for $10,000 in Grave." May 23, 1921, 1.

————. "Ghouls Strip Dead in Chicago, Is Claim." July 7, 1934, 4.

————. "Ghosts Prowl." March 8, 1907, 8.

————. "Girl Dies as Result of Terrible Dream." September 6, 1911, 4.

————. "Girl Pawned Body after Death for Ten Dollars." April 8, 1915, 6.

————. "Girl Slain, Friend Sought." April 16, 1934, 1.

————. "Girl's Body Mistaken for Effigy of Straw." October 24, 1922, 9.

————. "Girl's Death Is Solved by Confession." July 7, 1928, 1.

————. "Give Him a Cocktail." January, 19, 1884, 1.

———. "'Give Me Chance' Breaks 50 Year of Silence." June 20, 1939, I, 1.

———. "The Glenn Family." January 25, 1889, 2.

———. "'Good-Bye,' Says Polly . . ." May 8, 1917, 8.

———. "Grant Is Facing Death 8th Time." January 4, 1925, I, 7.

———. "Grant Is Given Reprieve to April." January 9, 1925, 2.

———. "Grant Slayer Fires Clothes to Kill Self." July 1, 1925, 1.

———. "Grave Robbed." September, 18, 1878, 4.

———. "Grave Robbers." November 15, 1878, 1.

———. "Grave Robbers Held." September 14, 1886, 1.

———. "Grave Robbing." August 11, 1878, 4.

———. "Ground to Death in Asphalt Plant." November 6, 1910, I, 8.

———. "Guarding Against Ghouls." May 5, 1885, 3.

———. "Guilty Plea for Slayer Considered." March 6, 1928, 1+.

———. "Gun Father Used to End Life, Kills Son." March, 19, 1920, 1.

———. "Hanging Futile." October 10, 1905, 1.

———. "Hammer Murderer Is Careless of Future." December 11, 1927, I, 1+.

———. "Hangs Self with Cord from Christmas Package." December 26, 1916, 1.

———. "He Was a Cool One." November 30, 1896, 6.

———. "Head and Legs Cut Off Woman's Body." May 2, 1928, 1.

———. "Head Found for Mutilated Body of Murdered Man." October 4, 1923, 8.

———. "Headless Body Is Proving a Mystery." October 8, 1923, 2.

———. "'Hello, Bill,' Comes from Supposed Corpse." December 14, 1910, 1.

———. "His Wife Lived to Spite Him." June 21, 1914, III, 12.

———. "Hit-Run Driver Suicide after 'Hearing' His Case." August 4, 1938, II, 8.

———. "Holds Breath to Kill Self." February 4, 1916, 5.

———. "Home for Skinny Girls Is Planned." March 13, 1927, II, 14.

———. "Hoppe Murder Trial June 25." June 3, 1928, I, 7.

———. "Horrible Mode of Suicide." July 9, 1895, 2.

———. "Human Hand Received through Mail." December 20, 1902, 3.

———. "Husband Slayer of Flapper Era Flees Prison . . ." June 20, 1939, I, 1.

———. "Hyena Still at Large." June 17, 1897, 3.

———. "Hymn-Singing Ghost Terrorizes Neighbors of Felons' Graveyard." July 27, 1932, 12.

———. "Identified Too Much." April 1, 1896, 2.

———. "Illinois Ghosts." March 10, 1890, 5.

———. "In Capsules." January 15, 1904, 8.

———. "In Honor of Himself." June 3, 1899, 6.

———. "Indiana Infidel Erects a Shaft, Is Asphyxiated." December 23, 1919, 1.

———. "Indiana Negro Is Held for 2 Murders." January 13, 1935, I, 1.

———. "It Loosened His Tongue." November 1, 1885, 12.

———. "Jabs Stick down Throat." May 27, 1916, 7.

———. "Joking to the Last." June 9, 1900, 10.

———. "Jumped into Lake at Wife's Bidding." August 13, 1905, II, 8.

———. "'Just Watch Me' . . ." October 13, 1907, I, 8.

———. "Killed Her Husband." April 29, 1898, 3.

———. "Killed by Rats." July 14, 1887, 4.

———. "King Sacrifices Man on Altar of Cult." November 21, 1932, 1.

———. "Last Man Club, Born in Spirit of Levity . . ." July 20, 1930, I, 1+.

———. "Last Man Club, Reduced to 4 Vets of Bull Run . . ." July 22, 1923, 1+.

———. "Last Man to Speak Toast." June 24, 1931, 19.

———. "Latest Ghost Story." January 11, 1886, 2.

———. "Lecturer on 'Why Worry' Ends Life in Indiana." July 21, 1921, 3.

———. "Letters from a Ghost." December 28, 1887, 4.

———. "Life and Death Touch." November 16, 1913, III, 10.

———. "Living or Dead?" April 30, 1889, 3.

———. "Loses Bet on Chair." February 4, 1939, II, 1.

———. "Lover's Fourth Attempt at Suicide Successful." May 27, 1914, 4.

———. "Lured to Death." October 11, 1884, 3.

———. "Makes Burial Robes; Then Kills Family." August 3, 1910, 2.

———. "Man, 62, Ill, Kills Self Comfortably." August 8, 1930, 4.

———. "Man Assails Social Order at Execution." March 27, 1938, I, 3.

———. "Man Bites Torpedo . . ." July 6, 1934, 22.

———. "Man Breaks in Harrison Tomb." June 11, 1934, 4.

———. "Man Buries, Then Kills Himself." May 6, 1932, 12.

———. "Man or Devil?" July 5, 1885, 2.

———. "Man Dies Playing Harp in Coffin." August 3, 1931, 3.

———. "Man Is Found Cut, Poisoned." August 20, 1933, I, 1+.

———. "Man Hangs Himself from Cross in Parlor." July 21, 1921, 8.

———. "Man to Hang, Opposes Daylight Saving Time." April 14, 1921, 1.

———. "Man Kills Two, Wounds Another in His Home." November 4, 1937, II. 5.

———. "Man Laughs Self to Death at Movie." August, 19, 1923, I, 4.

———. "Man Meets Awful Fate in Metal Pit." September 3, 1905, I, 4.

———. "Man Overlooked by Death Spends Days Polishing Tomb." June 23, 1939, I, 5.

———. "Man Predicts Death; Dies 3 Hours Later." November 8, 1922, 8.

———. "Man Shows Ingenuity in Committing Suicide." October 4, 1938, I, 1.

———. "Man Shoots Self as Toothache Cure." September 15, 1933, 4.

———. "Man Stranded at Altar, Silent 50 Years, Dies." May 25, 1939, I, 9.

———. "Man Suspected of Cannibalism." January 15, 1935, 1+.

———. "Man Ties Himself to Horse to End Life." October 15, 1922, V, 3.

———. "Man's Death Research Fatal, Data Valueless, Experts Say." November 27, 1936, I, 14.

———. "Man's Funeral Stopped to Await Wife's Death." April 26, 1921, 3.

———. "Master and Dog in One Coffin." December 6, 1903, V, 4.

———. "May Return to Life." March 5, 1889, 5.

———. "The Medical College Authorities Say . . ." August 9, 1878, 1.

———. "Melancholy Monkey Commits Suicide." April 22, 1910, 5.

———. "Midget Ends Life by 3-Inch Jump." September 16, 1934, I, 1.

———. "Ministers Killed by Bolt at Revival." August 11, 1920, 7.

———. "Minor Topics." September 26, 1878, 3.

———. "Missing Tooth Clew in Slaying." May 30, 1928, 1.

———. "Monkeys Heirs to Farm." August 21, 1910, I, 10.

———. "Monument to Satan Erected by Anti-Religious Fanatic in Detroit." November 11, 1905, 4.

———. "More Ghouls." November 14, 1878, 4.

———. "Mother and 5 She Slew Buried in One Grave." November 3, 1937, II, 5.

———. "Mr. Cave's Thumb." June 22, 1886, 5.

———. "Mr. Newberry's Body." December 31, 1885, 4.

———. "Mummified Remains." March 22, 1888, 2.

———. "Murdered in a Chair." December 23, 1895, 2.

———. "Mutilating a Corpse." May 27, 1884, 2.

———. "Mysterious Triple Tragedy . . ." March 23, 1903, 3.

———. "Nail Pierces Negro's Skull . . ." October 20, 1922, 3.

———. "Names Two Men." June 16, 1906, 8.

———. "Negro Admits Cannibalism." January 17, 1935, 2.

———. "Negro Gets Life for Drowning Man in Vat." March 14, 1936, 16.

———. "Negro Ghoul to be Hanged." February 5, 1935, 9.

———. "Negro to Face Skulls Today." February 15, 1927, 3.

———. "Negro Regards Hanging as Mark of Honor." January 31, 1912, 4.

———. "New Clews Show Groom Killed Self, Police Say." January 8, 1939, I, 2.

———. "News Gleaner." April 15, 1881, 3.

———. "No Flowers? Go Ahead Then . . ." June 22, 1919, I, 1.

———. "Not Dead, but in a Trance." May 5, 1889, 10.

———. "Not Poisoned, but Thought She Was." December 23, 1903, 2.

———. "Note Says Suicide Murder Alternative." June, 18, 1938, I, 3.

———. "Odor of Gas Revealed Corpse of Louisville Woman." June 30, 1903, 1.

———. "Offers to Hang as a Substitute." August 24, 1905, 4.

———. "Ohio Ghouls." June 5, 1881, 3.

———. "Ohio Man Died on Date He Predicted." August 22, 1910, 5.

———. "On His Sweetheart's Grave." December 14, 1896, 1.

———. "One Grave for Two." March 11, 1916, 5.

———. "One Hundredth Day of Dora Meek's Sleep." January 8, 1903, 2.

————. "One of Mr. Hyde's Victims." March 3, 1889, 16.

————. "One of U. S. Richest Men's Tomb Is Sacked." March 14, 1922, 1.

————. "Orator at His Own Funeral." February 2, 1905, 7.

————. "Outgrew His Coffin." October 20, 1901, II, 4.

————. "Overlooked Shell in 'Prop' Gun Kills Actor." March 30, 1936, 2.

————. "Packed in Ice Alive." August 7, 1892, 3.

————. "Parole for M'Dermitt." January 11, 1901, 2.

————. "Paroled Life Termer Dies First Day at Home." June 14, 1921, 4.

————. "Part of Second Torso Found in New York." March 31, 1931, 1.

————. "Pays for His Burial with Bogus Money." December 12, 1920, I, 1.

————. "Peculiar Method of Suicide." March 17, 1903, 2.

————. "Pelvic Section Added to Grim Collection." April 13, 1931, 12.

————. "Pennsylvania Hills Combed for Slayers." July 1, 1930, 1.

————. "Perspiring Man Electrocuted." September 14, 1938, I, 9.

————. "Photographer Drank Chemicals on Dare." November 26, 1913, 1.

————. "Pigeon Fluttering into Court Becomes Issue in Murder Case." August 9, 1934, 2.

————. "Police Believe the Girl Was Murdered." October 2, 1904, II, 4.

————. "Police, Opening 2 Graves . . ." January 9, 1922, 1.

————. "Police Will Dig Up Bodies . . ." January 8, 1922, I, 11.

————. "Prepares Own Funeral Sermon." June 28, 1914, III, 12.

————. "Preserved in a Grave." April 15, 1891, 1.

————. "Prisoner Ends Life in Cell." January 26, 1919, 1+.

————. "Problem Faced in Ohio Hanging." April 10, 1927, II, 7.

————. "Quarry Pool Mystery Solved as Physical Deformity Bared." January 9, 1939, I, 3.

————. "Queer Taste Is exhibited . . ." April 16, 1880, 3.

————. "Radio Set Is Made Machine for Suicide." May 12, 1932, 4.

————. "Rats Bite Woman Paralytic to Death." December 29, 1923, 1.

————. "Ravenous Rats." March 7, 1880, 6.

————. "Release Sought for Velma West." December 12, 1927, 3.

————. "Remarkable Collection in a Woman's Stomach." November 23, 1898, 4.

————. "Returned to Life." June 12, 1886, 4.

————. "Rev. Nevil D. Fanning . . ." February 2, 1891, 1.

————. "Rucker and Hoppe, Slayers, Executed." December 1, 1928, 1.

————. "Runaway Revives Corpse." November 11, 1912, 4.

————. "'Safe' Explosive Kills Inventor." July 15, 1932, 21.

————. "Saved From the Sea." December 29, 1885, 4.

————. "School Boy, 'Too Lazy to Live,' Blows Out Brains." April 3, 1920, 1.

————. "Second Killing Ends 24-Year Vendetta." July 6, 1931, 1+.

————. "Self-Destruction." November 14, 1881, 4.

————. "Sentenced to Sleep in Morgue." July 25, 1923, 1.

————. "Seven Pairs of Twins." December 27, 1895, 7.

———. "Sex Slayer Is Sought by Gotham Cops." June 1, 1931, 1.

———. "Shot the Ghost." March 3, 1889, 13.

———. "Skeletons of Giants Found in Wisconsin." September 1, 1905, 1.

———. "Skull Trunk His, Negro Admits." February 14, 1927, 1+.

———. "Slain Woman Lure of Thieves." January 16, 1928, 1.

———. "Slayer of Parents, Brother Given Life." November 6, 1938, I, 12.

———. "Slayer Stabbed in Prison Is Dead." June 23, 1925, 16.

———. "Slayer Starts Life Term Today." March 7, 1928, 1.

———. "'Sleep Killer' Found Guilty in Michigan." September 27, 1928, 1.

———. "Small Reprieves Bernard Grant." April 15, 1925, 12.

———. "Smallest Marker on Barber's Grave." May, 19, 1929, I, 8.

———. "Smith Died of Fright." October 20, 1891, 1.

———. "Snow Pens Slayer in Cabin with Victim." February 7, 1935, 1.

———. "Solves Lethal Jigsaw." May 13, 1936, 11.

———. "Some Strange Suicides." August 24, 1890, 12.

———. "Sorority Initiates Girl after Death." October 10, 1928, 3.

———. "Spanked Her Son; His Pocket Exploded." September 2, 1907, 1.

———. "Spectacular to the Last." January 22, 1896, 3.

———. "Stealing from a Corpse." May, 18, 1882, 4.

———. "Strange Delusion." March 13, 1877, 1.

———. "Strange Request in Will." October 23, 1931, 27.

———. "Strange Story of a Brakeman's Death." December 11, 1902, 6.

———. "Suicide Asks to Wear His Glasses to Grave." August 7, 1921, V, 10.

———. "'Suicide Club' Testing Resistance to Noose Blamed . . ." June, 19, 1934, 1+.

———. "Suicide Hides Poison in Salts; Sister Victim." March, 19, 1923, 11.

———. "Suicide Identified." July 2, 1907, 3.

———. "Suicide's Body Reeled in at End of Fishing Line." July 4, 1939, I, 11.

———. "Suicide's Head Carried 340 Miles by Train." June 22, 1908, 10.

———. "Suspected of Murder of Cincinnati Girls." September 15, 1907, I, 4.

———. "Suspended Animation." December 3, 1883, 5.

———. "Suspicion of Murder." August 10, 1878, 4.

———. "Sweethearts Agree to End Their Existence." September, 18, 1904, I, 5.

———. "Sword Swallower Victim of Best Trick." June 5, 1936, II, 1.

———. "Taxi Driver Admits Slaying Girl, 7." May 31, 1928, 1.

———. "Telling Time." April 17, 1911, 2.

———. "This and That." November 9, 1881, 4.

———. "This Woman Was Full of Snakes." October 3, 1899, 4.

———. "Thus Saith a Larned, Kans., Dispatch . . ." Editorial. August 15, 1901, 4.

———. "Toledo." January 31, 1878, 1.

———. "Tongue Clew to Slaying of Man." August 28, 1927, I, 1.

———. "Too Much Realism Kills Student Actor." January 26, 1938, I, 4.

———. "Torpedoes for Grave Robbers." July 29, 1878, 1.

———. "Torso of Man Found in River." November 25, 1930, 1.

———. "Torso Partly Identified." December 4, 1930, 2.

———. "Trapped, Tries to Sever Foot." October 6, 1912, II, 4.

———. "Tries Suicide at 122." September 2, 1901, 4.

———. "Troops to Protect Negro at Gallows." March 4, 1935, 9.

———. "Turk Vengeance Seen in Murder." October 7, 1923. I, 8.

———. "Two Men Die in Electric Chair." November 11, 1930, 1.

———. "Two Murderers Hanged in Chicago." February 17, 1906, 2.

———. "Unknown Fisher Commits Suicide." July 1, 1907, 1.

———. "Unparalleled Suicide." December, 18, 1885, 4.

———. "Use of Diary Leads to Double Tragedy." June 25, 1906, 2.

———. "Uses Wedding Dress as Noose to End Life." October 1, 1910, 3.

———. "Velma West Has Pleaded Guilty . . ." Editorial. March 27, 1928, 4.

———. "Velma West Is Denied Bond and Held to Jury." December 13, 1927, 1.

———. "Velma West Is Indicted for Murder." January 13, 1928, 1+.

———. "Victim of Nightmare Is Smothered to Death." April 15, 1918, 2.

———. "Voice from the Dead Testifies at Inquest." June 24, 1911, 8.

———. "Wanted Her Death Assured." April 30, 1900, 4.

———. "Wanted to Show His Gameness." July 21, 1896, 2.

———. "Was He Alive?" November 17, 1885, 1.

———. "Was the House Haunted?" July 8, 1888, 5.

———. "Was It a Ghost?" November, 18, 1888, 17.

———. "Watches Master's Grave." May 4, 1914, 10.

———. "Wedding Eve Slaying of Man Stirs Farmers." January 6, 1939, I, 10.

———. "What Dr. Tanner Said." May 7, 1889, 4.

———. "What Is It?" December 1, 1887, 1.

———. "Wife Pays for Poison Used by Husband." October, 19, 1905, 6.

———. "Wife Trapped in a Rail Frog . . ." September 3, 1919, 1

———. "Wilhelmina Stahl Buried." May 4, 1889, 5.

———. "Wolves Robbed Graves in Ohio." February 11, 1901, 4.

———. "Woman Admits Killing Spouse with Hammer." December 8, 1927, 1.

———. "Woman Dies in Midst of Minister's Sermon." March 15, 1909, 2.

———. "Woman Gets $100,000 by Will, Dies Next Day." May 23, 1922, 1.

———. "Woman Suspect Held in 'Tape Murder.'" January 17, 1928, 1.

———. "Woman Weds a Maltese Cat." March 7, 1901, 1.

———. "Woman's Ashes to be Scattered." August 4, 1909, 1.

———. "Woman's Body Found in Cemetery Lake." April 29, 1911, 9.

———. "The Work of Ghouls." September 14, 1886, 5.

———. "Workman Finds Headless Body." August 27, 1927, 3.

———. "Worry Drives Mother to Kill 5 of 7 Children and Herself." November 1, 1937, 1.

———. "Wraith Forces Man from Home." July 17, 1927, V, 3.

———. "Young Millionaire Suicide Was Insane, Says Jury." November 13, 1915, 5.

———. "Youth Explores Life After Death." January 24, 1927, 1.

———. "Youth Follows Lead of Friend in Suicide." January 25, 1927, 1+.

———. "Youth Practices to Drown Self." August 9, 1932, 2.

———. "Youth, Sweetheart Admit Love Slaying." May 9, 1936, 10.

Louisville Times. "Arrest Is Expected This Afternoon." November 4, 1904, 1.

———. "Bulletins." November 7, 1904, 1.

———. "Cincinnati's Murder Mystery Still Unsolved." November 5, 1904, 7.

———. "From Peculiar Cause." June 1, 1900, 5.

———. "Four Killed in Death Orgy." February 20, 1918, 4.

———. "Gives His Reasons." September 22, 1908, 5.

———. "No Solution . . ." November 4, 1904, 4.

———. "Suicide Keeps Schedule." April 23, 1937, IV, 7.

Marietta [OH] *Daily Record.* "A Record Kept by the Suicide . . ." December 1, 1896, 1.

Mason City [IA] *Globe-Gazette.* "Motion Filed in $60,000 Action." April 7, 1936, 22.

Nash, Jay Robert. *Open Files.* New York: McGraw-Hill, 1983.

National Police Gazette. "Vice's Varieties." February 1, 1879, 15.

Newark [OH] *Daily Advocate.* "A Woman's Will." April 26, 1900, 1.

New Brunswick [NJ] *Daily Times.* "Samuel Buxton, Tired of His Victim, Killed Her." October 30, 1894, 3.

New Orleans Picayune. "Cincinnati Mystery." October 12, 1911, 2.

———. "Defense of Mrs. Lindloff Known." November 1, 1912, 11.

———. "Dragnet for Carmichael." January 11, 1909, 11.

———. "House of Death Gets Last Victims," March 20, 1913, 13.

———. "Michigan Authorities Puzzled Over the Carmichael Mystery." January 8, 1909, 1+.

———. "The Michigan Church Crime." January 12, 1909, 1+.

———. "The Michigan Church Tragedy Mystery Takes a New Turn." January 9, 1909, 1.

———. "Michigan Town Stirred by a Dark Crime." January 7, 1909, 1+.

———. "Other Members of Family Poisoned." October 20, 1912, 2.

———. "Seers See Ghosts as Mrs. Lindloff Battles for Life." October 29, 1912, 1.

———. "Woman Accused of Five Deaths." June 15, 1912, 1.

New York Clipper. "Cincinnati's Latest." November 17, 1888, 570.

New York Sun. "Cora Stickney's Death Trance." February 20, 1887, 2.

New York Times. "A Service Interrupted." June 1, 1886, 2.

——. "Autopsy Held on Torso." May 3, 1928, 9.

——. "Backs Dead Girl's Story." November 4, 1928, 29.

——. "Believe Pastor Not Slain, but Fugitive." January 8, 1909, 1.

——."Body of Man Found Headless in Queens." August 27, 1927, 15.

——. "Bronx Laundry Marks Torso Murder Clues." November 26, 1930, 2.

——. "Carmichael Was Insane." January 15, 1909, 1.

——. "Clues Fail in Identity of Headless Body." August 30, 1927, 4.

——. "Confesses Knaak Burning." November 29, 1928, 22.

——. "Death or a Trance." February 21, 1887, 2.

——. "Dismembered Body of Man Is Found." November 25, 1930, 56.

——. "Family of Six Slain by Detroit Maniac." July 4, 1929, 32.

——. "Find Parts of Body and Clue to Murder." June 1, 1931, 36.

——. "Finds Burned Woman Was Own Torturer." November 11, 1928, 27.

——. "Furnace Death Case Recalled by Arrest." August 14, 1929, 14.

——. "Held Limbs in Fire, Burned Woman Says." November 1, 1928, 31.

——. "Hold Woman for Five Deaths." June 15, 1912, 1.

——. "Identify Slain Man as Former Convict." August 29, 1927, 4.

——. "Kin Hires Detectives in Immolation of Girl." November 5, 1928, 29.

——. "Life in the Dead." February 13, 1887, 7.

——. "Man Held in Slaying of Six in Detroit." *New York Times*, July 5, 1929, 2.

——. "Miss Knaak Dies Saying 'They Did It.'" November 3, 1928, 21.

——. "Mrs. Hanks Not Alive." December 4, 1883, 2.

——. "Nude Woman Found Burned in Furnace." October 31, 1928, 3.

——. "Offer $1,000 Reward in Woman's Burning." November 6, 1928, 29.

——. "Parts of Body in River." July 24, 1927, 22.

——. "Preacher a Suicide; Confessed Murder." January 12, 1909, 1+.

——. "Record of an Old Murder." January 12, 1889, 2.

——. "Reopens Knaak Mystery." August 15, 1929, 20.

——. "Search Chicago for Carmichael." January 10, 1909, 4.

——. "Seek Carmichael for Church Murder." January 9, 1909, 16.

——. "State Seeks Test for Burned Woman." November 2, 1928, 27.

——. "Thinks Letter Clue to Burning Mystery." November 14, 1928, 29.

——. "To Exhume Bodies for Poison." June 21, 1912, 14.

——. "Topics of the Times: Murders and Hypnotism." Editorial. January 13, 1909, 8.

——. "Torso of Woman Found in the Bay." May 2, 1928, 27.

——. "Visit Scene of Murder." August 31, 1927, 23.

——. "Woman Murdered: Crime a Mystery." March 28, 1931, 3.

——. "Woman's Torso in River." July 22, 1927, 40.

New York Tribune. "Grave-Robbing in Ohio." October 4, 1884, 1.
Niagara Falls Gazette. "Mystery Shrouds Four Skulls in Trunk . . ." February 12, 1927, 26.
Nickel, Steven. *Torso.* Winston-Salem, NC: John F. Blair, 1989.
Oakland [CA] *Tribune.* "Chicago Girl Thrusts Head, Body into Fiery Furnace." February 16, 1929, 3.
Omaha Daily Bee. "Barrett Scott Brutally Lynched." January 2, 1895, 1.
Pittsburgh Chronicle Telegraph. "Headless Body Found in Dressing Room at Pool." October 3, 1923, 1+.
———."Headless Body Is Not Identified." October 4, 1923, 1+.
———."Nurse Says She Gave Picture to Charles McGregor." October 5, 1923, 1+.
———. "'That's My Son,' Parent Exclaims on Seeing Body." October 7, 1923, 1+.
Pittsburgh Dispatch. "She Was Talked to Death." August 21, 1891, 6.
Pittsburgh Gazette. "In All the Strange Freaks of a Disordered Mind . . ." July 15, 1876, 1.
Pittsburgh Leader. "Detroit." September 5, 1875, 1.
———. "The Devilish Doctors." July, 18, 1876, 3.
———. "Woman's Body Stands Erect in River Ice." December 23, 1913, 10.
Pittsburgh Press. "Tried to Butcher the Family." December 27, 1891, 2.
Pittsburgh Telegraph. "Personal." September 30, 1873, 2.
Porter, T. R. "Ex-Kentuckian Won Case with Steeple Picture." Louisville *Courier-Journal*, May 13, 1928, magazine section, 6.
Richmond [KY] *Register,* "Buried Alive," August 20, 1886.
Riverside [CA] *Daily Press.* "Coroner Believes Elfrieda Murdered." November 3, 1928, 1.
———. "Death Relives Furnace Victim." November 2, 1928, 1.
———. "Mystery Still Inexplicable." November 1, 1928, 1.
———. "Police Puzzled by Girl's Burns." October 31, 1928, 1+.
Sahs, Harry C. "Evangelista Clue Given by Woman." *Detroit News*, August, 18, 1935.
San Francisco Examiner. "Mysterious Murderer Who Hides among the Grave Stones." *American Magazine*, supplement, November 27, 1904, 8.
Semi-Weekly South Kentuckian [Hopkinsville, KY]. "Of General Interest." August 20, 1886, 1.
St. Louis Republic. "Coffin Decorated with Cornstalks." December 2, 1903, 1.
St. Paul Globe. "In One Room 38 Years." April 30, 1899, 19.
Stark County [OH] *Democrat.* "Somnambulism as a Murder Defense." August 4, 1905, 2.
Sumner [IL] *Press.* "Eccentric Vow." October 11, 1900, 10.

Tesch, Jeffrey K. "'Murder Zone' Killer Paralyzed the Queen City in Ripper-like Fear." *Louisville.com*. October 4, 2004, http://louisville.com/indexdisplay.html?article=9339 .

Thomas [OK] *Tribune*. "Cure for Sleeping Girl." November 27, 1902, 4.

Times and Democrat [Orangeburg, S.C.], "Alive in His Coffin," August 5, 1886.

Tyrone [PA] *Daily Herald*. "Hangs Himself from Cross." July 21, 1921, 1.

University of Iowa Libraries. "Traveling Culture, Circuit Chautauqua in the 20th Century." May 17, 2000. February 6, 2006, http://sdrcdata.lib.uiowa.edu/libsdrc/Details.jsp?id=/hitchcockc/5.

Urbana [IL] *Courier-Herald*. "Runaway Saves Man's Life." November 9, 1912, 2.

Utica [NY] *Herald-Dispatch*. "Dora Meek of Centralia, Ill . . ." October 17, 1904, 1.

Wallis, Charles L. *Stories in Stone*. New York: Oxford University Press, 1954.

Washington [PA] *Reporter*. "A Horrible Story." (Reprint of *Indianapolis Sentinel* article) February 5, 1873, 6.

Washington Times. "Save Cake for Their Boy Who Went to War in '99." January 26, 1916, 14.

Weekly Argus News [Crawfordsville, IN]. "Waiting to be Murdered." October 4, 1890, 2.

Weekly Wisconsin [Milwaukee]. "At the Hearing at Saukville . . ." November 14, 1885, 2.

———. "Careless Guard Permits Escape." October 4, 1890, 7.

———. "Young Man at Sturgeon Bay Narrowly Escapes Being Buried Alive." January 28, 1899, 5.

Windsor [MO] *Review*. "A Revolting Crime." November 1, 1894.

KEVEN MCQUEEN IS AN INSTRUCTOR IN THE DEPARTMENT of English at Eastern Kentucky University. He is the author of numerous books, including *The Kentucky Book of the Dead*, *Murder and Mayhem in Indiana*, and *The Axman Came from Hell and Other Southern True Crime Stories*.

CPSIA information can be obtained
at www.ICGtesting.com
Printed in the USA
SHW052016151022
'725JS00002B/86